Under Foreign Eyes

Western Cinematic Adaptations
of Postwar Japan

T0308608

Under Foreign Eyes

Western Cinematic Adaptations of Postwar Japan

James King

Winchester, UK
Washington, USA

First published by Zero Books, 2012
Zero Books is an imprint of John Hunt Publishing Ltd., Laurel House, Station Approach,
Alresford, Hants, SO24 9JH, UK
office1@o-books.net
www.o-books.com

For distributor details and how to order please visit the 'Ordering' section on our website.

ISBN: 978 1 78099 048 4

Design: Lee Nash

Printed in the United States by Offset Paperback Manufacturers

We operate a distinctive and ethical publishing philosophy in all
areas of our business, from our global network of authors to
production and worldwide distribution.

CONTENTS

For my grandson, JACKSON

LIST OF ILLUSTRATIONS

With the exception of Figure 25 (by kind permission of Women Make Movies), all the images in this book have been provided by Photofest Digital.

PREFACE

This narrative, which provides a cultural history of some sixty films set in postwar Japan by foreigners, is intended as a comprehensive survey of a significant film genre of which no book-length study exists. In the eyes of the West, Japan is seen in many different guises, and the films examined here portray that country in a variety of ways. In looking at how Western films construct the idea of Japan, we see reflections of our own contradictory feelings about the Land of the Rising Sun.

I was inspired to write this book because of Donald Richie, who, more than any other *gaijin*, has sought to make Japanese cinema known in the West.

Although this book is intended for a popular audience, I would like to thank the graduate students at McMaster with whom it has been my privilege to discuss the films considered here: Aaron Andrews, Jessie Arsenault, Aida Boutine, Cassel Busse, Anna Daniels, Asha Joseph, Erin Julian, Katrina Lagacé, Amanda LeBlanc, Eleni Loutas, Barbara MacDonald, Vinh Nguyen, Simon Orpana, Kimberley Service, Marquita Smith, Adela Talbot, Jennifer Tasker, and Carolyn Veldstra. I am grateful to all the help given by Marty Gross and Roger Macy.

CHAPTER ONE

UNDER FOREIGN EYES

THE OTHER

This book is about the perception of Japan in the sixty films set there by *gaijin* (foreigners) — outsiders who almost always do not speak or read Japanese. My area of interest is centered on films depicting post World War II Japan and the Japanese, and, in many cases, films showing how foreigners in the same time frame respond to Japan. Why have a substantial number of films been set there by strangers? As a body of work, what do they tell us about contemporary Japan and about cinema? These films certainly provide a new cultural history of the West's *reaction* to Japan, but, even more, they are constructions that demonstrate how the West gazes at Japan. As such, more information can often be derived about the onlookers as on those looked-upon.

As a form of mass media, films influence the ways in which a culture is seen, and, generally speaking, in these films the exotic of Japan is characterized as something that has not only the potential to be liberating (in the sense that it is has values different from the West) but also as an entity lacking safe, Occidental values. From the outset, this issue becomes an often double-edged sword wherein Japan is both valorized and castigated.

Furthermore, most of the films under consideration seek to create a version of a "true" Japan that they will attempt to portray realistically. The storytelling may be of various kinds, but all the films repeatedly tell of Japan from the perspective of outsiders: what it is, what it should be, and what it is capable of being.

My basic approach has been to create a comprehensive, interpretive history for the general reader, arranged generically, of the constructions of postwar Japan in foreign-made films (mainly by American and European directors). In the first instance, my method has been to analyze the films themselves by providing close readings incorporating clear plot summaries. Since just over sixty films are involved, I have not given equal weight to each. Rather, I have tended to emphasize those that require detailed treatment because they raise significant artistic and cultural issues.[1] Again, because so many films are treated, I have felt it crucial to provide the reader with a synopsis of the plot trajectory of each because, to do otherwise, might make it difficult for the reader to follow my arguments.

The discussions of individual films arise from the contexts in which each evolved. Since these films have extremely varied ways of coming into being, I have tried to be pragmatic in order to provide the best way into each narrative. Any Orientalist project such as mine has theoretical implications, and mine venture in the direction of postcolonial in that I emphasize the fact that the filmmakers—no matter what their personal or political convictions—tend to objectivity Japanese experience in order to speak of its differences from their own. (I sometimes mention other kinds of critical approaches in this book, but I do not offer a specific, theorized reading of these film texts because they contain far-ranging, often-contradictory views of Japan.)

Specifically, I define postcolonial to refer to that area of academic discourse that focuses on the fact that so-called advanced Western (technologically superior) nations, cultures or races have for three centuries colonized and exploited weaker nations, cultures or races in order to extract natural resources or other advantages from the resulting relationships. For example, countries such as England, France, and Germany took over large portions of land in Africa and the Americas to benefit themselves economically. In the case of Japan, the situation is more complicated because up until 1853 the Tokugawa regime had been successful in closing the country off from the world. With the arrival of Matthew Perry and his black ships, Japan was forced by the United States to become part of the community of nations. The Meiji restoration followed and so did the Westernization of Japan.[2]

In postcolonial terms, Japan is a form of the Other, the exploited.[3] In *Orientalism*, Edward Said argues that Western knowledge about the East is not generated from facts or reality, but from preconceived archetypes which envision all "Eastern" societies as fundamentally similar to one another, and fundamentally dissimilar to "Western" societies. This "a priori" knowledge establishes the Oriental as antithetical to the Occidental. Said's conjectures are best applied to the Middle East, but they can also be useful in studying Japan, which has been seen as both gloriously different and treacherously different from the West.

Orientalism began in the West as the collecting of objects— mainly ceramics and furniture—from Egypt, Arabia, India and the Far East. This accumulating of objects fetishized the East by assigning a mysterious quality to those things. In one sense, they were glorious artifacts, the ownership of which ennobled both the collector and the collected. Of course, this almost always means that a great distance is maintained between the East and the West, a distance that ultimately allows the adult West to condescend to the beautiful but ultimately childlike East.

The Other is also often figured as feminine. This is because colonial regimes often see themselves as masculine entities coercing reluctant females into submission. This point of view reflects how male, hegemonic power looks upon women in society, and a correlation has been developed in postcolonial studies between women and subjugated states.[4] In the male eyes of the West, Japan is often gazed upon as female.

Japan retains a unique place in the Occidental consciousness because it was the Asian country that most influenced the course of art in Europe and the United States in the late nineteenth and early twentieth centuries and subsequently became fetishized in the West as a civilized, advanced society.[6] Then, beginning especially in the Thirties, Japan was seen as a rogue nation that had bitten the hand that had nourished it.[7]

In the imagination of the West, Japan has been perceived as a different kind of Other than, say, Barbados, a British colony, but this status nevertheless means that it is in a subordinate position to a more powerful entity: it is condescended to, seen as someway inferior, and, in general, conceived of as subordinate. This subordination means that Japan remains the Other and is perceived as a satellite, a moon to the West's sun.

Japan's special Other status makes it unique, and leads filmmakers from the West to gaze upon it differently than they do, for instance, China. In the case of Japan, modernization led to a rejection by nativists of this status and the desire to be a nation that looked upon rather than being looked at.

Thus, many Western intellectuals and artists classified Japan as a place of Enlightenment; during and well after the Pacific War, the Japanese were stereotyped as barbarians. However, some forms of pigeonholing can provide useful tools in demarcating what is Occidental from what is Oriental or Japanese. (In saying this, I am also aware that the concept of the West is a huge term with all kinds of possible meanings; in this book, I employ the word to refer to American and European attitudes towards Japan.) Ultimately, works of art create their own distinct realities, and this is certainly the case in the Western interpretations of Japan studied in this book.

These films sometimes emphasize variants in customs (the Japanese addiction to politeness; the removal of footwear when entering a home; the fact that kissing in Japan is only erotic and never social; the prevalence of bowing; the veneration of experience and, sometimes, age and position; the valorization of community over self), but they almost always treat these customs *as differences*, not as sources for comedy, sarcasm or contempt. Paul Schrader put it this way: "Japan is a very codified little moral universe with very strict rules which govern all forms of behavior and decorum."[5] That is not to say that the West does not suffer from pernickety rules—the rules are merely different. Most filmmakers studied here attempt in various ways to go beyond the superficial in order to contemplate significant issues of discrepancy and, thus, no overriding reading can be assigned as to how cinematic foreign eyes reimagine and reinvent Japan.

In this book, I show how Western filmmakers adapted this distinct Otherness of Japan. Moreover, I attempt to contextualize accurately the films under consideration so that their individual and varying treatments of Japan are brought to the fore. What, I am asking in each instance, is being claimed about this Other? (In this book, two non-Western films about Japan are included: Pramrod Chakravorty's *Love in Tokyo* (1966) and Hsiao-Hsien Hou's *Café Lumière* (2003). Although Takashi Shimuzu directed *The Grudge* (2004), I include it in this book because it is an American-produced film using American actors.)

This introductory chapter focuses on Japan as a locale that exerted an enormous, benign influence on the West and, during the Meiji reign, attempted to become the paradigm of an advanced, Western state. So successful was this transformation that Japan became a colonial nation that pursued China and Russia for disputed territory; later, it challenged the United States and its allies for domination in the Far East; after Japan lost that war, the United States, during the Occupation, attempted to make it once more a model Western state.

In many ways, then, Japan was seen to be a simulacrum of Western ideals and values and yet one that attempted to resist such influences. For the West, Japan became a Prodigal Son. The West desired conformity; the Japanese rebelled. That opposition of values is paramount. However, a filmmaker must take a position on this issue when he or she makes a film about Japan, and it is those shifting points of view that I have sought to elucidate in the films studied in this book. Although it may be futile to make any general statement about how Western filmmakers have situated Japan, it is certainly possible to see how a number of such filmmakers have imagined—or attempted to encapsulate—the entity of Japan.

In reading the various films, I have attempted to provide as much relevant information as possible on its accuracy or inaccuracy in displaying Japan. That is, I attempt to look at the appropriate surviving evidence to see how convincing or true a film is to historical evidence.

I use Japanese films in the first seven chapters mainly as a contrast to the "foreign" movies that are my real subject matter. Thus, the Japanese films have been employed as intertexts; they have been selected to show how Japanese directors treat or handle a subject under discussion in a given chapter; the contrast between how Japanese directors treat topics differently from their Western colleagues often throws into high relief how foreigners see and imagine Japan. The Japanese films are used, therefore, solely as guides or signposts. This approach has been abandoned in Chapters Eight and Nine because Japan in the films discussed there is now seen as part of a worldwide global village, an active participant in globalization. This phenomenon means that Japan (and some other nations) once perceived as the Other have seen their underdog status revised and sometimes eliminated. In any event, the introduction of Japanese films as intertexts does not serve a useful purpose in these two chapters.[8]

ADAPTATION

In film studies, "adaptation" is an area in which there has been renewed conjuncture as to how a literary text can be made into a film text. For years, it was postulated that a film text of a novel would invariably be a failure because the language of film could not capture the inner reality of a printed text. Such approaches have long been discarded. Of course, film has its own narrative logic, but it possesses strengths that the written word does not. For a long time, the printed was simply privileged over the visual.

In this book, I am arguing that Japan as a nation can be adapted, with varying degrees of success, by filmmakers and that this constitutes a sub-genre within adaptation theory as applied to cinema. Robert Rosenstone's caveat on how to distinguish between printed and film texts is useful for my purposes:

> It is time ... to stop expecting films to do what (we imagine) books do. Stop expecting them to get the facts right, or to present several sides of an issue, or give a fair hearing to all the evidence on a topic, or to all the characters...

Like written histories, films are not mirrors that show some vanished reality, but constructions, works whose rules of engagement with the past are necessarily different from those of written history.[9]

He also adds: "...we must admit that film gives us a new sort of history, which we might call history as vision....Film changes rules of the game and creates ... a multi-level past that has so little do with language that it is difficult to describe adequately in words."[10]

The "sort of truth" that Rosenstone eulogizes is a challenging one to unlock. What are the criteria by which an adaptation is judged? Basically, successful film adaptations respond imaginatively, intuitively and truthfully to a printed text, but they most always do so by using the language of cinema. In looking at cinematic adaptations of Japan, the standards are similar. How successfully and accurately does this film display an aspect of Japanese life or history? Does the film show us something different from our previous conceptions of Japan? Does the film reveal something significant about how Japan is perceived as the Other?

Film offers the possibility of revealing new insights, as Christian Metz has argued, because cinema "tells us continuous stories; it 'says' things that could be conveyed also in the language of words; yet it says them differently."[11] Since its inception, its *different language* has remained a stumbling block for many. For instance, as a medium, Virginia Woolf labeled film as a "parasite" feasting on its victims: literary texts. Yet, she recognized that "cinema had within its grasp innumerable symbols for emotions that have so far failed to find expression" in words.[12]

Although there are some exceptions, Japan is usually treated by Western filmmakers as a space that is so different from the United States and Europe that central notions about existence, belief, and community acquire radically different perspectives when films are set there.

Like no other genre, as I have suggested, film's reality presents itself as a new form of truth telling. But there are many problems in this approach. For example, Alain Resnais, a great enthusiast for the paradoxical, argues that the bombing of Hiroshima and its after-effects cannot be captured in cinema. If not on film, where does the truth of Hiroshima reside? Aleksandr Sokurov deliberately flattens the complex story of Hirohito's involvement in the Pacific War. Films about the Occupation tend to show Japan as a place rescued from its tendency towards self-destruction.

In the case of the representations of geisha and yakuza, the situation has an additional complexity because Western filmmakers are often at pains to position these Japanese "realities" next to Western conceptions, respectively, of female sexuality and organized crime. Films that depict post-1970 Japan have extremely diverse aims. For instance, in their documentaries Wenders and Marker attempt to reveal Japan to a Western audience while highlighting cultural differences.

Paul Schrader uses an unusual form of biopic to display the novelist Mishima's dissatisfaction with what Japan had become after the War; he shows us the inner world of the novelist by the introduction of highly-stylized sequences, indebted to Nô drama, which interrupt the depiction of the day on which Mishima committed suicide. Films like *Babel, Lost in Translation,* and *Cherry Blossoms* emphasize both the continuities and discontinuities between East and West. There is always, unfortunately, the tendency to simplify the Other. For example, stereotyping the Other is a common practice. It distinguishes Us from Them. It is often a way of imposing the power of the Us over the Them. Adapting Japan obviously poses myriad problems.

SIMPLIFYING THE OTHER

Despite good intentions, representing Japan in films is often both reductive and objectifying. Virtually every Western filmmaker dealing with Japanese culture does one of several things explicitly or implicitly: s/he valorizes or castigates Japan in contrast to the West, or there is the point-of-view that Japan is so vastly different from the West as to be a cipher. The latter point of view is crystallized in the anthropologist Ruth Benedict's *The Chrysanthemum and the Sword: Patterns of Japanese Culture* (1946), a book commissioned by the American government in June 1944. An even-handed report in the main, it isolates differences—some of them irreconcilable—between American and Japanese views of the world:

> Any attempt to understand the Japanese must begin with their version of what it means to "take one's proper station." *Their* reliance upon order and hierarchy and *our* faith in

freedom and equality are poles apart and it is hard for us to give hierarchy its just due as a possible social mechanism. [italics mine][13]

These twains remain on a collision course, she argues, unless ideas of freedom and equality are introduced into Japanese society.

In 1991, Edith Cresson, the French prime minister, made a remark that caused a considerable stir. She told an interviewer that the Japanese "work like ants....[the French] cannot live like that. I mean, in those tiny flats, with two hours of commuting to get to work....We want...to live like human beings as we have always lived."[14] The differences could not be greater, she implies, between the two cultures, between a humanistic society and a mechanical-based one, between the prizing of individuality and a willingness to see oneself as part of a community. The statement is racist, but it reflects the thoughts of many Westerners about Japan. In this book, we shall see some of these situations replayed.

However, others highlight the fact that the West has a great deal to learn from Japan. In an arresting imitation of a dialogue by Plato, Oscar Wilde in *The Decay of Lying* (1905) allows Cyril and Vivian to discourse over a wide range of topics. Among the most salient points raised is the observation that "Life imitates Art far more than Art imitates Life." At one point Vivian informs Cyril:

I know that you are fond of Japanese things. Now, do you really imagine that the Japanese people, as they are presented to us in art, have any existence? If you do, you have never understood Japanese art at all. The Japanese people are the deliberate self-conscious creation of certain individual artists. If you set a picture by Hokusai, or Hokkei, or any of the great native painters, beside a real Japanese gentleman or lady, you will see that there is not the slightest resemblance between them. The actual people who live in Japan are not unlike the general run of English people; that is to say, they are extremely commonplace, and have nothing curious or extraordinary about them. In fact the whole of Japan is a pure invention. There is no such country, there are no such people. One of our most charming painters went recently to the Land of the Chrysanthemum in the foolish hope of seeing the Japanese. All he saw, all he had the chance of painting, were a few lanterns and some fans. ...He did not know that the Japanese people are, as I have said, simply a mode of style, an exquisite fancy of art. And so, if you desire to see a Japanese effect, you will not behave like a tourist and go to Tokio. On the contrary, you will stay at home, and steep yourself in the work of certain Japanese artists, and then, when you have absorbed the spirit of their style, and caught their imaginative manner of vision, you will go some afternoon and sit in the Park or stroll down Piccadilly, and if you cannot see an absolutely Japanese effect there, you will not see it anywhere.[15]

Put another way, Wilde is suggesting that Japan would have to have been invented if it did not exist. Furthermore, he is commenting accurately on the extraordinary effect that the flat planes and lively color values of Japanese woodcuts had had upon artists such as Monet, Van Gogh and Whistler. As people the Japanese have a humdrum existence, Wilde observes; their artists, however, are a different matter: their "exquisite" sense of Art has infiltrated how people in the West look at Nature.

Wilde makes his observations coolly and precisely. In contrast, Van Gogh was rhapsodic about how his art had been transformed by looking at Japanese woodcuts. In September 1888 he wrote from Arles to his brother, Theo: "The weather here remains fine, and if it was always like this, it would be better than a painter's paradise, it would be absolute Japan."

Van Gogh did not need to visit Japan because, in Wildeian terms, he stayed at home and remade Arles in the image of the Land of the Rising Sun. He equates Japan with paradise. When he journeyed there in 1966, the theorist Roland Barthes had a similar reaction. He found a land completely free from Western preoccupations that he loathed: "in the ideal Japanese house, stripped of furniture (or scantily furnished), there is no site which designates the slightest propriety in the strict sense of the word – ownership."[16] In Japan, he discovered that there was no terrible innerness as in the West; there was no soul, no God, no fate, no ego, no grandeur, no metaphysics, and finally no meaning. For Barthes, Japan is a society where things possess innocence. For instance, in Japan, Barthes declares that "sexuality is in sex, not elsewhere; in the United States, it is the contrary; sex is everywhere, except in sexuality." Similarly, the famous flower arranging of Japan (ikebana) is an art not concerned with symbolism but with gesture. There, the point of a gift is not what it contains but the exquisite package that encloses it." Barthes titled his book *Empire of Signs*, but his Japan is one liberated from the tyranny of signs – it is land of the senses.

In privileging the Japanese as people who accept the surface of existence, Barthes sensitively provides a way of reading that country and its inhabitants as substantially different from the West. Whether he wished to do so or not, he also, at the same time, revived the notion of Japan as the exotic Other.

Very recently, the term "techno-Orientalism" has come into vogue to describe books and films in which the Japanese, in particular, are constructed as robotic or android-like; it arose in response to Western anxiety about Japan's technological wizardry combined with that country's collective sense of itself. This approach to Japan was common during the Seventies and Eighties, before the economic bubble burst. Such a construction of Japan is taken up in Chapter Eight, but an excellent example of this sub-genre can be found in *Blade Runner* (1997), which is set in a futuristic, in-part Japanese-looking Los Angeles filled with Japanese corporate logos and neon signs in kanji. (To be fair, the film incorporates other "styles," i.e., quasi-Mayan/Aztec.)

Writers such as Wilde and Barthes bestowed unqualified praise because they perceived Japan as possessing essentially different values from suspicious Western ones. For Gilbert and Sullivan in 1885, Japan proved especially fertile ground. They recognized Japan as an essentially foreign culture and decided to turn that to their advantage. In *The Mikado*, they combined lavish costuming, elaborate sets, stirring music, and social satire (directed at English institutions). Their Japan is a comic, benign place full of delightful, eccentric personalities. For Gilbert and Sullivan, it was not a place veering between the chrysanthemum and the sword; it was not a place to be valorized because it incorporated neglected aesthetic and sensual ideas. Rather, it was a place to be exploited because it was fashionable and exotic.

The collaborators were in a sorry way when they hit upon Japan as a setting. The year before, their previous opera, *Princess Ida* was not a box office success. In March 1884 Richard D'Oyly Carte demanded a new opera within six months. Sullivan was in bad health and wanted to devote himself to more serious music. The two men quarreled; no salvation was at hand. When an enormous Japanese sword decorating a wall fell to the ground in his study, Gilbert picked it up and started to think about the recent Japanese Exhibition. Mike Leigh uses this anecdote in *Topy-Turvy* (1999), but the Japanese Exhibition in Knightsbridge did not open until 1885. More accurately, Gilbert had decided to capitalize on the fascination in England for all things Japanese. In fact, when interviewed, he could not give a good reason for his new piece being set in Japan, except that it afforded scope for exceedingly picturesque scenery and costumes.

Gilbert and Sullivan combined engaging tunes, wonderful bits of satire and a glamorous Far East destination. Ten years later, Puccini would turn to Japan for one of his most successful operas, but his use of Pierre Loti's *Madame Chrysanthème*, as we shall see, is much more problematic than the issues raised by *The Mikado*, where the widely-recognized exquisiteness of Japan is used a vehicle for beautiful melodies and trenchant satire. The social criticism of *The Mikado* is obviously made stronger by being clad in Japanese dress, but Japan itself survives as a place of gentle—although obviously foreign—beauty.

In the Western imagination, Japan remains fixed as a place vested with important issues about race, about aesthetics, about sensuousness and beauty of a kind vastly different from the West. In all these instances, however, a false notion of Japan is often invented, and such misapprehensions haunt all attempts by Westerners to make films there.

There often remains, for example, a strange mixture of admiration and condescension (as well as possible racism) in the West's construction of Japan. For instance, the writer Henry Adams, while visiting Japan in 1886, wrote to a friend in the United States:

> [John] La Farge and I ... were playing baby, and living in doll-land. Just now we are established in our doll-house, with paper windows and matted floors, the whole front open towards ridiculously Japanese mountains; and as it is a rainy day we expect our child-owners to come and play with us; for we think ourselves rather clever dolls as dolls go. As to the temples, I will enclose a photograph of one. You will see that it is evidently a toy, for everything is lacquer, gilding, or green, red and blue paint. I am still in search of something serious in this country, but with little more hope of success.[17]

This can be read in a negative but extremely reductive way: Japan has the effect of making James and his friend childish. There is also the implied contrast between the child and the adult, which we have seen is central to Said's conception of Orientalism. On the other hand, James seems a willing participant in the activities of "doll-land," and this is largely because he has many faults to find with the industrialized (adult) society of the West. Another way to read this passage is in the Barthes manner: Japan is a world where appearance is everything and symbolism can be disregarded.

Can there ever be a "true" Japan? Or must the adjective always remain in quotes? As argued above, the answer to the second question is yes. After all, Japanese scholars have long disagreed about what is distinctly Japanese. Moreover, this idea is always in the process of being redefined and reinvented.

Nevertheless, it is possible to talk about what might constitute ideas of authenticity as applied to the Western recreation of Japan in genres such as novels and films. This task must be undertaken gingerly because there is no simple binary between the West and Japan: as already indicated, films set in post World War II Japan have a particularly complex pedigree because there is a cultural memory of indebtedness to Japan for its many gifts to the West, and then there is the fact that Japan was the enemy during the Pacific War. In the West's cultural memory, there are three main divisions: a recollection of Japan as it once was in the nineteenth century; a remembrance of what Japan became in the early twentieth century; and an impression of how Japan came to exist after World War II.

In addition to looking at the issues of adaptation and the Other, this introductory chapter examines three additional background issues: 1. How was Japan presented in films made during the time period leading up to the Pacific War and during the war itself? How do Western directors after the War portray Japanese soldiers? This issue will be treated by looking at Sessue Hayakawa's career as a pre-War Hollywood matinee idol, Arnold Fanck's *The Daughter of the Samurai* (1936-7), Josef von Sternberg's

Anatahan (1953) and Clint Eastwood's *Letters from Iwo Jima* (2006). Before examining how the Japanese depict post-War Japan in its cinema, Nagisa Ôshima's *Merry Christmas, Mr Lawrence* (1983) will be analyzed to see how it differs from *Anatahan* and *Letters from Iwo Jima*; 2. This section will concentrate on how the residue of the War can be glimpsed in the films of Ozu and Kurosawa, two directors who heavily influenced the Western directors studied in this book; and 3. How do cinematic adaptations of Japan function? This issue will be treated initially by evaluating *Bridge to the Sun*, a non-fiction/fiction film set before, during and after World War II.

The remainder of this book is divided into sections dealing with Hiroshima (Chapter Two); biopics (Chapter Three) the Occupation (Chapter Four); the depiction of geisha (Chapter Five); the portrayal of gangsters and practitioners of the martial-arts (Chapter Six); the use of the documentary format (Chapter Seven) and contemporary Japan (Chapter Eight).

SESSUE HAYAKAWA: HOLLYWOOD MATINEE IDOL

The remarkable success of the young Sessue Hayakawa in Hollywood demonstrates the complexities of racism. Born Kintaro Hayakawa in Chiba in 1889, he was the third son of the governor of the prefecture. A bit of a misfit as young man—he failed his training as a naval officer and made a suicide attempt—he then immigrated to the United States in 1911 to study political economics at the University of Chicago, where he played quarterback on the football team. A chance visit to the Japanese Theatre in Little Tokyo in Los Angeles turned his attention to acting and to adopting his stage name of Sessue (snowy island). His first major role was in Thomas Ince's *The Typhoon* (1914). He became a star the following year when he appeared in Cecil B. DeMille's *The Cheat*.

Hayakawa's austere, exotic appearance soon made him into a male star who exuded sexual appeal, but a sexual appeal that suggested forbidden love. Women could be attracted to him, but they knew at the same time that it was dangerous to be seduced by such a dangerous male. He was a matinee idol but, in his films, he never obtained the white women he courted. By 1918, unhappy with this kind of typecasting, he formed his own company, Hayworth Pictures Corporation, which made twenty-three films in three years. Four years later, in 1922, as racial animosity towards the Japanese increased, Hayakawa left the United States for Europe and, subsequently, Japan.

Part of Hayakawa's success in the United States had to do with the craze for things Japanese that had been so prominent there and in Europe from the last part of the nineteenth century. However, by 1905, Japan was seen as a major military power and a potential threat to the States. As Yunte Huang has proposed, "The acclaim for Hayakawa, then, oddly suggested a strange mixture of xenophobia and xenophilia."[18]

There was also the lurking issue of miscegenation. Daisuke Miyao points out that one "strategy was to locate Hayakawa in the moveable middle-ground position in the racial and cultural hierarchy between white American and nonwhite Other. On the one hand, Hayakawa's (and his characters') status had to be raised and distinguished racially or culturally from other nonwhite actors (and their characters) in order for the American middle-class audience to sympathize with, identify with, or even desire Hayakawa more easily. On the other hand, Hayakawa's status had to be clearly differentiated from white Americans in terms of race. Any sexual relationship between Hayakawa's characters...and white women must be avoided in order not to cause any anxiety around miscegenation." In other words, Hayakawa could appear to be very masculine, even enticingly so, but he remained the Other.[19] Women could look at him, but they most certainly should not imagine sleeping with him.

In 1924, the Johnson-Reed Act excluded the Japanese, among other groups. Within a decade, a vehement racism against the

Japanese was firmly in place. Hayakawa did not return to the United States until 1948, when he agreed to play the villainous Baron Kimura opposite Humphrey Bogart in *Tokyo Joe*.

DEMONIZING THE OTHER: JAPAN IN WESTERN CINEMA, 1938-1945

In the late 1930s, in response to Japan's aggression in China, a host of American films began to portray the Japanese in a sinister light. For example, Clark Gable and Rosalind Russell in *They Met in Bombay* (1941) are con-artists in Hong Kong who protect Chinese evacuees from Japanese troops. In its advertisements, Universal Studios dubbed Japan as "the Beast of the East."[20] In *Prisoner of Japan* (1942), Japanese soldiers murder an innocent native boy and a wounded American Naval officer for no apparent reason. Insidiously, Twentieth Century-Fox's *Little Tokyo, U.S.A.* (1942) accentuated the fact that anyone of Japanese descent, whether an alien or an American citizen, was loyal to the Emperor and thus an enemy of the United States.[21]

In 1945 the War Finance Division of the US Treasury released *My Japan* in which an obviously Caucasian actor, using a fake Japanese accent, talks about the beauty of his homeland and how "his" people are different (and superior) to naive American soldiers. The film's opening titles proclaim: "The Japanese viewpoint —Japanese doctrine —with captured Japanese film. This is the way the enemy looks at the war —thinks it —fights it—to him, this is — MY JAPAN." According to the narrator, who insults his viewers as stupid, a US invasion of Japan would not succeed due to the superior fighting power of the Japanese people who, if forced, would retreat from their islands and take up refuge in caves on mainland China. Intended to eradicate complacency on the part of its viewers, the speaker presents "his Japanese" as a nation of thoroughly cynical, cruel, would-be world conquerors. So far, he warns, only "second-rate troops" have been deployed against "your finest. We are a people," he asserts, who "rule the weak and laugh at Americans, who will soon be led to slaughter."

The full force of the Japanese threat is best imagined in the twenty-minute short, *Our Enemy — The Japanese* (1943), produced by the United States of War Information, Bureau of Motion Pictures as a training film for the United States Navy. In order to combat the Japanese effectively, they must be understood properly, the narrator assures the viewer. This is not an easy task because the Japanese mindset is so different from that of the West. Significantly, the Japanese are not logical: their weapons may be modern, but their thinking is two thousand years out of date. Tokyo desires to establish itself as the capital of the world; the Japanese feel they owe everything to the Emperor and have a sacred duty to impose his order upon the world; those who die in battle are assured an immortal life among the Shinto gods. Painting its message in such broad strokes, the film shows example after example of Japanese fanaticism.

"A stronger nation than ever before thanks to its slavish adaptation of Western technology, its economy is totally war-driven," the viewer is instructed. "Never an inventive or creative race," the Japanese have now turned to Nazi Germany for economic solutions. In addition, the media in Japan is heavily censored; every military disaster is reported as a victory.

The Japanese are a supremely ungrateful people, the narrator points out, because in 1923—at the time of the Great Earthquake—it was the United States, more than any other nation, that rushed to Japan's rescue. Now restored, thanks in large part to American generosity, the same people are working for the destruction of the States.

The final third of the film reminds the viewer that "against the madness" of the well-disciplined Japanese war machine with its "samurai code," total sacrifice must be exerted on the part of American troops. The Japanese soldier, the narrator observes, compensates for his small physical size by his fanaticism.

Against such a "primitive" and "murderous" force, extraordinary measures must be taken to assure victory. In fact, Japanese "ingratitude" extended to a cinematic collaboration between Hitler's Germany and Hirohito's Japan.

THE PERILS OF COLLABORATION

In 1936, Japan, in the process of colonizing large portions of Asia, formed a strong alliance with Germany. Soon they signed the Anti-Comintern Pact, and cinematic co-operation seemed a likely way to help cement cultural exchange between the two nations. The outline of a proposed film emphasized "the unity of the Nazi group-spirit and the racial spirit of the Japanese as opposed to the weak spirit of the democracies." The "volcano-like sacrificing spirit" of Japan was also to be underscored.

The German director chosen to make the resulting film was Arnold Fanck, a former geologist famous for quasi-mystical mountain movies such as *The Holy Mountain* (*Der Heilige Berg*, 1926), which starred Leni Riefenstahl. The script, written entirely by Fanck, was to be called *The Daughter of the Samurai* (*Die Tochter des Samurai*)—its name was later changed to *The New Earth* (*Atarashiki Tsuchi*)—and centered on the protagonist's renunciation of Western democracy in favor of Japanese home truths.

Teruo (Kosugi Isamu) returns home from an extended stay in Germany, a country he worships for its many scientific accomplishments. On board ship he meets and falls in love with Gerda (Ruth Eweler). His fiancée in Japan, Misuko (Setsuko Hara), becomes distraught at his betrayal and attempts suicide by throwing herself into Mount Aso. Teruo rescues her. After Teruo has a heart-to-heart talk with his future father-in-law (Sessue Hayakawa) about the glories of Japan, the couple marry, move to Manchuria, which had been opened to Japanese settlement. In the finale, Terou places his newborn baby in one of the furrows on their land and predicts his offspring "will become a child of the land." In the background, a Japanese soldier, armed with rifle

and bayonet, stands at attention. Teruo has finally gotten a grip
on himself and his Japanese ideals. According to Fanck's film, the
warring aspect of the Japanese – the samurai side – was
completely congruent with the aims of National Socialism.
Throughout his career, Fanck was renowned for his capri-
ciousness and temper tantrums. Before arriving in Japan in 1936,
he had approached Kawakita Nagamasa and his wife Kashiko of
Towa, Japan's leading importer of foreign films. They were
enthusiastic about assisting Fanck find a co-director. After
looking at a number of films, the German chose Itami Mansaku,
the style of whose *Kôchiyama Soshun* reminded Fanck of René
Clair. However, Itami did not like Fanck's script and turned the
Kawakitas down three times before mysteriously agreeing to co-
operate. Possessing a much more cultivated and apolitical mind
than Fanck's, he obviously thought the script was a horrendous
blend of racism and condescending Western notions of the
Orient.

Kawakita Kashiko would recall to interviewers many years
later that Itami disliked Fanck's script, and he threatened to
reject the project out of hand if not allowed to participate in
its revision. Itami did in fact come up with a script of his own,
a perfectly delightful one about Japanese children. Fanck,
however, would have none of this, insisting that his first real
Japanese-German film collaboration have a clear, pro-Fascist
political message. Fanck won out.[22]

But a strange compromise was agreed to: each director would
make his own version of the film. Fanck shot during the day,
Itami at night. The cinematographer Richard Angst and the
actors had to work day and night; studio costs were, of course,
doubled.

Fanck's film, which begins with the subtitle, "This film is
about Japan seen by a foreigner," is crammed with stereotypical

images: in addition to Fuji, a volcano and earthquakes, there are the Kamakura Buddha, a Japanese garden complete with torii and stone lanterns, shrines, temples, tea ceremonies, flower ceremonies, sumo wrestling, Kabuki, and geisha. For good measure, Misuko and her father demonstrate archery and sword fighting. In one scene, Misuko's father urges her not to wear a Western dress when meeting with Teruo. The music is by Yamada Kosaku, an internationally known composer.

Both versions were premiered in Tokyo in February 1937— first, Itami's and then a week later, Fanck's. The latter was a commercial success although Sawamura Tsutomu in the *Eiga Hyoron* dismissed *New Earth* "as no more than an attempt to form Nazi propaganda out of Japanese raw materials." One of the reasons that Fanck had gone to Japan was that he had been in the bad books of Joseph Goebbels, who was delighted with the film's excellent press in Germany. He should not have been surprised since in a circular he had declared the film vital for public relations and ordered critics to praise it highly.[23] Fanck's film offers splendid visuals, especially of mountains and is the fifth film to feature the now legendary Setsuko Hara, later celebrated for her appearances in various Ozu films.

After World War II, Fanck's films were proscribed. He wound up employed as a lumberjack. Working on *New Earth* took its toll on Itami: his film received a bad press and he succumbed to TB. Until his death in 1946, he wrote criticism and screenplays. After the war ended, another visitor to Japan, Josef von Sternberg faced a vast number of problems when he went to Japan to make *Anatahan*.

EVERY MAN REMAINS AN ISLAND: *ANATAHAN*

Josef von Sternberg's *Anatahan* (1954) is a curious—and idiosyncratic—portrayal of Japanese soldiers by a Western director. Although born to a Jewish family in Vienna, von Sternberg spent most of his childhood in New York City and Lynbrook, New

Jersey. From 1925 to 1929, he made eight silent films. After his first talkie, *Thunderbolt*, was released in 1929, his career went into decline and this led him to Germany, where he made the first German-language talkie *Der blaue Engel* (1930) and, simultaneously, its English-language version, *The Blue Angel* (1930), both with Emil Jannings as the doomed Professor Rath. Two years earlier in America, von Sternberg had directed Jannings in *The Last Command*.

The role of Rath is justly regarded as the finest in Janning's career, but the film is even more renowned for von Sternberg's casting of Marlene Dietrich as Lola, the vamp role that made her an overnight celebrity. Director and actress furthered their collaboration, one of the greatest in the history of cinema, in *Morocco* (1930), *Dishonored* (1931), *Shanghai Express* (1932), *Blonde Venus* (1932), *The Scarlet Empress* (1934) and *The Devil is a Woman* (1935).

Von Sternberg was in his late fifties when he arrived in Japan in 1952, where the Kawakitas assisted him (Yoshio Osawa and Nagamasa Kawakita produced the film for Daiwa-Towa Productions). The script derives from a book by Michiro Maruyama based on an actual incident reported in *Life* magazine. In 1944, twelve survivors, including Maruyama, from the Japanese Imperial Navy were stranded on the volcanic island of Anatahan south of Japan. At first, they attempted to remain vigilant to protect their assigned turf. Quite soon, however, they became aware that there were two other inhabitants of their new home: a man and woman who worked on what was once a plantation. Since each other's spouse had been transferred a while back to a new locale, the man and woman lived as husband and wife. Keiko (Akemi Negishi) and Kusakabe (Tadashi Suganuma) made a virtue of necessity. At first, they do not wish their retreat to be invaded by the military riff-raff, but Keiko bathes in the nude at a spot not far from where the soldiers can gaze on her; then she beguilingly rests her foot on the shoulder of one of the men.

A diligent researcher, Von Sternberg delved "deeply into [his] subject, not only discussing it with length with [Michiro Maruyama] but reading endless newspaper accounts published at the time, including psychiatric studies of all the survivors." During the first few weeks, he recalled, while working on the script, "rumbles of protests" reached his ears: "not many Japanese were fond of the idea that a foreigner was to exploit an ignominious episode in their national history."[24]

Anatahan was made on a huge soundstage (a former airplane hangar) in an exhibition hall in Kyoto's Okazaki Park. The sets look like they were created out of cellophane and paper, and this is correct. In fact, von Sternberg so wanted to avoid "realism" on his Pacific island that he was angry when forced to use water. He designed the light units, background projectors, camera booms— even the heat units. "Giant cryptomeria roots were hauled in and turned upside down to form a jungle that existed only in my imagination. Leaves and palms were added and huts on stilts erected, and all of this sprayed with aluminum paint."[25]

The single woman in the film, Keiko, "was hauled out of a chorus line," von Sternberg observes, "after every geisha in Tokyo had been paraded before me." (Akemi Negishi later had a distinguished career in films, including parts in Kurosawa's *Ikimono no kiroku* (*I Live in Fear*), 1955; *Donzoko* (*The Lower Depths*), 1957; and *Akahige* (*Red Beard*), 1965.) Three of the men were Kabuki veterans, the rest from dance schools; one was discovered in a restaurant.

Although the film is spoken in Japanese, the audience's attention is focused on the booming English-language voice-over by von Sternberg annunciated in a harsh-sounding Brooklyn-accent. The narrator is brash: he offers philosophical reflections on isolation, bravery, sexuality and a wide variety of topics. Often he states that he does not know how a certain event unfolded, but then the camera shows exactly what occurred. The implication is that the omniscient narrator may not know the entire story but that the camera never lies; the discrepancy might have occurred, however, because of von Sternberg's own confusion as to what he was attempting to accomplish. In any event, the sentiments espoused are voiced in a no-nonsense, omniscient manner:

> At first, she was only another human being stranded on this pinpoint on the map. Then, she was to become a female to us, and finally a woman—the only woman on earth.
>
> [Keiko] was a pretty woman—she was a Japanese woman—trained to obedience. When she was young, she followed her father—never dreamt of walking at his side. When she married, she walked behind the husband— obedience to a husband is considered to be the prime virtue of Japanese womanhood.[26]

Reflections such as these inform the viewer how to interpret what is being shown; in addition, the reflections have an indomitable art of certainty: no room is left for interpretation.

FIGURE 1 Keiko (Akemi Negishi) takes obvious enjoyment in cavorting lasciviously for the stranded Japanese soldiers in *Anatahan*.

At first, one soldier, Kusakabe, blocks his comrades from gaining access to Keiko, but he cannot do so once two guns are discovered on a plane washed ashore. At that point, "the Queen Bee" establishes a relationship with Kusakabe and the two men who have taken possession of the firearms. One of the gun-holders murders the other in plain sight, although the voice-over tells us "we can only guess" how the murder victim died. Then Kusakabe is murdered, and, afterwards, the other gun-holder is killed. Eventually, the cook becomes the "new king." Then he is killed in a storm. Meanwhile, when pamphlets shower down on the sailors announcing that the war has long ended, they are convinced that this is an enemy trick.

Then Keiko disappears. Somehow she makes her way back to Japan and notifies the families of the soldiers that they are alive. The exile of the five remaining sailors comes to an end. As each emerges from the plane that returns them to Japan, their countenances are shown in medium-shot and the narrator points out that they may have survived, but that they had "lost the battle of Atanahan." At the film's conclusion, von Sternberg's voice-over states that Keiko must have been among the group that witnessed the return of the men; this reflection allows the film to end with a close-up of the enchantress.

From the outset, von Sternberg had determined to "picture the Japanese exactly as they were, not as they imagined themselves to be, and I wished to show that they were no different from any other race of people, much as they would like to be considered apart from the rest of mankind." Asked why he had gone to Japan to make this film, he shrugged his shoulders: "Because I am a poet." Later, he more realistically pointed out, that he had chosen "this readily understandable series of events to carry out a not easily understood experiment in indirect mass psycho-analysis, to alert all of us, to put it simply, to the necessity of reinvestigating our emotions and the reliability of our controls under unfavorable conditions."[27]

The film becomes an investigation of what happens to mankind when it returns to "the level of the cave man." As von Sternberg also observed, "The men I pictured were not the Japanese of a counterfeit folklore, they were ordinary human beings subject to the ordinary strains without which there is no life."[28]

Anatahan demonstrates how patriotic Japanese sailors forget their obligations to their homeland in their pursuit of a beguiling *femme fatale*. The stranded sailors—over five years— think constantly of survival and, mainly, of Keiko. If the film has an argument, it seems to be that even the most inner-directed of individuals will eventually forget the ties of patriotism in lieu of self-interest and, especially, the promise of sexual pleasure. That point is made repetitiously because Keiko is shown as a vamp in the Marlene Dietrich tradition. Her nude body, her bewitching smile, and her flirtatious eyes overwhelm the film because von Sternberg has no interest in developing his plot line in any but an uncomplicated, uninflected manner.

The voice-over is ineffectual because it simply tells rather than shows, almost as if von Sternberg had forgotten some of the most basic rules of filmmaking. Attracted though he may have been to developing a story about castaways, the film contains no intrinsic subject matter that could properly be called Japanese. Von Sternberg may have been thoroughly educated in every aspect of the craft of making films—especially his use of lighting, soft lens shots, and overall success in establishing mise en scène—but his genius resided in dramatizing female sexuality, a talent on obvious display in his films with Dietrich. In *Anatahan*, he attempted to infuse Akemi Negishi with a Dietrich-like vigor, and only to a limited extent was he successful.

Overall, the film offers trite observations on the plight of the stranded Japanese, who are presented as a rather humdrum, tawdry group of individuals. Placed in desperate circumstances, the Japanese act without valor or intellect. Von Sternberg claimed that he wanted to portray the Japanese *exactly* and not as *they imagined themselves* to be, but then why did he make the film? By his own admission, he offers little or no insight into the Japanese character. He does his best to exploit an ignominious episode in the history of the Pacific War. Part of the answer may rest in the simple fact that he found in Japan collaborators willing to work with a celebrated auteur. Von Sternberg said it best when he remarked: "I used my emotions rather than my reason in choosing to make this film."[29] In making *Letters from Iwo Jima*, Clint Eastwood conjoined emotions with reason.

REJECTING STEREOTYPES: *LETTERS FROM IWO JIMA*

Like von Sternberg, Clint Eastwood was a well-established director when he travelled to Japan. Unlike, his predecessor, he was determined to make a film that vanquished mindless generalizing about the Japanese. In some earlier films, Eastwood had consistently taken a stereotype and then punctured it. For example, in *The Unforgiven* (1982), a reformed killer, returns reluctantly to his trade in the defense of justice, thus blurring the lines between heroism and villainy.

On October 20, 2006, Eastwood's *Flags of our Fathers* was released in the United States; three weeks later *Letters from Iwo Jima* was shown in Japan (the film's first showing in the United States was on January 12, 2007). The first film depicts the Battle of Iwo Jima (February 19-March 26, 1945) from the American point of view; the second from the Japanese. What is perhaps more significant is that both narratives seek to undermine stereotypical views. *Flags of Our Fathers* recounts how the Marines hoisted the American flag on Mount Suribachi on February 23 but that the celebrated photograph by Joe Rosenthal of five Marines and one Navy Corpsman raising the flag was re-staged later that day at the request of James Forrestal, the Secretary of the Navy. Three of the six later died in battle at Iwo Jima, and the film chronicles the subsequent lives of the survivors, two of whom had a great deal of difficulty dealing with their celebrity status.

If victory can come with a heavy and complicated price, defeat can be accompanied by simple heroic glory. Such is Eastwood's view of the Japanese at Iwo Jima. If previous Western films had shown Japanese soldiers as mechanical-acting and savage-like followers of Hirohito and Tojo, Eastwood in one stroke attempted to undo that cinematic past.

In his portrayal of American soldiers fighting the Japanese in the 1942 battle of Guadalcanal in *The Thin Red Line* (1998), Terrence Malick allowed his narrative to unfold from the perspective of a number of soldiers; he also moved his camera Stateside to show the lives of soldiers before they were sent overseas. In a similar way, Eastwood depicts the Japanese struggle to survive from extremely different vantage points, and he weaves in some significant flashbacks to life before and during the war. The incorporation of multiple viewpoints and flashbacks allowed Malick and Eastwood to layer their war films so that the differing life experiences of the various participants are juxtaposed. The viewer sees various reasons for fighting and comes to appreciate that there is no single point of view.

Since Japanese soldiers had previously been dealt with as stereotypes, Eastwood's methodology cracks the mould. The film, in blending real-life characters with invented ones, constantly strives for authenticity. Lieutenant General Kuribayashi (Ken Watanabe), the actual commander of the Japanese at Iwo Jima, sketches touching *etegami* (picture letters) to his son; the simple baker Saigo (Kazunari Ninomiya), the fictional Everyman, writes longingly to his wife. The interactions between these two characters give coherence to the story line (Kuribayashi rescues Saigo at the beginning, middle and end) and, as Eastwood has pointed out, "we see General Kuribayashi through the eyes of a conscriptee."[30]

FIGURE 2 General Kobayashi (Ken Watanabe) is the embodiment of deportment, courtesy, bravery and military skill in *Letters from Iwo Jima*.

In general, Eastwood avoids the appearance of coherence because he wants to capture the total disruptiveness of war. Plans of defense are made but have to be jettisoned when the enemy counters. The trauma of war unhinges some men: some act their worst while the best in others comes to the surface. At the beginning of the film, Saigo is a complainer; later, he attempts to surrender but is thwarted; at the end, convinced he is soon to die, he resolves to fight bravely for his country's cause.

Consistently, the film dramatizes the differences between reality and fantasy. Two real life characters (Kuribayashi and Baron Takeichi Nishi) had spent extended periods in the United States. Kuribayashi served as a deputy military attaché in Washington, DC, travelled across the United States and briefly studied at Harvard. Nishi won the gold medal in equestrian individual jumping at the Los Angeles Summer Olympics in 1932; his easy-going playboy personality endeared him to many celebrities including Mary Pickford and Douglas Fairbanks. Both these men are fearless fighters against their American foes, but they obviously have no preconceived notions of the enemy as "devils." Most of the enlisted men do. Private Saigo's previously held sentiments are shattered when he hears Naishi translate a letter to a dying captured American soldier from his mother. That woman's heartfelt concerns for her son's fate and the incidents she recalls from their daily lives allow Saigo to identify completely with his foe. "My mother could have written that letter to me," he confides to a comrade.

The film shows a wide range of emotions regarding national-istic labeling. The General and the Baron knew the States first-hand, and they therefore are not predisposed to think of its citizens in black-and-white terms. Enlisted men from both Japan and the United States were *taught* to think in racist terms that reduced the enemy to the level of evil scum.

In another telling incident, a former member of the *kempeitei* (military police) peremptorily arrives to serve with the enlisted men. Saigo, certain this man has been assigned to spy on him and his colleagues, develops an elaborate fantasy about this possi-bility until one day his new comrade tells him that he was expelled from the military police because he refused to shoot a dog that had annoyed his superior.

One of the commonly held opinions about Japanese soldiers was that they always placed duty to the Emperor over personal considerations. The problem with such a belief-system is that it would lead to the unacceptable pre-supposition that American soldiers would place self before country. Some of the Japanese in the film conform to the stereotype, but most do not. At one point Kuribayashi states: "I promised to fight to the death for my family, but the thought of my family makes that a difficult task." At another point, Nishi commands his charges: "Do what is right because it is right."

When an enlisted American is captured, Nishi orders the medics to treat him exactly as if he were Japanese. Later, two

Japanese deserters surrender to American soldiers who decide not to trouble themselves by returning them to their base camp; instead, they shoot them in cold blood. Atrocities occurred on both sides, and, in this instance, the Americans are shown in a negative light.

When he arrived at Iwo Jima, Kuribayashi determined that it would be unwise to contest the Allied beach landings. Fully aware that he was in a no-win situation, he determined that the Japanese defense had to be placed underground, where there were more then eighteen kilometers of tunnels and five thousand caves. This kind of fighting, he felt, would challenge the American forces dearly but, without the hope of reinforcements and further supplies, he knew his position was hopeless. This battle—the first on Japanese Home Islands—was symbolically important: it had to be waged in the most determined, aggressive manner to promote the Japanese cause, although any reasonable expectations of success had by the winter of 1945 been eradicated. The fighting environment in which the Japanese existed— the caves—are shown as they were: eerie, dark, claustrophobic and air-deprived. When the Japanese venture outside, they see the huge American armada that has arrived to destroy them. To accompany the foreboding air of menace, Eastwood has deliberately restricted his colour palette, almost as if the film was shot in brown and white.

Kuribayashi is characterized as a determined man who realizes that he has been given an impossible task. He demands the very best of those in his command and is shown as a warm-hearted but tough soldier. For example, he gently dismisses one admiral from Iwo Jima when it is obvious that man will not follow his orders thoroughly. In moments by himself, the General composes his tender picture letters to his son, Taro.

Letters from Iwo Jima begins with a group of archeologists searching within the caves at Iwo Jima—the film ends with the discovery of a cache of letters saved by Kuribayashi and buried by Saigo. As the letters are held up in the air, they flutter to the ground accompanied by a polyphony of excerpts spoken in Japanese. This underscores the fact that Eastwood's film allows a multi-voiced perspective on the Japanese to emerge from the debris of time.

More of a commercial success in Japan than in the United States, the film was generally praised in Japan for its empathetic view of the Japanese, although the Association for the Advancement of Unbiased View of History questioned the accuracy in the presentation of the Japanese military police. It received the Japan Academy Prize for Outstanding Foreign Language Film.

WESTERN AND JAPANESE REPRESSION: *MERRY CHRISTMAS, MR LAWRENCE*

Throughout his career Nagisa Ôshima had a fascination with the psychosexual and, not surprisingly, he centers *Merry Christmas, Mr Lawrence* on the hidden, compulsive feelings of his protagonists. The setting is a Japanese prisoner-of-war camp in Java in 1942. Colonel John Lawrence (Tom Conti) is a dapper, well-educated Englishman who speaks fluent Japanese; he is paired off opposite brutal, proletarian Sergeant Hara (Beat Takeshi), who takes every opportunity that presents itself to contrast Japanese bravery—in his opinion, any Japanese soldier who is captured is by definition an utter failure—to English cowardice (demonstrated by their acceptance of the fact the fact that they, despite their best efforts, have been imprisoned by the enemy).[31]

During the course of the film, Hara acquires a grudging admiration for Lawrence and, towards the end, prevents Lawrence from being executed on Christmas Day. Having drunken too much sake and filled with good cheer, he decides to play Santa Claus by allowing him to live. "Merry Christmas, Mr Lawrence," he proclaims. The film concludes in a postscript from 1946 in which Lawrence visits Hara the night before he is to be executed for war crimes. Lawrence disagrees with Hara's fate: "You are the victim of people who think they are right just as you and [the camp commander] once believed you were right. Of course, no one is right."

At the very beginning of the film, Hara peremptorily summons Lawrence to witness a vile event. A guard — of Korean descent — has raped a Dutch prisoner and is about to be forced to commit seppuku. Lawrence is appalled: "Do you want me to hate the Japanese?" Hara offers the prisoner the opportunity to escape the required death penalty for this offence if he displays "how he used his thing" on the Dutchman. The suggestion is that the resultant spectacle will somehow humiliate the offender sufficiently to mitigate his punishment. Hara, it turns out, has somewhat ambiguous feelings on this topic. At one point he observes that "all British are homosexuals," but he also claims "samurais accept homosexuality."[32]

Hara does not see himself as a would-be samurai, but he certainly sees his commanding officer Captain Yonoi (Ryuichi Sakamoto) as one. (Like David Bowie in the Western world, Ryuichi Sakamoto, who composed the film's score, was a celebrated pop music star in Japan.) In fact, he attempts to keep this incident secret from Yonoi, but that hope is thwarted when Yonoi, clad in his kendo outfit, arrives on the scene. Disgruntled not to have been informed of the event, he decides to postpone imposing a solution because he has just been called away to serve on a military tribunal in Batavia [Jakarta].

That trial has been convened to deal with Major Jack Celliers (David Bowie), a South African who has been acting as a guerilla operative. The court martial must decide if Celliers has been acting as a renegade and thus worthy of execution or if he is an enemy officer performing his duty against the Japanese and thus to be deemed a prisoner of war. From the moment he glances at the pale skinned, exceedingly blonde Celliers, Yonoi is taken with him. He asks questions that seem to suggest that he considers that Celliers has acted appropriately. Yonoi begins his interrogation by quoting Hamlet: "To be or not to be"; this signifies that the ensuing drama will be about both identity and indecisiveness.

Deemed guilty, Celliers is brought before a firing squad, which opens fire. But they have been shooting blanks. From the shadows behind Celliers emerges Yonoi, who, it transpires, is returning to his camp with Celliers as a prisoner. Yonoi has had his way, and the verdict has been postponed.

Celliers, who is both stroppy and arrogant, does not mind showing his contempt for the Japanese. When an officer asks him, "Can you guess what I'm thinking?," he responds: "No. Can you guess what you yourself are thinking?" At the camp, Yonoi renews his strong interest in Celliers, who he determines will become the new prisoners' chief officer, much to the anger of Group Captain Hicksley (Jack Thompson).

Lawrence tells Celliers: "If Yonoi has something on his mind,

FIGURE 3 David Bowie (Celliers) and Ryuichi Sakamoto (Yonoi) in *Merry Christmas, Mr Lawrence*.

why doesn't he come out with it?" This is the first explicit reference to the fact that Yonoi is sexually attracted to Celliers. Later, Lawrence tells Celliers: "Yonoi has taken a shine to you." In fact, Yonoi's attraction to Celliers is so evident that one of Yonoi's officers attempts to murder Celliers. When Yonoi asks him his motivation, the subordinate replies: "That man is a devil destroying your spirit." When Celliers attempting to escape is confronted by Yonoi, he refuses to fight him. Yonoi tells Lawrence: "Your friend is a disappointment to me." On the issue of his use of homosexuality in this film Ôshima claimed that such an inclination "is the synthesis of friendship and violence: military men are attracted by their enemies, as men, in compensation for their frustration."[33]

These largely unresolved tensions come to a head when Yonoi, acting more and more irrationally, orders all prisoners to appear before him. When they are assembled, Yonoi becomes enflamed when the severely disabled prisoners are not there. He insists they too be brought forward. Yonoi's behavior suggests that he is acting upon the paranoid assumption that the prisoners are deliberately dishonoring and thus publicly shaming him. When one of the prisoners collapses and dies, Hicksley confronts Yonoi, who is about to execute him for his insubordination. At that moment, Celliers strides towards Yonoi, embraces him and kisses him on both cheeks. Yonoi is about to kill Celliers in retaliation for this public insult but faints before he can do so.

He swoons for two reasons: his sexual fantasy has been brought to life, but he is deeply ashamed of having those feelings made public. The issue is Yonoi's sense of himself as an honorable Japanese male and warrior. Can such a person be truly masculine and an effective warrior if he is governed by strong sexual feelings for members of his own sex? (This issue is central to Paul Schrader's *Mishima*: see Chapter Three).

For his act, Celliers is buried in sand with only his head exposed. This public act of humiliation is supposed to represent

Yonoi's distance from the kiss and its implications. Celliers is left to die but one evening Yonoi walks over to him, bends down and cuts a lock of his hair. When Lawrence and Hara meet in the film's coda, it is disclosed that Yonoi, before he was executed, had this lock of hair sent to a shrine in his hometown in Japan. Ultimately, Yonoi decided that Celliers was a person to be emulated as well as loved.

Very little of Yonoi's past is revealed in the film, although he does express his regret that he was in Manchuria at the time the Two Twenty-six Incident took place in Tokyo on February 26, 1936 when twenty-two junior officers of the First Division attempted to overthrow the government. Yonoi is haunted by the fact that he was not able to assist his brother officers.

Celliers is also haunted by a youthful incident that is shown in flashback. He considers himself to be a traitor because he did not assist his younger, vulnerable brother from being hazed at school. Completely unforgiving of himself, he led a barren life until he joined the army. In battle he found meaning to his existence. Just before he dies, he imagines a conversation in which his brother forgives him.

Yonoi and Celliers have severely wounded masculinities. Yonoi attempts to deal with his sexual feelings, with which he is obviously uncomfortable, by idealizing the South African as a brave person whom he can rescue and place in a position of authority. However, his sexual feelings are strong. One evening, shortly after Celliers has arrived at his camp, he visits the infirmary secretly to gaze at him.

When Lawrence tells Celliers his sexual fantasy about a woman, Celliers, who does not respond with a similar anecdote, simply notes that he does not have any memorable experiences of that kind to share. He may be homosexual, but the script is deliberately hazy on this point.

What the film makes clear is that homosexual activity can be a life-threatening experience. The Korean soldier ultimately dies a gruesome death. Celliers looses his life for bestowing the kiss on Yonoi, who is deeply ashamed of his feelings.

At one point, Lawrence offers this interpretation of Japan and Japanese militarism: "They are a nation of anxious people. They went mad—or worse—because they could do nothing." This observation can be extended to both Yonoi and Celliers, both of whom are trapped men who seek in battle the solutions to their personal problems.

Ôshima has no hesitation in showing the brutality of the Japanese guards towards their captors, but the context of the film suggests that a Western camp would manifest the same behavioral patterns. Rather, the film demonstrates that the roots of war and war-like conduct stem from feelings of inadequacy enacted on both national and personal levels by persons from *each* side of the conflict. Probably because of being Japanese, Nagisa Ôshima had no difficulty in displaying the brutality of the Japanese prisoner-of-war camps, but he had no hesitation in demonstrating that the cause of the war resided on both sides. As can be seen in the films of Ozu and Kurasawa, the Pacific War fundamentally changed how the Japanese viewed themselves.

NOTHING IS THE SAME: POSTWAR JAPAN IN KUROSAWA AND OZU

Most postwar Japanese cinema takes into account both the physical devastation Japan suffered and the monumental psychological and socio-economic changes imposed by MacArthur's Occupation. In this section, I shall focus only on two examples: Akira Kurosawa's Stray Dog (*Nora inu*) from 1949 and Yasujirô Ozu's Tokyo Story (*Tokyo monogatari*) from 1953. I choose these two because both directors heavily influenced some of the Western films to be considered later in this book and because both films encapsulate—in very different but significant ways—the fragile, fractured postwar Japanese sensibility.

The soldier returned from battle became a staple in Kurosawa films. There is Yuzo in *One Wonderful Sunday (Subarashki nichiyobi,* 1947), Matsunaga in *Drunken Angel (Yoidore tenshi,* 1948)*,* Fujisaki and Nakata in *The Quite Duel (Shizukanuru ketto,* 1949) and Kamada in *The Idiot (Hakuchi,* 1951). In *Stray Dog,* both the homicide detective, Murakami (Mifune Toshiro) and his prey, the murderer Yusa (Kimura Isao), have served as soldiers in the War.

The credit image for *Stray Dog* shows a dog panting for air. This sequence consists of one long shot, followed by a shorter one. The dog's open mouth, sharp teeth, and extended tongue confront the viewer; the dog does not have a collar and is thus a stray; the sound of the dog's heavy breathing begins and ends his appearance with strong dramatic music filling the middle portion of the sequence. No dog appears in the film's remaining diegetic space.

The film's story centers on Murakami and his efforts to recover his stolen handgun. The overzealous young police officer is ham-fisted in this endeavor. He then partners with the older, fatherly Sato (Shimura Takashi). Eventually, at the film's climax, Sato is shot by Yusa, and only then does Murakami—and the audience—confront the criminal face-to face. After a tussle, Murakami handcuffs Yusa.

In the film's most celebrated sequence, Murakami disguises himself as a homeless veteran. "Yet because he was a returned soldier," as Mitsushiro Yoshimoto observes, "he is not really in disguise but plays the role of himself."[34] In a nine-minute sequence, he roams through the black market. With almost no dialogue but accompanied by documentary montage with wipes, dissolves, superimpositions, diegetic sounds, and a variety of close-ups, he searches for his lost weapon. Symbolically, this city landscape becomes postwar Japan: chaotic, orderless, and ruthless.

Murakami wants his gun back because it has been stolen from him. As the story progresses, however, he becomes aware that

Yusa is using that weapon to kill. There is a sense that he wants his property restored to him at the same time he feels that his personal honor has been blackened because his gun has been used as a murder weapon. The Japanese word for "bullet mark" (*dankon*) also means penis or phallus. Therefore, it can be argued that Murakami's manhood has been threatened by the loss of the gun. Only by re-possessing his property can he regain his sense of a shattered masculinity.

Murakami's partner, Sato, a much calmer, more logical pursuer of those who commit evil, has very clear ideas about good and evil. When the pair visits Sato's home about halfway through the film, the older man's obvious pleasure in his wife and children are highlighted. As far as Sato is concerned, he is a good man whose job is to catch evil ones. Neither Murakami nor Kurosawa is comfortable with this uninflected point of view.

FIGURE 4 Murakami (Toshiro Mifune), left, and Sato (Takashi Shimura) stalk a suspect in *Stray Dog*.

Murakami's constant state of agitation—his sometimes-overpowering feelings of guilt—stem from his sense of identification with Sato, who functions as a kind of doppelgänger, a ghostly likeness or double. Both Murakami and Sato have served their country in the war. In returning to civilian life, Murakami wants to fit into postwar Japanese society, although, as the film shows, he is having a great deal of difficulty doing so. Noma Hiroshi, a writer who emerged during the Occupation as an important intellectual, argued that returned soldiers were treated as stray dogs both by their former master (the Emperor) and by the new democratic government.[35] In obviously seeing a strong reflection of himself in Yusa, Murikami is appalled.

One of the film's central ironies is that Yusa began his crime spree because his girlfriend Harumi (Keiko Awaji) craved a Western-style dress that she saw in a shop window: such an alluring entity is beyond her reach in Occupied Japan and the sly suggestion might be that Yusa's criminal behavior is linked to his pursuit of a Western-made commodity.

At the film's conclusion, when Murakami visits the wounded Sato in hospital, the older man assures him that the memory of Yusa will eventually fade from Muramachi's consciousness. However, he cannot accept this bland assurance, and this is obviously Kurosawa's point: Japan has become a place steeped in moral ambiguity.

Kurosawa (1910-1998) served his apprenticeship with PCL, which was re-named Toho, during the war years whereas the older Ozu (1903-63) was a fairly well established filmmaker when he was conscripted in 1937 (he served in China). He returned to filmmaking in Japan but was then drafted again in 1943 to make a propaganda film in Burma. However, he spent most of his time in Singapore, where he saw a number of American films, including Walt Disney's *Fantasia*. The technical brilliance of that film convinced him that the United States would win the war.

Ozu's films are often said correctly to be infused with *mono no aware* (a sense of the impermanence of all things), and he used the genre *gendai-geki* (family stories) to comment on the state of the Japanese family and thus to reflect on the intricate, far-ranging changes introduced into Japanese society during his lifetime. For him, like Kurosawa, uncertainty invaded every aspect of Japanese existence after World War II.

However, Ozu's postwar films are not so much about the destruction of the family unit as they are about the changes introduced during the Occupation and afterwards into that most fundamental of all social structures. Ozu may have had a conservative eye that felt change had not been beneficial to family values, but he was very accepting of the fact that his fellow Japanese had to adapt to a changing world. His may be a searching, critical viewpoint but it was also a deeply compassionate one.[36]

Tokyo Story is seemingly straightforward. An elderly couple from Onomichi—Shukichi (Chishû Ryû) and Tomi (Chieko Higashiyama)—leave their single daughter Kyoko (Kyoko Kagawa) behind and travel to Tokyo to visit their son, Koichi (So Yamamura) and daughter, Shige (Haruko Sugimura). However, it is only Noriko (Setsuko Hara), the widow of their son Shoji, killed in the Pacific, who seems genuinely pleased to see them. In fact, brother and sister, anxious not to have to deal with their parents, send them to a spa at Atami. The old couple finds that place noisy and unrestful and return to Tokyo, where they have no place to stay. Mother visits Noriko whereas father goes out drinking with old friends. They eventually set out for home, but mother becomes ill in Osaka. Shortly afterwards they reach home, where mother dies. The children arrive for the funeral but head back to Tokyo quickly. Only Noriko remains to help. As she leaves, father thanks her, urges her to remarry and gives her his wife's watch.

Koichi and Shige lead busy lives and seem engulfed in the Tokyo rat race. Koichi is not as successful as he would like to be, and his two sons are disrespectful, self-centered little boys. Hard-working Shige is doing everything to make her hairdressing salon a success. There is one hint of discord about the past that is voiced by Shige: she remembers her father coming home drunk and these events may have frightened or traumatized her as a child. In any event, she is not pleased when father shows up drunk at her home after a night on the town. The scene is played comically, but it has melancholic reverberations.

The fallout from excessive drinking is indirectly referred to in the long sequence during which Tomi stays with Noriko in her small, cheaply furnished tenement apartment. Concerned about her daughter-in-law, Tomi tells her to marry if she has a chance.

FIGURE 5 Tomi (Chieko Higashiyama) and her daughter-in law Noriko (Setsuko Hara) in *Tokyo Story*.

(Before the War, under the idealized *ie* system, a widowed daughter-in-law would have been taken in by her husband's family; this convention became defunct after the war.) Shoji has been dead for nine years, and yet his photograph holds pride of place in the flat. This is not right, Tomi reflects. "I feel sorry for you. You're young." Reluctantly, Noriko agrees to consider remarrying. Tomi then makes a reference to the fact that Noriko's marriage gave her "more trouble than happiness." Then she makes an even more oblique statement: "We should have done something." From earlier references in the film, it is clear that Shoji was a heavy, perhaps abusive drinker. Tomi obviously feels that she and Shukichi should have intervened. (Of course, the film may be indirectly talking about alcoholism as a destructive force in pre-War Japan).

After Koichi and Shige rush back to Tokyo after their mother's funeral, Kyoko and Noriko have an exchange. The younger woman denounces the insensitive behavior of her siblings. Noriko reminds her that children drift away from their parents. "I may become like that in spite of myself."

Kyoko: Isn't life disappointing?
Noriko (smiling): Yes. It is.

People are who they are, Noriko is reminding Kyoko. Not much can be done to alter that fact. The words have an added force because Noriko has, up to this point in the film, seemed to be suffused with both a tender melancholy and a stoic resignation. Even she, it would seem, is capable of bitterness and regret.

In the film's penultimate long scene, Shukichi, having been informed by his deceased wife of her conversation with Noriko, reiterates Tomi's admonition that their daughter-in-law re-marry.

Shukichi: Thank you for everything. You have been a great help...[My wife] was worried about your future. I want to see you married soon. It hurts me to see you going on like this.
Noriko: I'm not always thinking of your son, although you think I am.
Shukichi: I'll be happy if you forget him.
Noriko: Often I don't think about him for days.

Sometimes I feel I can't go on like this forever. Often, when going to sleep, I wonder what will become of me if I stay this way. I'm selfish.

"No, you are not," Shukichi admonishes her. He reminds her that she has been far more generous to him and his wife than his own children in Tokyo and then gives her his wife's "old-fashioned" pocket watch: "Take it for her sake." Overcome by the gift, Noriko bursts into tears.

On the train back to Tokyo, a very sober faced Noriko looks at the face of the watch, puts it away and then stares ahead, the slightest of smiles crossing her face. Whether she will accept the freedom bestowed upon her by her in-laws remains a mystery.

Both Kurosawa and Ozu conclude their films with austere uncertainties. Murakami is very hesitant in accepting the simple black and white morality of Sato: he feels that he now lives in an increasingly complex and perhaps destructive world. Noriko has been made aware that she can change her style of existence, but it is impossible to know if she will be able to take advantage of the freedoms of the new postwar social culture of Japan. In *Bridge to the Sun*, the changes visited upon Japan in the Thirties and Forties are also closely examined.

MARRIED TO THE ENEMY: *BRIDGE TO THE SUN*

Despite a surfeit of melodramatic moments, the American-made *A Bridge to the Sun* embraces some of the complexities examined by Kurosawa and Ozu. A film centered on adaptation, it is told from the viewpoint of an American woman who falls in love with a Japanese diplomat, marries him, and subsequently lives in Japan during World War II. The director, Brussels-native Etienne Périer (b. 1931), who had directed three films before *Bridge to the Sun* and went on to have a prolific career in both movies and television, excels at establishing mise en scène and moving the film along crisply.

45

At a cocktail party at the Japanese Embassy in Washington, D.C. in the summer of 1935, twenty-one year old Gwen Harold from Johnson City in the blue mountains of Tennessee meets Hidenari Terasaki, the Ambassador's private secretary. Smitten by Gwen, Terasaki [Terry] comes to her assistance when she drops her lipstick into some food and cannot retrieve it. Theirs is a whirlwind romance, although at the outset she is "a bit ashamed" of the strong attraction she feels for a Japanese man. The opening sequences make it clear that the Japanese are seen in racist terms by some Americans at the party. One woman, when looking for a washroom, observes: "they must have a powder room even if they are Japanese." When her aunt frets when Gwen has wandered off with Terasaki, the young man accompanying them comments: "Except for politics, they [the Japanese] are harmless little people."

As the courtship enfolds, Gwen's aunt becomes perturbed. She does not welcome such an alliance, although she concedes: "He is a lovely man for an Oriental, so clean and proper." Gwen retaliates: she loves him because he is strong, tender, and fearless. Ambassador Debuchi summons Gwen in order to express his strong disapproval of inter-racial marriage. In tears, she rushes out of his office and then telephones Terry to tell him that the marriage is off. About to set off by train for Tennessee, one of the Ambassador's assistants rushes up to Gwen and announces that Terry, who had just learned of her encounter with Debuchi, had informed his boss he will leave the foreign service if he is not allowed to marry the woman he loves. Then Terry appears. Gwen, overcome with happiness, rapturously embraces him.

This outline of the film's first twenty minutes is at odds with the written memoir, where the meeting, courtship and subsequent engagement of Gwen and Terry are presented as much more matter-of-fact events. There were ripples in the courtship; for instance, Ambassador Debuchi did object to the marriage. However, in her memoir, Gwen stresses personal, rather than racial, differences between her and Terry: "I realized that whoever married Terry would have to get her way by indirect means; he was a forceful, dominating person."[37]

In order to make a successful adaptation—one which would tell the "true" story of a successful marriage between an American woman and a Japanese man—the filmmakers obviously felt that they would have to hit hard at certain events, particularly the impact of Pearl Harbor on the lives of the two protagonists and their subsequent harsh existence in wartime Japan. In order to do this, racial conflict was highlighted in a manner absent from the printed text. When the now-married Gwen and Terry arrive in Japan in 1931, the film emphasizes the xenophobia visited upon Gwen by the Japanese, and Gwen is also portrayed as a somewhat gauche American rebuffing stuffy Japanese customs in etiquette and social behavior. Japan is revealed to be a culture where women are very much in second place and accept their sorry lot. One evening, angry at the male "fraternity meeting" that keeps women at a safe distance, Gwen voices her displeasure at Japanese militarism.

A bit earlier, the movie introduces a cactus, given to Gwen by her mother, into the story line. The plant is kept by Gwen as a souvenir of the United States. In the midst of the heated argument following Gwen's outburst, Terry hurls the plant outdoors. Later, repenting his behavior, he returns it to his wife, who apologizes for forgetting her place and acting like a "shameless hussy." Terry tells her: "I don't want a Japanese wife—I want you!" During the same encounter, Gwen reveals to Terry that she is pregnant. When Mako is born, Terry hopes that she will be a "bridge across the Pacific" and thus be a physical embodiment of their marriage across races. Symbolically, the cactus represents the thorny status of this inter-racial marriage—the fact that the couple comes from divergent backgrounds—but its restoration suggests that this merging of opposites can work. "Advanced" attitudes Gwen may have in her memoir, but she does not act upon them: she never "shames" her husband and his friends publicly.

The film then fast-forwards ten years to Pearl Harbor. Terry has been re-assigned to the Embassy in Washington. On that fateful day in December 1941, Gwen, accompanied by her aunt and Mako, attends a matinee. When the small group arrives back at their hotel, passers-by in the lobby exclaim, "They don't know what's happened!" Terry telephones and orders her and Mako to stay behind in the States while he returns to Japan. Meanwhile, Gwen's maid leaves, shouting at her: "No yellow rats are going to slit my throat!" When an FBI agent appears at her door and tells her that she is free to remain behind, Gwen tells him: "What American wife would not wish to go with her husband?" Her aunt intervenes: "They'll tear you to pieces over there!" On her way to the rail station, someone shouts: "She's no Jap! She's a white woman!"

As far as Gwen is concerned, there is no question of remaining behind. At the rail station, she reminds her husband, "We were here before." Back in Japan, angry students accost Gwen and demand that she walk on the American flag. An official at the War Office demands she be shipped back to the States. During a bombing raid, Gwen frantically searches for Mako, who, it is revealed, is being hazed by schoolmates for being "American." All these events are absent from the memoir. Film and text diverge the least when it comes to the war years, although the film consistently introduces fictional elements: a female servant betrays peace-activist Terry; Mako comes perilously close to dying during another bombing raid—her close friend is killed; Gwen becomes furious at Terry for giving precious rice to an underling. In that encounter she asks him if she and Mako count for anything. She then remonstrates against a culture that places duty before humanity. Terry becomes irate, at which point she apologetically beseeches him, "Love me a little, Terry. Please." Later, Terry is sought by the police and escapes. Then the bombings of Hiroshima and Nagasaki are mentioned; the Emperor makes his radio broadcast; and, at last, there is peace.

The last ten minutes of the film are devoted to Terry's increasingly bad health and his desire for Gwen and Mako to return to the United States. He does not explain his reason for wanting them to leave, although it is clear that he knows he dying and does not wish them to see him in his increasingly frail state. A Japanese friend tells Gwen: "Death may be beautiful; dying is not." Mother and daughter leave Japan aboard an ocean liner: this scene compliments that in which Gwen first arrived in Japan with Terry. Before she departs, Terry maintains he has given Gwen "a bad life." She assures him she "wouldn't have had it any other way." The film closes with a close-up of Gwen's face suffused with melancholic stoicism.

When she arrived in Japan in November 1960, thirty-year old Carroll Baker was no stranger to controversy. Four years before, she had starred in Elia Kazan's *Baby Doll* (1956), variously labeled by critics as salacious, revolting, steamy, morally repellent and provocative. *Time Magazine* dubbed it: "Just possibly the dirtiest American-made motion picture that has ever been legally exhibited." New York's Cardinal Spellman declared the film "evil in concept... certain to exert an immoral and corrupting influence on those who see it." This stark Southern drama was so viciously denounced by the Legion of Decency upon its release with a "C" (for condemned) rating that many theaters were forced to cancel their showings. The advertisements and posters featured a sultry young "Baby Doll" curled up in a crib in a suggestive pose, sucking her thumb. The young actress portraying the precocious, 19 year-old Baby Doll received a Best Actress Academy Award nomination. Filmed on location in rural Benoit, Mississippi, the film was based on Tennessee Williams' first original film screenplay, interweaving and adapting two of his earlier one-act plays: *Twenty-Seven Wagons Full of Cotton* and

The Long Stay Cut Short (aka *The Unsatisfactory Supper*). Five years earlier, Kazan's film version of *A Streetcar Named Desire* had been released to acclaim.

Middle-aged Archie Lee (Karl Malden) and Baby Doll live in a dilapidated plantation house in Tiger's Tail County, Mississippi. Their two-year marriage has not been consummated because Archie promised her father he would not touch her until she was "ready." Archie is forced to peek at his squirming, half-dressed child bride through a hole in her bedroom wall. Archie's self-esteem is further punctured by Silva Vaccaro (Eli Wallach), a business rival. Silva and Baby Doll play hide and seek in the absence of her husband and, later, they flirt openly in front of Archie, who then attempts to kill Silva. At the end of the film, Archie is carted off to prison, and Silva decides he is more interested in his business than in Baby Doll, who now has to wait what the future will bring.

Two years younger than Baker, James Shigeta was born in Hawaii of Japanese ancestry. He studied drama at New York University and then won first prize on a television talent show. During the Korean War, he enlisted in the Marines and subsequently moved to Japan where he starred in four musical films.

In 1959 he played Detective Joe Kojaku in Samuel Fuller's *The Crimson Kimono*. In Shigeta's first American film, Sugar Torch, a Los Angeles stripper, is shot in the neck by a man dressed in a fedora and trench coat. Homicide detectives Charlie Bancroft (Glenn Corbett) and Kojaku, who happen to be roommates, investigate. A variety of clues, including a painting with a bullet hole in it, lead them to Los Angeles' Little Tokyo and to an attractive artist Chris Downs (Victoria Shaw). As the case builds to a climax, Charlie and Joe's partnership is threatened by an interracial love triangle. Chris chooses Joe over Charlie, and the relationship between the two men barely survives.

In casting Baker and Shigeta in *Bridge to the Sun*, Warner Brothers chose two actors who had excellent credentials: Baker's celebrity status had been established by playing a young woman married to a middle-aged man, and Shigeta had been the victor in Fuller's film where he vanquished his white-skinned competitor. In order to ensure that the film would fully exploit the tensions in an inter-racial coupling, two fictional characters were introduced into the film: Jiro (Tetsurô Tanba) and Ishi (Hiroshi Tomono).

FIGURE 6 The theme of cross-racial love is emphasized in this poster for *Bridge to the Sun*.

Jiro, a long-time friend of Terry, works for the foreign office. When he first meets Gwen, he expresses his disdain for her and, in a moment of great insensitivity, suggests that his friend find comfort in the arms of a Japanese woman rather than in those of outspoken Gwen. Later, depicted as a rabid supporter of Tojo during the last days of the War, he attempts to blackmail Gwen by requesting that she appear with the traitor, Tokyo Rose. There is no such villain in the memoir, but the filmmakers obviously felt they needed one in order to give tension to the story line.

Ishi, a young relative of Terry, is first characterized as a naïve young man; during the war he becomes a kamikaze who upbraids Gwen for her pacific inclinations; in a later scene, he is shown dying. The young man's face is filled with anguish, but he sends his wife away so that he can die alone (this foreshadows Terry's separation from Gwen at the end of the film).

Although Gwen Terasaki's book makes it clear that her husband was—and remained—a peace activist before and during the War, the film—except for one instance—downplays this central aspect of the memoir. Just before Pearl Harbor, Terry and some colleagues enlisted the assistance of the Rev. E. Stanley Jones, a prominent Methodist, an internationally known peace activist, and a friend of Franklin Delano Roosevelt, to approach the President early in December 1941 to request he send a cable directly to Emperor Hirohito. By so doing, it was hoped that that the Emperor would order Tojo to cease his aggressive stance towards the United States. The cable was not sent until two days before Pearl Harbor. The film toys with this event in a manner implying that there was a distinct possibility that such an intervention could have prevented Pearl Harbor.

Gwen Terasaki's memoir is carefully, sometimes densely written. She makes no attempt to proselytize miscegenation. In fact, her agenda is to tell the story of her marriage in a straightforward manner, although she recognizes that her life as an American woman living in Japan during the Pacific War is the obvious selling point of her autobiography. The film is never so content. At one point in her memoir, Gwen goes to the hairdresser to have a "charcoal permanent" (in which heated charcoal was substituted for electricity). "As the operator began to remove the ash-filled clips, I held my breath. Everyone was silent again, watching the operator work. They could not have been more attentive had I been Medusa having my snakes arranged. The hair was unrolled, and the curls were elastic and radiant."[38] In the film, Gwen has her hair done as some sort of appeasement to Terry with whom she has been quarrelling. She is appalled by the hairdo and rushes home to wash it out.

In the film, Gwen, somewhat bumptiously, refuses to look down when the Emperor Hirohito's procession goes by. Later, an archival clip of the Emperor, along with some of Hitler and Mussolini, is introduced. Gwen Terasaki actually met the Emperor twice after the war, but this encounter is of no interest to the filmmakers. Also, a lengthy section of the book describes the degrading living conditions and starvation in Japan after the surrender. This is excised from the film.

As Gina Marchetti has observed, this film is also careless about period details: "Throughout most of the film, Carroll Baker wears billowy A-line skirts, tight at the waist, often cut low at the bodice, characteristic of women's fashions of the late 1950s and early 1960s."[39] A similar lack of due diligence so invades the transformation of printed memoir into film text that of necessity the question must be asked: does the film do justice to its source? This query could be more precisely focused: does the film— despite manifest and important deviations from its source— still manage to capture its essence?

Terasaki's memoir is consistently even-handed—it disdains sensationalism. The strength of the book lies in large part on the author's sympathetic depiction of her adopted country. In many ways, this is an immigration narrative that proposes, as does the title, that bridges between nations and races can be crossed.[40] The same can be said of the film but the question remains: does the film ultimately betray the book? The easy answer is that it does. On balance, however, this may not be a just response.

Without doubt, the memoir was intended to celebrate an unusual marriage between an American and a Japanese. Both the film and the printed text highlight the fact that sensibilities that *could* be labeled nationalistic were present in each person. Gwen tends to be more outspoken than her husband. Throughout their marriage, Terry craved personal space apart from his wife, but he extended this sense of privacy to his wife: throughout their marriage he always, to her dismay, knocked before entering her bedroom.

At the beginning of the film, Baker's Southern drawl accentuates her naivety. She modulates her accent as the film progresses and, at the very same time, her performance becomes more controlled and deliberate: this is a woman who determinedly makes her way through uncharted waters. Shigeta does not deviate in his rendering of Terry: he has the capacity to become violently angry with Gwen, but his habitual state of mind is tranquil. In the book and in the film, Terry's desire that Gwen and Mako leave Japan when he becomes gravely ill is never sufficiently explicated.

Bridge to the Sun reminds its viewers that racism cuts both ways and that such attitudes impair understanding. Before the viewer's eyes, Gwen changes from a slightly flirtatious, frivolous young woman to a person of substance. She retains her American identity, but she attempts to understand and adopt Japanese customs. Her task of living as an alien in Japan during the War is assisted by the fact that her husband is sympathetic to the Allies. Her Japan remains a "foreign" land, but she leaves there enabled by her experiences.

In order to draw the viewer into the action on screen, the filmmakers decided to embroider their source with melodramatic moments that keep the narrative line emotionally charged. The end result produces a completely different kind of narrative from the book but one that does succeed in showing a successful inter-racial marriage. In essence, the film, although a heavily fictionalized version of Gwen Terasaki's autobiography, succeeds in establishing the same emotional truths established in the printed text. (Two years after *Bridge to the Sun* appeared, Betty Friedan's *The Feminine Mystique* was published, and the film may reflect issues raised by the Women's Movement in the 1950s.)

If, as Walter Benjamin claimed, "storytelling is the art of repeating stories"[41], this film version's art is to repeat the story with intriguing fictional components. *Bridge to the Sun* recreates the printed text with considerable verve: it recasts the story of the non-fiction memoir in cinematic terms and, in the process, infuses the book with a new quasi-fictional existence. The film may have a vastly different notion than its source of what is authentic in recreating Gwen Terasaki's life, but the result nevertheless respects the idea of Japan as a nation with vastly different values from that of the West. In this film, the Other of Japan is rendered neither superior to nor inferior to the West. As the film takes its course, exoticness becomes an irrelevant issue, and cultural dissimilarities are validated.

CHAPTER TWO

FILMING THE UNTHINKABLE

In *Bridge to the Sun*, Gwen Terasaki, then resident in Japan, does not refer to Hiroshima when the reader would expect it to occur in her narrative. Rather, she mentions a visitor—"a three-hundred-pound faith healer"—whom she met in the postwar years:

> He was a survivor of Hiroshima. When the bomb was dropped he was awaiting his *shôsen* (tramcar) at the railway station and had fallen unconscious into a drainage ditch. Sometime later he awoke. The siren was stilled, the planes were gone, and there was only emptiness where the station had been, but as he related it to us it appeared his greatest concern was that his clothes had been burned off. He arose and ran to his little house four miles away. When he got there his surviving child did not recognize him for his skin was a livid black. Having no medicine, he put potato juice in a mixture made from tea leaves on his burns. His wife and one child had been killed along with almost everyone he knew. He wondered why he had been spared. He came to think that the homemade remedy he had concocted had saved him and believed that he had been endowed with special curative powers and had a mission to perform. That was how he had become a faith healer. I remember his face, covered with keloids and scars from the after-effects of the bomb.[1]

As well, the movie version of *Bridge to the Sun* makes passing reference to what happened in Hiroshima and Nagasaki, almost as it would be inappropriate to dwell on this subject.

That problem did not deter the US War department from

releasing "A Tale of Two Cities" in 1946, nor did any such obstacle prevent Universal Newsreels from showing "Atom Blast at Hiroshima," (1946) taken from Japanese footage. In the former, various American soldiers, acting as tour guides, wander around in the debris left by the bomb. Buildings and bridges are examined as to how they withstood its impact. Very little mention is made of the loss of human life, almost as if the film is dealing with uninhabited terrain. Hiroshima became, the narrator moralistically observes, "the funeral pyre of an aggressive nation." In the later film, the footage was "taken," the voice-over states, "by the Japs." Both films are obviously meant to serve as warnings about the consequences of war-like behavior towards the Western allies by any future warmongering nation.

After six months of fire-bombing various Japanese cities, President Harry S. Truman, apparently frustrated because the Japanese government had ignored the ultimatum given in the Potsdam Declaration, ordered the nuclear weapon, "Little Boy" (evidently a reference to the late Franklin Delano Roosevelt) to be dropped on Hiroshima on August 6, 1945. Three days later, "Fat Boy"(named after Churchill) was detonated over Nagasaki. Within the first two to four months after the bombings, 90,000-165,000 persons died in Hiroshima, 60,00 to 80,000 in Nagasaki. Half of the deaths in each city occurred on the actual day of bombing. Approximately sixty per cent of those in Hiroshima were killed from flash or flame burns, thirty per cent from falling debris and the remainder from other causes. Afterwards, large numbers of people died of radiation sickness, flash burns and from various cancers.

Six days after the detonation over Nagasaki, the Japanese surrendered to the Allies; the Instrument of Surrender was signed on September 2.

The bare facts of Hiroshima can be put on paper or they can be made into newsreel footage, but what are the psychological implications of this incident? What kind of transgression was perpetrated on the Japanese? These are the difficult questions.

Alain Resnais felt that the issue of Hiroshima had to be handled with considerable restraint. According to him, Hiroshima presented a paradox: it was an event that deserved to be examined cinematically and yet, at the same time, it could not really be filmed. How, he asked, can that which is ultimately "unthinkable" be placed on celluloid? Ultimately, he made a film about not making a film about Hiroshima. Shôhei Imamura paid a heavy psychic price when he decided to show the unshowable. In this chapter, I shall look at his later *Black Rain* before examining *Hiroshima Mon Amour*. Both directors, in their vastly different ways, took enormous risks in daring to ask meaningful questions about nuclear holocaust.

FICTIONALIZING HIROSHIMA: SHÔHEI IMAMURA'S *BLACK RAIN*

Previous to making *Black Rain* (*Kuroi Ame*; 1989), Shôhei Imamura was no stranger to controversy. Before he studied Western history at Waseda University after the war, he sold cigarettes and liquor on the black market. A perpetual malcontent, he disliked the Japanese studio system; he also found considerable fault with Ozu, to whom he served as an assistant on *Tokyo Story*. In 1958-9 he completed four B-movies for Nikkatsu within eighteen months before beginning work on what could be called his first signature film, *Pigs and Battleships* (*Buta no Gunkan*), released in 1961. This tragi-comedy about yakuza dealing in black-market pigs at a US Navy base in Yokosuka went seriously over-budget, and Immamura was not allowed another project for two years.

In *The Insect Woman* (*Nippon Konchûki*; 1963), Tome is a born survivor who becomes a prostitute and, ultimately, a madam: she has a strong animal-like ability to exploit the men who would exploit her. *The Pornographers* (*Jinruigaku Nyumon*) of 1966 is about a seller of blue movies who eventually abandons all human contact. The lengthy, exploit-filled 1979 *Vengeance is Mine* (*Fukushu Suru-wa Ware ni Ari*) recreates in grim detail the manic sprees of a real-life sociopath. In the 1970s Imamura directed two documentaries: *History of Postwar Japan as Told by a Bar Hostess* (*Nippon Sengoshi-Madama onboro no Sikatsu*) and *Karayuki-san, the Making of a Prostitute*. He once claimed that he liked making messy films and added: "I've always wanted to ask questions about the Japanese because they're the only people I'm qualified to describe."

Imamura's career, therefore, had been devoted to both the sensational and the chaotic when he undertook work on *Black Rain*, but he restrained himself in recreating the events of August 1945. That day occupies relatively little of the film's time — most of the action takes place in 1950 — and the events of the fateful day are presented in a melodramatic, almost hackneyed manner that cannot compete with newsreel footage. Also, Imamura had a great deal of difficulty ending the film. First, he shot the film in high contrast black and white with a twenty-minute coda in color. When he decided to cancel the coda, he had to reassemble many of the actors to re-shoot an ending in black and white.

Shizuma Shigematsu (Kazuo Kitamura) and his wife are the guardians of their niece Yasuko (Yoshiko Tanaka). On the morning of August 6, Yasuko hitches a ride with a neighbor in order to transfer her family's ancestral clothes for safekeeping to a friend's home on a nearby island. During a tea ceremony there, Tasuko and her companions experience a blinding flash of light. They hurry outside to see a huge mushroom cloud. Concerned about her guardians, Yasuko boards a boat to Hiroshima and, along the way, encounters the radioactive fallout (black rain) from the bomb. Arriving in Hiroshima, she finds her relatives. They walk through the ruins of the city en route to seeking a safe refuge at the factory where Mr Shizuma works.

Five years later, the trio attempt to rebuild their lives in the rural village of Takafuta. Husband and wife are demonstrating initial symptoms of radiation poisoning, although Yasuko appears to be symptom free. However, she cannot find a husband because it is suspected that she, like so many others who were in Hiroshima on the fateful day, has somehow been contaminated. Despite the fact that her uncle produces certificates attesting to her good health, she begins to warn off suitors. In fact, the only male with whom she forms a bond is Yuichi (Keisuke Ishida), a poor man who carves *jizô* (statues of the mendicant Buddha); as a result of his experience as a soldier in the war, he suffers from a form of post-traumatic stress disorder which compels him to attack passing motor vehicles as if they were tanks.

Ibuse Masuji's novel (on which the film is based) ends with the extremely ill Yasuko being taken to hospital, from which she will presumably not emerge. Before shooting began, however, Imamura decided to end the film with a twenty-minute color sequence in which all of the members of her family having died, Yasuko sets off at the age of forty on a pilgrimage of atonement. On her journey, she encounters an old man she had met on the day of the Hiroshima explosion and travels with him until he passes away.

One day, she comes across a studio where Yuichi is carving; she hides from him, but she overhears a conversation in which she learns that he is patiently awaiting her return. In the final sequence in which she appears, Yatsuko comes across a glade in which there are statues of the various people from her past; they come briefly to life and then return to their mineral state. Then, the viewer is transported to present-day Hiroshima, where women are hawking souvenirs: roof-tile fragments from the atomic blast. Then, as the camera moves back to the Hiroshima Museum, the voice-over states: "Yes, indeed, an unjust peace is still better than a just war." The camera view soars into the sky, presumably to the same altitude at which the bomb was detonated.

Throughout filming, Takashi Miike, who served as second

assistant director, saw Imamura as a man constantly in battle with others (particularly Ibuse Masuji) but really, Miike felt, the director was struggling with his own inner demons. The younger man felt the director "forged me into something," but he nevertheless did not appreciate his boss's constant bad temper.

Yoshiko Tanaka had been impressed with the director's resolve that she and the other cast members live in an isolated rural village during the filming—he did not want them returning to Tokyo lest they be contaminated by the metropolitan environment. Having returned to her "normal" life in Tokyo, she was startled when informed that the color sequence was to be cancelled and that a "new" black and white ending filmed.

The decision—an astounding reversal—to end the film in accordance with the novel's conclusion seems to have been Imamura's. He may have realized that the coda gave a sense of closure to Hiroshima whereas no such resolution should really be possible. The kinds of dilemmas that confronted Imamura during the making of his Hiroshima film haunted Resnais earlier in the making of *Hiroshima Mon Amour*. Like Immamura, making a film about Hiroshima unleashed his inner demons. Before that, he had taken on the Holocaust.

THE VARIETIES OF UNKNOWING IN *NIGHT AND FOG*

Alain Resnais has never shirked away from challenging projects. His early career as a maker of short documentary films led to high words of praise from Jean-Luc Godard:

> If the short film hadn't existed, Alain Resnais surely would have invented it.... From the blind, trembling pans of *Van Gogh* to the majestic travelling shots of *Styrène*, what in effect do we see? A survey of the possibilities of cinematographic technique, but such a demanding one, that it finishes by surpassing itself, in such a way that the modern young French cinema could not have existed without it. For Alain Resnais

more than anyone else gives the impression that he completely started over at zero.[2]

Beginning from scratch is certainly what Resnais attempted with both these short films.

Resnais rather proudly claimed that *Van Gogh* (1948) "incurred numerous criticisms." The chief offense for many was that he presented the artist as someone who, completely committed to his work, "felt the appearance of things escaping him." Nature struck him in the face because paradoxically his entire identity was subsumed into it. Unable to bear his separation from Nature and thus endure the loss of the ability to paint, he killed himself. Resnais selected paintings by Van Gogh to show the gradual blurring of the painter's sense of self-identity. The commentary states that he took his life as a free choice, but the repeated, bludgeoning close-ups of the sun contradict this assertion. In describing the technical problems associated with *Van Gogh*, Resnais wrote:

> [The film] concerns itself, in effect, with finding out if painted trees, painted houses, can, in a narrative, thanks to the montage of the cinema, serve to take the place of real objects, and if, in this case, it is possible to substitute for the spectator, and almost without his knowledge, the internal or interior world of an artist, a world such as is revealed by photography. [3]

Capturing an "interior world" is one of the most difficult tasks in filmmaking, Resnais is asserting, but it is a task to which he has committed himself throughout his career. He even bestows the semblance of an interior world on plastic.

Le Chant du Stryène (1958) traces the manufacture of polystyrene backwards from the manufactured product, "across the desert of pipe work, towards the raw material, towards the abstract matter."[4] The commissioned poem by Raymond Queneau reads in part: "D'où viens tu? Qui es-tu? et qu'est-ce qui explique/ Tes rares qualités? De quoi donc es-tu fait?/ D'où donc es-tu parti?" (Whence come you? Who are you? and who can explain/ Your rare qualities? Of what, in fact, are you made?/ Where, in fact, do you come from?)[5] Scientifically, these questions can be answered but ontologically, the poem and film are suggesting, it is a different matter.

Toute la mémoire du monde (1956) uses what became Resnais' trademark long tracking shots to explore the treasures of the Bibliothèque Nationale. Since human beings have fragile memories, books have been written and then stored in libraries, where they are imprisoned, the film argues. The books—each of which has a distinct personality—must be catalogued because otherwise they would exist in fortresses in which they could not be located.

In *Guernica* (1950), about Picasso's monumental anti-war canvas, the point is made that the people of that Spanish town were treated as objects that could easily be destroyed: "We read it all in the papers, drinking our coffee: somewhere in Europe a legion of assassins were crushing a human ant-heap." Even if the world in 1937 was not indifferent to the Spanish Civil War, how could they "hold back death"? How could they "explain to a mother the death of her child?"

Les Statues Meurent Aussi (1950-3), co-directed with Chris Marker, was commissioned by Présence Africaine and is about the decline in the quality of indigenous Black art as a result of contamination from Western influences; it was banned in France until 1965, although it was shown at the Cannes Film Festival in 1953. In his early career, Resnais remained committed to controversial social causes.

Like *Les Statues Meurent Aussi*, *Night and Fog* experienced censorship problems. Initially, it was withdrawn from Cannes in 1956. The stated motive was that the French government did not want to offend West Germany. The real reason, however, is that French complicity in war crimes was highlighted by a five second shot which showed the Pithiviers assembly camp: in the control tower a French gendarme was readily visible. A film about châteaux was inserted into the Cannes lineup in place of Resnais' film. Then, the newspapers accused the government of cowardice, and eighteen members of the selection committee for the festival threatened to resign. Finally, after two months of negotiations, the producers agreed to alter the image by covering the gendarme's uniform, and *Night and Fog* was granted a slot out of competition.

How does one capture the reality of Auschwitz as a concentration camp? Resnais tackles this problem head-on with the tracking shots that begin the film. The present (always in color) is in many ways an unsatisfactory fragment of the past. The buildings of torture remain, but they look like factories or storage facilities. Nature has intervened and softened this landscape.

From the glare of the present, the film moves into combining black and white documentary footage and still photos showing the disappeared "reality" of the camps. In black and white, the viewer is shown various architectural styles of camps: watch-towers were "Swiss style, garage style, Japanese style." Some camps were even decorated with quaint rustic signs. One had a zoo, another an orphanage on its grounds. There was the facade of normality. Such outer trappings can be filmed or photographed; the interior remains a different matter.

As the film moves back to color, the viewer has a sense of escaping, as if s/he has been given some sort of balm or restorative. Of course, no such bounty was granted the inmates of the camps. The interweaving of black/white and color also disorients the viewer, making it impossible to establish a constant point of view. That is exactly Resnais' point. Such an outrage in human history has not a shred of logic to it. He is also implying that it can be filmed, but it cannot be captured. The narrative underscores this. Although information is presented in a loose chronological order, it consists of a series of observations that supplement the camera's eye. Facts can be gathered about what happened at Auschwitz but a coherent narrative trajectory is not only impossible but also undesirable.

Examining the present, the voice-over tells us: "We go slowly along...looking for what?" The interrogative remains the dominant mode in the black and white sections: "Is it in vain that we try to remember?" The viewer is told that it is "useless to describe what happened in these cells," and "words are insufficient." Soft, lyrical lute passages on the soundtrack are in stark contrast to the harrowing images and heighten the tone of inquiry—and absurdity.

The meaning of the film's title is derived from the dwarf Alberich's claim in Wagner's *Das Rheingold*:

Nacht und Nebel—
Niemand gleich!
Night and Fog—
No one remains as he was!

From this source, Heinrich Himmler, Reichsführer SS of the German Reich, invented the term, a "night and fog" prisoner: for him such an ideal person enters the camp at night and in fog and then quickly vanishes. A person exists and then is made to disappear. More specifically, the screenwriter, the novelist Jean Caryol, had been incarcerated at Mauthausen and in 1946 had published *Poèmes de la nuit et brouillard*. This makes the choice of title doubly appropriate.

For Resnais and Caryol, the title is a metaphor of the human condition, of the impossibility of attaining any real knowledge about what is labeled history, especially the history of trauma. We can talk about such things, but we cannot really comprehend them.

FICTIONALIZING TRAUMA IN *HIROSHIMA MON AMOUR*

By 1958, when he was asked by Anatole Dauman to make a non-fiction film about Hiroshima and the atomic bomb, Resnais hesitantly accepted and then, after some months, firmly declined to make *Picadon* (*Flash*). He had reached his own personal limit in his documentaries in recording barbarism.

Only a fiction film—in which a form of unknowing was foregrounded—he came to realize would be an acceptable way of dealing with this particular atrocity. That solution became a possibility when Dauman reached an agreement with Daiei Studios to change the contracted Japanese-French co-production documentary to a fiction film with the following requirements: one major character must be French, the other Japanese; in addition, at least one major sequence had to be filmed in each country using technicians of that nation.

The producers asked the popular novelist Françoise Sagan to write the script, but she declined. Resnais then proposed that the invitation be extended to the experimental novelist, Marguerite Duras, who accepted the challenge. At that time, Resnais said that he "wanted to make a film for women.... She was an essential factor in the 'grand opera style' I wanted to achieve."[6] He also requested her to keep in mind Griffith's epic *Intolerance* as a possible model for their collaboration.

Duras completed the script in the summer of 1958. Then Resnais and his script girl, Sylvette Baudrot, went to Tokyo and Hiroshima where Michio Takahashi filmed the exterior and studio shots; simultaneously, Sacha Vierny filmed the exterior Nevers sequences according to Resnais' instructions; the studio sequences in France were filmed by Vierny only after Resnais and Emmanuelle Riva had returned from Japan.

Riva (Elle), who was born in Chénimenil in the Vosges in 1927, had been principally a stage actress until Resnais hired her to play the co-lead in his film, in which role Duras envisioned her as a woman "giving this Japanese—*at Hiroshima*—her most precious possession: herself as she now is, her *survival* after the death of her love at Nevers."[7] For Resnais, it was crucial that an "unknown" play Elle; he selected Riva's photograph from an agent's files.

Seven years older than Riva, Eiji Okada had appeared in twenty films when he made *Hiroshima Mon Amour*. He was chosen using very exacting standards imposed by Duras:

> A Japanese actor with pronounced Japanese features might lead people to believe that it is especially because the protagonist is Japanese that the French actress was attracted to him. Thus, whether we liked it or not, we'd find ourselves caught again in the trap of "exoticism" and the involuntary racism inherent in any exoticism. The spectator should not say: "How attractive Japanese men are," but "How attractive *that man* is."

Duras's statement is making it clear that she wanted her film to be read symbolically and hoped that any taints of racism could be exorcised by having Lui be a "Western-looking Japanese actor."[8] (That decision, however, can be used to argue that the resulting film is too Euro-centric.)

Although Elle compliments Lui on his perfect French, Okada had to learn all his lines phonetically. Working relationships on set were harmonious, and Resnais was in constant touch with Duras by phone and mail. The director asked the two actors to simply live their parts and to leave the rest to him.

The scenario is divided into five parts. At the outset of Part One, the shoulders and arms of Elle and Lui are intertwined in an embrace of pleasurable agony "as if drenched with ashes, rain, dew, or sweat.... The main thing is that we get the feeling that this dew, this perspiration, has been deposited by the atomic 'mushroom' as it moves away and evaporates." Duras's words signify that the viewer should obviously see the bodies coated by "black rain." Then Lui announces: "You saw nothing in Hiroshima. Nothing." Elle responds emphatically: "I saw *everything. Everything.*" She recalls visiting the hospital where she visited victims of radiation sickness and the museum that contains countless photographs and other mementoes. At the museum, she saw both explanations and reconstructions ("authentic as possible"); she specifically recalled pieces of metal as vulnerable as flesh. Still, Lui is emphatic in contradicting her. He is a survivor—but of a radically different strain from her.

The pieces of evidence Elle witnessed appear on screen. Then there is a crosscut to the lovers, whose skin now appears normal.[9] At this point, fictional cinematic reconstructions of the events of August 6, 1945 are introduced (these sequences are garish and even more unconvincing than the recreation in Imamura's *Black Rain*.) Elle recalls weeping over the events in Hiroshima. Lui simply says: "No."

Attempting to make her assertions more valid, the woman shifts ground. She recalls newsreel footage made from August 7 onwards. As Elle makes this claim, the viewer is shown the evidence. As the newsreel footage becomes more and more gruesome, she states:

> Hiroshima was blanketed with flowers. There were cornflowers and gladiolas everywhere, and morning glories and day lilies that rose again from the ashes with an extraordinary vigor, quite unheard of for flowers till then.

Lui remains unimpressed. Elle then introduces love into the equation:

> Just as in love this illusion exists, this illusion of being able never to forget, so I was under the illusion that I would never forget Hiroshima. Just as in love.[10]

Elle alters her strategy: if love is an illusion, perhaps Hiroshima can be treated as such. She also states that their abilities to remember and to forget are on an equal footing. Changing tactics once again, Elle confesses:

> You destroy me.
> You're so good for me.
> You destroy me.
> You're so good for me.[11]

Their conversation becomes more centered on the present. Lui tells her that his family was in Hiroshima on the fateful day, but he was away fighting the war.

Elle is in Hiroshima to make a film. Before that she was in Paris. Previously, she was in Nevers. And why did she want to see Hiroshima?, Lui wonders. She responds: "Because it interested me. I have my own ideas about it. For instance, I think looking closely at things is something that has to be learned."

The fifteen-minute conversation that opens the film can be interpreted in a variety of ways. Lui may be stating that no one can understand the atrocity that occurred at Hiroshima. He may be privileging his male point of view over hers. Lui may also be implying that she is not Japanese and therefore cannot comprehend the tragedy of his native city. Of course, Lui is affirming Resnais' own position about both the Holocaust and Hiroshima as unknowable events.[12]

The second part of the film contains completely different kinds of interactions between two lovers who have met up, gone to bed precipitously and are soon to part. Lui humorously tells her that he approached her at the café because she looked ugly and bored. (Towards the end of the film, the viewer sees that this café is called the *Casablanca* and realizes that Elle is to be imagined as a form of the Ingrid Bergman figure and Lui as the Humphrey Bogart one from Michael Curtisz's celebrated romantic film from 1942.) Their behavior remains flirtatious.

However, looking at her lover lying on his back, Elle has a flashback to an earlier lover. When Lui asks her what "Hiroshima" meant to her, she observes that it signified the end of the war, but she makes this statement in a melancholic manner. Then, Elle remembers: she felt remorse, which then vanished. Lui offers the opinion that people in the West rejoiced at the news of "Hiroshima."

FIGURE 7 Elle (Emmanuelle Riva) is clad in her nurse's costume as she converses with Lui (Eiji Okada) in *Hiroshima Mon Amour*.

When Lui in a subsequent scene asks the woman, now in the costume of a nurse, what has brought her to Hiroshima, she tells him she is playing a role in a film: "A film about Peace. What else do you expect them to make in Hiroshima except a picture about Peace?" Elle's answer cuts in several directions. The actual Hiroshima film she is in is about much more than the concept of Peace; in addition, in Resnais' film she is playing an actress playing an actress. Elle then reveals that when she was young in

Nevers she was ripe with hate; at one point she thought she would make a "career" of hate. Finally, Elle tells her lover that she will be returning to France the next day. Lui wants her to stay. They part.

Elle's refusal to spend the coming night with Lui is infused with poignancy, almost as if something from the past is threatening to rise to the surface of her consciousness. Part Three opens with the dismantling of the set for the Hiroshima movie in which Elle is acting. (In a nice metafictional touch, her peace film is also obviously a French-Japanese co-production, and Elle has to film sequences in Paris.) She is napping on the ground when Lui approaches her. Elle goes back with Lui to his home (his wife is away). They make love. Afterwards, Elle reveals that the man she loved during the war was a German soldier.

At this point, the film shifts to Nevers, and the barns, ruins, and rooms where Elle conducted her clandestine affair with an enemy soldier. The style of filming changes significantly with brief, lyrical shots of meetings and partings; the music is sprightly. "Why are you asking about him?" Elle asks Lui. His answer demonstrates that he has come to understand her very well: "It was there, I seem to have understood, that I almost ... lost you ... and that I risked never knowing you." She tells him that she wants to leave his house.

Part Four begins as night falls over Hiroshima. The couple has returned to the café where they met the night before. As she speaks again of Nevers, Elle recalls being imprisoned in a cellar; the viewer sees her there, her hair shorn. She tells Lui: "I call your name softly." This is a crucial turning point in the film because the enemy soldier and Lui, also a former enemy soldier, become one in her mind.

As a rebellious young woman, Elle collaborated with the enemy in undertaking a love affair with a German and feels the repressed memory of the pain of that past in the company of Lui. Elle's narrative and the accompanying visuals move from effect to cause: she is imprisoned, but the viewer is told the full story only later. In that cellar, Elle becomes a madwoman in love with Lui. She is entombed. Her hair grows back and is shorn again. Her life is a living hell.

> I see the daylight.
> I see my life. Your death.
> My life that goes on. Your death that goes on.[13]

In these sequences, Resnais changes Elle's appearance so that she bears a strong resemblance to a Hiroshima victim. Early in the film, Resnais had displayed the clumps of hair that had dropped from the heads of Hiroshima victims; at this late point in the film he connects such losses to the symbolic castration of Elle by having her hair shaven. He also films Emmanuelle Riva in such a way as to make her look like the iconic image of Maria Falconetti, the heroine in Dreyer's *La passion de Jeanne d'Arc* (1928).

Then, Elle returns to the past. She was going to run away with the German; when she arrived at their rendezvous, "he wasn't quite dead yet. Someone had fired on him from the garden." Elle could not distinguish between his dead body and her own. That night Nevers was liberated, and her imprisonment began. Elle begins to shout, and Lui slaps her in the face to snap her out of her frenzy. Eventually, Elle became "reasonable" in Nevers. Her mother assisted her to leave for Paris, where two days later the name "Hiroshima" was in all the newspapers.

Lui is the only person Elle has ever told of her unhappy past in Nevers. "I want to have lived through that moment. That incomparable moment." Lui responds:

> In a few years, when I'll have forgotten you, and when other such adventures, from sheer habit, will happen to me, I'll remember you as the symbol of love's forgetfulness. I'll think of this adventure as of the horror of oblivion. I already know it.[14]

At the beginning of Part Five, Elle and Lui part, and Elle walks back to her room. The viewer overhears her interior monologue:

> You were not quite dead.
> I told our story.
> I was unfaithful to you tonight with this stranger.
> I told our story....
> Look how I'm forgetting you....
> Look how I've forgotten you.
> Look at me.[15]

The scene eventually shifts to a bench outside the café where Elle and Lui had met. Her interior discourse continues: "I'm going to stay in Hiroshima. With him, every night. In Hiroshima. I'm going to stay here. Here." Lui then appears, and Elle tells him: "Of course I'm going to stay in Hiroshima with you." Then she abruptly tells him to go away.

Elle appears again at the café, where another Japanese man attempts to pick her up (presumably very much in the manner of Lui the night before). In the last sequence of the film, Lui appears at her door.

> *Lui*: Impossible not to come.
> *Elle*: I'll forget you! I'm forgetting you already!

Suddenly, in amazement, Elle looks at him: "Hi-ro-shi-ma. Hi-ro-shi-ma. That's your name." Lui responds: "That's my name. Yes. Your name is Nevers. Ne-vers in France."

Elle suffered trauma when her German lover was killed and her parents imprisoned her. Since she left Nevers, she has closed herself off from those events. She retains a memory of what happened, but she does not wish to be emotionally engaged with this aspect of her past. Elle's affair with Lui forces her to confront that history and, in the process, to cure herself by remembering events with which she was not previously strong enough to deal. Confrontation with Lui for Elle becomes a form of healing.

More significantly, when Elle allows Lui to become her dead German lover, she conflates the Nevers of her past with the Hiroshima of Lui's past (this has been earlier signaled with the merging of her appearance as a Hiroshima victim into that of Falconetti as the tragic, heroic Joan of Arc).

At the beginning of the film, Elle had looked at only simulacra of Hiroshima and what she witnessed were largely representations of representations. In order to have the slightest understanding of Hiroshima, she must return to the memory of the loss of her German lover in Nevers. In that way, she comes to have a limited knowledge of what Hiroshima was when her Japanese lover becomes her German lover: this fusion allows her to feel again the earlier trauma and to experience Lui's sense of trauma. At that point she becomes a stand-in for all those who have endured profound losses.

At the conclusion of the film, Elle recognizes that she previously saw nothing of Hiroshima. Lui is Hiroshima and she is Nevers. Their love has permitted both to retain their individual identities (heightened them, in fact). Through the mingling of fiction and fact, Resnais allows the audience to experience through Elle what it was like to be a victim of Hiroshima. However, the film validates Lui's experience over Elle's She attains a certain knowledge of that event, but it can simply not be the same as his. What Elle and Lui do share as characters is a large measure of incomprehensibility.

FABRICATING TRAUMA IN *HIRSOHIMA MON AMOUR*

When describing the Loire on which Nevers stands, Elle recounts: "It's a completely unnavigable river, always empty, because of its irregular course and its sandy bars. In France, the Loire is considered a very beautiful river, especially because of its light. "[16] A place that seems welcoming but is impossible to traverse. Such paradoxes inhabit the entire film and the personalities of Elle and Lui. In this instance, the Loire could be either Elle or Lui: persons whose experience of trauma has cauterized them in the present. At one level, this is the love story that comprises *Hirsohima Mon Amour*, but, very significantly, there is no comma in the title separating *Hiroshima* and *Mon Amour*: the two elements have to be read as one. This is precisely what Resnais and Duras had in mind: that which is universal and public slides into the personal and private.

In her Synopsis, Duras emphasizes that the initial exchange between Elle and Lui "is allegorical. *In short, an operatic exchange.* Impossible to talk about Hiroshima. All one can do is talk about the impossibility of talking about Hiroshima. The knowledge of Hiroshima is being stated à priori by an exemplary delusion of the mind."[17] (The point about the Loire being "unnavigable" is meant to apply to the inner lives of Elle and Lui—and, by extension perhaps, to all persons.)

The primary delusion would be to think that one could make a film about Hiroshima or that one could make a film that linked Hiroshima and love. There is the possibility, however, of constructing a film that denies the possibility of making a film about Hiroshima but attempts to capture some of the feelings of trauma associated with it. In fact, if the love story is adhered to, Duras points out, "we'll end up with a sort of false documentary that will probe the lesson of Hiroshima more deeply than any made-to-order documentary." In other words, by concentrating on what might be ephemeral and fleeting, it might be possible to make a genuinely investigative film—the best one can hope for in dealing with Hiroshima.[18]

Lui's involvement with Hiroshima is never foregrounded in the film—the trauma Elle endured at Nevers emerges as the central, defining experience of her life. What about Lui? Rather than claiming that the film becomes centered on the Occidental as opposed to the Oriental, it might be well to reflect on what

Resnais felt about historical catastrophes such as the Holocaust. He increasingly came to the position that such events are beyond representation, that it was perhaps repugnant to deal with them. In foregrounding Elle, the film allows a view into her tragedy, and that tragedy helps her to get some basic understanding of what happened at Hiroshima. In the film's conclusion, therefore, she can alter her stance from the film's opening: she recognizes that Lui is Hiroshima, whatever that word signifies.

At the outset, Elle pronounces the word Hiroshima in an exaggerated manner—Hi-ro-shi-ma—, as if to imply she does not really know the word. When she pronounces it at the end in an even more broken-down fashion, the implication is that she has never really known the full meaning of the word and consigns it to her lover. Lui has always pronounced Nevers in a normal manner throughout the film, but at the conclusion, he says "Nevers," consigning the word to Elle.

In *"Hiroshima Mon Amour*: You Must Remember This," the historian Michael S. Roth argues that Resnais and Duras "explore the question of how one can be fully alive under the burden of a history that is not a stranger to trauma but that has not fully domesticated the traumatic."[19] In support of his argument, he cites Van der Kolk and van der Hart's "The Intrusive Past":

In the case of complete recovery [from trauma], the person does not suffer anymore from the reappearance of traumatic memories in the form of flashbacks, behavioral reenactments, etc. Instead, the story can be told, the person can look back at what happened; he has given it a place in his life history, his autobiography, and thereby his whole personality. Many traumatized persons, however, experience long periods of time in which they live, as it were, in two different worlds: the realm of the trauma and the realm of their current, ordinary life.[20]

I am sympathetic to this argument but would maintain that Elle is a victim of trauma as described in the above passage but that Lui is not. In fact, her interactions with Lui allow Elle to "domesticate" her trauma.

From the outset, Resnais and Duras wanted to make a "false documentary" because for them that is the only authentic form of cinema that can embrace trauma. Earlier, in *Nuit et Brouillard*, Auschwitz was Resnais' subject matter. He made a film of remembrance but became dissatisfied because he realized that any film commemorating the Holocaust would by its very nature do an injustice to subject matter which is *beyond* knowing. In *Hiroshima Mon Amour*, he constructed a film in which the viewer—through identification with Elle and her suffering in the past—comes to an *approximate* understanding of what Lui endured. In this allegorical context, Lui becomes Japan, the country against which the unspeakable was unleashed.

As the films of Immamura and Resnais bear eloquent testimony, no resolution can be imposed upon what happened in Hiroshima in August 1945. The topic can be talked *around* but it is difficult to talk *about*. Immamura was reduced to a state of despair by attempting to impose meaning on Hiroshima; he abandoned that approach. From the outset, Resnais accepted the limits of any genuine, comprehensible knowledge of that tragedy. In their different ways, both directors came to realize that only "traces" of this monumental event in Japan's past could be reconstituted. In Resnais's film, the Other of Japan is neither condescended to nor feminized. In fact, the tragedy of Hiroshima is restored to Japan, although that cataclysmic event is refracted in a Western eye.

CHAPTER THREE

UNIMAGINABLE EXISTENCES:
THE EMPEROR AND THE WRITER

The biography picture (biopic) has never been a genre favored by the Japanese film industry.[1] There are very few extant examples, although two will be discussed later in this chapter. Why do Japanese directors and producers avoid biography? This obvious question is difficult to answer. Much of it comes from a sense of reticence, from a feeling that individual sensibilities are not as celebrated in Japan as in the West because Japan is a consensus society. The rugged individual and the Romantic artist are not popular constructions there. Moreover, it could be argued that the great number of Japanese period films that celebrate with great nostalgia the by-gone culture of the samurai may have lessened any demand for forms of traditional film biography.

The two biography pictures by Schrader and Sokurov to be evaluated are of celebrated persons who in Japan would not be subject to close biographical scrutiny. Sokurov's film concentrates on the Emperor Hirohito's decision to make his declaration of humanity. This public event, Sokurov implies, was reached only after deep soul-searching, but a film that shows the inner torments of the Emperor would from the outset be a non-Japanese project: it investigates psychological terrain in a way that is simply too probing and, as a result, disrespectful of such a person.

Schrader's portrayal of Mishima is another venture the Japanese would probably not tackle. For many, Mishima, despite his extraordinary fame, was a man who courted publicity. He was also a deeply conflicted man: although Mishima's homosexuality was well-known in the West and had been written about openly there, this basic fact of his life was known to a relatively small group of people in Japan, despite the fact that Mishima was a celebrity (information about Mishima's sexual identity had been available in English since John Nathan's biography was released in 1974). In fact, Mishima's widow, Yôko, did everything in her power to keep information about her late husband's sexuality secret, although any reader of his obviously heavily autobiographical fiction would have known For her, there was a difference between a fact being known in a work of fiction and a fact being incorporated into any form of non-fiction available in Japan.

In both *The Sun* and *Mishima*, the unimaginable is enacted: the deeply-conflicted Emperor rejects his divinity and thus sets Japan on a new course following the conclusion of the Pacific War; in the other film, Mishima calculatedly stages his suicide as a media event. Most Japanese would consider his dogged pursuit of fame beyond death both shoddy and incomprehensible.

A PORTRAIT OF THE ARTIST AS NARCISSIST: *MISHIMA*

At a basic level, Schrader accepts Mishima's own account of himself as the artist as a dandy. However, as the film progresses, it becomes a complex account centered on a person who is obsessed with the fear of failure, about a man who is deeply afraid that he is not sufficiently masculine. Mishima's fears are the real cornerstone of his work—when all is said and done, his talent was to expose and explore his own anxieties and vulnerabilities—and the resulting film biography by Schrader continually elaborates this fraught interior landscape. The director refused to buy into the mythology that artists are persons who have suffered or experienced life in a profoundly different way from other people. In Mishima's case, however, Schrader was fascinated by how art and life had been often deliberately intertwined by his subject, who did believe that artists are incredibly dissimilar from most people.

In his screenplay for Martin Scorsese's *Taxi Driver* (1976) Schrader had explored in the central character Travis a man who is a hero and a monster, a rescuer and a killer. After completing *Cat People* in 1982, Schrader wanted to make a biopic of Hank Williams, the American country music singer, who died at the age of twenty-nine in 1953 in mysterious circumstances: much of his short life was taken up with the pursuit of suicidal glory. When the Williams project faltered, Schrader thought of Mishima as an artist of the same self-destructive bent as the American.

Surprisingly, Mishima's widow gave her support to the film project—and then withdrew it. Initially, in her role as guardian of the flame, she favored a film that would help spread the international reputation of her husband. She thought her "consultation rights" agreement gave her more power than it actually did. Later, when she realized how revealing the film could or would be, she withdrew her cooperation.[2]

Having decided to do all in her power to kill the film, Yôko Mishima approached the two companies—Fuji and Toho—who were providing approximately half of the film's five million dollar budget. (The other half came from Warner Brothers because Francis Ford Coppola and George Lucas had asked them to come on board.) However, the Japanese producer Mataichiro Yamamoto had invested some money of his own and when he was told by Fuji that they were withdrawing, he informed them he had a great deal to forfeit, might become despondent and commit suicide to release his family from further financial obligations. Realizing what the resulting publicity could do to their reputations, the two companies arranged for a representative to deliver the money in a paper bag to Mr Yamamoto. Subsequently, both firms insisted that they had never had anything whatsoever to do with the film.

When it became known that the project had incurred the wrath of Yôko Mishima and her circle, the casting of the role of Yukio

Mishima became difficult. Schrader's first choice was Ken Takakura, but he became physically sick at the idea of taking on this responsibility. Other actors declined; some because Mishima's right-wing attitudes were repulsive to them. Initially, Ken Ogata seemed like a bad choice: a larger man than the compact, muscular Mishima, Ogata had established his reputation playing extremely different lead roles—mainly of gangsters— from that in Schrader's proposed film. He appeared not to have the "right breeding." Most of the Japanese involved in the production did not really understand why anyone would wish to make a film about Mishima.

Schrader and his colleagues found it difficult to obtain the permissions they needed for exterior shots: those buildings were suddenly not available. The sound stages for the interior scenes were done at the Toho studio in Tokyo, but the sets for the fiction sequences were located in an annex that segregated them from everyone else. When the cinematographer John Bailey mentioned that he would like to meet someone like Kon Ichikawa, he was never told no, but he never was introduced to the famous director. The designer Eiko Ishioka felt that her Japanese colleagues distanced themselves from her: her sets for the fiction sequences (see below) were considered outlandish. Kazuo Takenaka, a distinguished Toho regular, designed the other sequences in the film.

Ishioka found Mishima a repulsive personality. Before Schrader hired her, she was frank about her feelings: the director told her that he did not care what she thought about Mishima because the film was going to be centered on his [Schrader's] view of the writer. Having reached an accord on that issue, they worked well together although she often thought Schrader too intellectual.

When he began work on *Mishima*, Schrader was well aware of the knocks routinely bestowed upon the biopic genre: it dealt only with externals, tended to be superficial in any assessment it provided, stripped lives down so much that the individual celebrated became unrecognizable. Of course, he also knew that this form was enormously popular in the West and, in some instances, extremely successful at the box office.

Eiko Ishioka is accurate in her assessment of Schrader's intellectualism, and there is perhaps no biopic so rationally and rigorously constructed. The film is in four parts: I. Beauty: "Temple of the Gold Pavilion"; 2. Art: "Kyoko's House"; 3. Action: "Runaway Horses"; 4. Harmony of Pen and Sword. Each of these four parts is told in three visual styles: 1. quasi-documentary-appearing color sequences restaging the events that took place on November 25, 1970, the day Mishima committed seppuku at Ichigaya, a military base[3]; 2. fiction sequences in Parts 1-3 in highly saturated color; 3. black-and-white flashbacks retelling the story of Mishima's life chronologically (this part of the film was made to look like the black and white films of auteurs like Ozu, Kurosawa and Mizoguchi; in particular, Schrader was heavily influenced by Ichikawa's *Enjô* (1958), an adaptation of Mishima's *The Temple of the Golden Pavilion*, although his way of narrating the same material is done in a completely different manner.)[4] However, Part 4 does not use a fictional source and moves between November 1970 and events in Mishima's more immediate past. Only when Mishima's theatrical death is completed at the conclusion of this part are the endings of each of the three fictional sequences inserted.

The fictional (hyper real) sequences in Part I emphasize green and gold; those in Part 2, pink; they are black and white in Part 3. Schrader told Ishioka that the sets for the fiction sequences should look like stage sets—their deliberate artificiality should harmonize with the pieces of fiction being dramatized. In the case of Part 2, he asked her to make the sets look as vulgar and crass as possible: she was happy to oblige because she felt Mishima a vulgar and crass person.

When Schrader commissioned the minimalist composer Philip Glass to write the music, the two reached an accord quickly. Glass, having immediately conceived of Schrader's Mishima as a deeply romantic person to the core, wrote music encapsulating the resulting intensity. At the time Ishioka showed the composer her drawings, Glass realized that she was creating dream worlds, and he wanted his music to have a corresponding otherworldly sound. There were further refinements: for example, flashbacks are played to string quartet accompaniment whereas the suicide day is orchestrated.

Ishioka and Glass may be visceral artists, but they are also ones who are intimately acquainted with the histories of design and music, respectively. Schrader is an auteur deeply involved with the history of film. A great admirer of Bertolucci's *The Conformist* (1970), for instance, he paid similar attention to color values in establishing the character of a man cut off from his own feelings. The highly-charged efforts of Schrader, Ishioka and Glass were brought together in order to redefine the biopic as a genre, and Yukio Mishima was the perfect subject because he separated, divided and compartmentalized his own existence as if it were a staged biography.

Mishima was born in 1925 in the Shinjuku area of Tokyo. His father was a government officer, his mother the daughter of a school principal. His maternal grandmother, Natsuko, who removed him from his immediate family, dominated Mishima's childhood. She was the illegitimate daughter of a *daimyo* and had been raised in an aristocratic household. The illusion of being an aristocrat consumed her, and she passed on that heritage to her grandson, whom she mollycoddled. As a student, Mishima was precocious and bookish and, as a result, he felt deeply separated from his peers who preferred traditional masculine-stereotyped activities such as sports.

When he was drafted into the Army, Mishima had a cold

during the medical check up but suggested to the examining doctor that he might have TB. He was declared unfit for military service. Later, he felt deeply guilty about this subterfuge and tried to make up for it.

He became a prolific writer. One early novel, *Confessions of a Mask*, is a semi-autobiographical account of a latent homosexual who must hide behind a facade in order to fit into society. At the age of twenty in 1955, Mishima took up bodybuilding and frequently deplored the emphasis given by intellectuals to the mind over the body.

Mishima's sexuality was much more homosexual than heterosexual, but he married Yôko Sugiyama in June 1958; the couple had two children. In 1967, Mishima enlisted in the Ground Self Defense Force and underwent basic training. A year later, he founded the Tatenokai (Shield Society), his own private army composed of young men who studied martial arts and physical discipline under his tutelage and swore to protect the Emperor. However, Mishima had mixed feelings about an Emperor who had renounced his divinity since, for him the Emperor was the embodied essence of Japan.

In addition to his writing and military lives, Mishima acted in films and even directed one. In 1960 he played the role of Takeo, a yakuza, in Yasuzo Masumura's *Afraid to Die* (*Karakkaze yarô*). The film opens with a botched assassination attempt on Takeo while he is in prison. The assassin gets the wrong man because, while playing volleyball, Takeo has a fellow inmate sub for him when a visitor calls on him. The hit was ordered by a rival gang leader, whom Takeo had knifed in the leg—that incident sent him to prison. Reluctant to leave the relative safety of jail, Takeo is nevertheless released the next day and manages to sneak a ride in a police car to safety. The wily ex-con returns to his old haunts, where his uncle Gohei Hirayama (Takashi Shimura), looks upon him with contempt for not immediately going after his rival and gives him a gun.

Since his Asahina gang is down to himself, his uncle, and his cynical longtime friend Aikawa (Eiji Funakoshi), Takeo needs time to get money together to build a new gang and sees his singer girlfriend Masako (Yoshie Mizutani) to tell her that he is dropping her because his rival will be watching her closely. He then hides out in a flophouse, fearing for his life, after discovering his rival has brought in an out-of-town hit man named Masa (Shigeru Kôyama) who has a severe case of asthma and while, stalking his victims, clutches on to an inhaler.

Takeo's gang also owns a movie house in a seedy neighborhood, where he meets pretty theater cashier Yoshie Koizumi (Ayako Wakao) and offers her cash when she asks for a pay raise. When she turns down his money, he falls in love with her and gets her pregnant (after saying women are just toys). Given to temper tantrums, Takeo slaps Yoshie around when she refuses to have an abortion, but this only makes her love him more. Her labor activist brother Shoichi (Keizo Kawasaki), who despises the yakuza, is snatched by Takeo's chief rival and beaten and held for ransom. This, however, is in response to Takeo snatching the boss's young daughter earlier to raise money in order to buy a massage parlor.

When Takeo finally thinks he has settled things with his rival and has opted to move with Yoshie to Osaka and lead a normal life, the asthma hit man shoots him when he is purchasing things for his expected child. Takeo dies on a crowded mall escalator, exclaiming, "I never expected this."

The film—which is done very much tongue-in-cheek—nevertheless portrays a deeply divided person. Takeo is "afraid to die" in the sense that he does not pursue his opponent; on the other hand, he accepts the twist of fate that deprives him of life. Mishima actively collaborated with Masumara in portraying a yakuza capable of divided feelings. In that sense, a significant aspect of the famous writer's character is captured.

The pursuit of death is the focus of Mishima's own half-hour film of 1966, *Patriotism* (*Yûkoku*). Two days after the Two Twenty-six Incident in Tokyo on February 26, 1936, when twenty-two junior officers of the First Division attempted to overthrow the government, Lieutenant Shinji Takeyama (Mishima), assisted by his wife Reiko, commits ritual suicide. He is strongly motivated by the fact that his fellow junior officers, aware of his recent marriage, did not ask him to join them; he has also been summoned by his superiors to fight against his compatriots. The couple make love one final time, and then Takeyama endures the "bliss" of seppuku whereupon the widow drives a dagger through her heart. (In *Merry Christmas, Mr Lawrence*, Captain Yonoi is sympathetic to the same group.

When filming the final moments of Mishima's death, Schrader enacts it following the depiction in *Patriotism*. The third fictional adaptation—"Runaway Horses"—is derived from another Mishima account of the failed Two Twenty-six Incident. Schrader, in setting up how the three fictional sequences were to be rendered, was also following Mishima's lead in using sets inspired by the conventions of Nô theatre (there is even a film within a film sequence in which the filming of *Patriotism* is re-staged).

Up to a point, Schrader allowed his subject to guide him through the maze of his personal and professional lives—and the glaring fact that they were so chaotically intertwined. And yet, Schrader saw his biographical subject as lacking a great deal of self-knowledge and, certainly, any sense of irony, and he rightly conceived his role as biographer as one in which he makes some connections perhaps not easily made by Mishima.

In 1972, Schrader had published *Transcendental Style in Ozu, Bresson and Dreyer*, but in making *Mishima* he had to find a style that went in the completely opposite direction of the minimalist approaches of those three auteurs. The result is a deliberately elaborate, baroque film. However, *Mishima*'s aesthetics are indebted in part to Schrader's definition of transcendental style:

...if you reduce your sensuous awareness rigorously and for long enough, the inner need will explode and it will be pure because it will not have been siphoned off by easy or exploitative identifications; it will have refined and compressed to its true identity...the divine sense...The more you define the world and the tinier the aperture, then the more blinding the light of faith becomes in its brilliance.[5]

In *Mishima* Schrader wanted the suicide to be such "an emotionally blinding moment."[6]

In Part I in the flashback sequence, the viewer sees an observant, withdrawn boy who is not allowed to play with friends. In the fictional sequence, the protagonist is crippled with a bad stammer and cannot, under the tutelage of a friend with a similar disability, use his deficiency as a ploy to seduce young women. He sublimates his sexual feelings into a fascination with the remarkable beauty of the Temple of the Gold Pavilion, a structure so beyond life that he burns it. (Mishima resented the fact that art resided in a sphere beyond mundane human existence.) In Part 2, the protagonist's eroticism is unleashed when he sees a reproduction of the almost naked St. Sebastian in Guido Reni's painting. In the accompanying fictional sequence, the young man becomes devoted to improving his body but becomes entrapped in a sado-masochistic relationship with a woman to whom his mother owes money; she inflicts damage to his body and finally kills him. The fictional sequence in Part 3 reenacts the activities of the cadre that attempted the failed Two Twenty-six Incident: the ringleader commits seppuku.

The film can be read in the way Mishima invented his life. He discovered that he belonged to the world of Beauty from a young age. This alienated him from his peers, but he nevertheless dedicated his life to putting Beauty on to paper (Art). Having come to that realization, he knew that he had cut himself off from the world of Action, whereupon he took up bodybuilding and military activities. Then he sought the Harmony of Pen and Sword in his pursuit of right-wing causes, including a highly overzealous anachronistic devotion to the Emperor. After the Occupation, he felt, Japan had become a second-rate nation. By killing himself, he would demonstrate how Beauty, Art and Action could be united and thus become a role model for a restored Japan. He had intended—after committing seppuku and before being beheaded—to write a poem on his chest. However, he was not able to fulfill this wish in his final moments of life.

Schrader enacts Mishima's scenario, but he invests it with considerable irony. In the November 1970 and appropriate flashback sequences, Ken Ogata plays the role of a sophisticated man-of-the-world, although he is deeply affronted when a lover refers to his "flabby" (pre-bodybuilding) body. The protagonists in all three fictional sequences are young men deeply unsure of themselves.

Man's desire to be beautiful is a wish for death, claimed Mishima. Schrader examines this proposition carefully. As mentioned above, the adolescent boy's sexual awakening occurred when he came across a reproduction of the Reni painting; as an adult in 1970, Mishima posed for a photographic restaging of the painting by Kishin Shinoyama. For the homosexual, the decay of the body was the greatest treason imposed by life, Mishima once claimed. He obviously wanted to avoid the ravages that time would impose upon his physique.

"Words had separated me from my body," Schrader's protagonist also asserts. Yet the claim can be easily made that Schrader shows a man who never escaped his sense of being different from others—from feeling inferior; in the film he becomes a person who never really knows who he is and, as a result, constructs a highly artificial symbolical world to hold himself together. He makes himself into an iconic object in order to evade the pain of his own subjectivity.

At a press conference, Mishima once espoused Elvis Presley as

FIGURE 8 Ken Ogata as Yukio Mishima posing as Saint Sebastian in
Mishima; the iconography is based on a painting by Guido Reni.

his great contemporary hero, and he was not being comical. He
wanted to be a media star, one who staged his finest role.

Mishima warned the media that a major event was to take place at Ichigaya. He spoke to a group of assembled soldiers, who mocked him. Mishima died as he thought he wanted to live. Schrader captures the full theatricality of his subject, but he also puts on display a deeply vulnerable human being. The director's scrutiny may be merciless but it is tinged with mercy. A similar compassion inhabits Mizoguchi's portrait of Utamaro.

A PORTRAIT OF THE ARTIST AS AESTHETE: *UTAMARO AND FIVE WOMEN*

Kenji Mizoguchi's 1947 *Utamaro and Five Women* (*Utamaro omeguru gonin no omna*) was made under trying circumstances at the outset of the Occupation. [7] The director pleaded with the censors to be allowed to make it. He assured them: "The common man loved Utamaro, he was a great cultural object, really sort of a pre-occupation democrat." After debating this proposition, the censors gave the go-ahead provided Mizoguchi make another film, this one contemporary, in which the emancipation of women was emphasized.

Kanji Kuneida, the writer of the novel on which the film is based, had emphasized human freedom through the pursuit of the erotic. Yoshikata Yoda, who wrote the screenplay, later claimed that, despite good intentions, the film was confusing on this topic, "its ideas not aesthetically integrated."[8] There is certainly a marked discrepancy between the original story and the film, but this is because Mizoguchi imposed his own vision on the raw material with which he began work.

Very little is known of the life of Utamaro Kitigawa (1753-1806), one of the most productive and talented Ukiyo-e woodcut artists. He worked in most of the print genres associated with the floating world including actor prints, landscapes and erotica, but he is especially known for his *bijinga*, representations of beautiful women. Many of these women were courtesans who worked in the Yoshiwara, the licensed pleasure quarter. He had a close association with the publisher Tsutaya Jûzaburô; in 1804 he was punished by the shogunate for contravening the ban on representing the shogun Toyotomi Hideyoshi. He was sentenced to fifty days in manacles.

Mizoguchi's film alludes briefly to Utamaro's visit to a publisher and his establishment, but the name Tsutaya is assigned to the owner of a brothel. Although the reason for Utamaro (Minosuke Bandô) attracting the displeasure of the authorities is not mentioned, the artist is placed in fetters towards the end of Mizoguchi's film. In terms of narrative space, more than half of the film concerns the five women: the courtesan Oishin who becomes engaged to Utamaro's assistant, Take; the courtesan Okita, upon whose back Utamaro designs an image for a tattoo artist to engrave; she falls in love with a young man, Shozaburo; the courtesan Takasode, who also falls in love with Shozaburo; the courtesan Oran, who falls in love with another artist; the young beauty Yukie, who loves the same artist (he runs away with Oran).

At the outset of the film, a young artist of the Kanô school, Seinosuke (Kotaro Bando), purchases some woodcuts to show a mentor and is scandalized to see that Utamaro has emblazoned on one print an attack on the Kanô school emphasizing its use of unnatural colors that make women look freakish. Against the wishes of his fiancée, Yukie, the daughter of Kanô, he decides to challenge Utamaro to a duel. Oshin warns Utamaro of the danger posed by the young man, but Utamaro is not concerned: he goes in search of Takasode, whom he hears is about to be tattooed. When Seinosuke finally meets up with Utamaro, they decide to settle their differences by a painting challenge. Seinosuke makes a drawing of a woman and then Utamaro infuses it with his personal touch ("She's not alive. I'll fix it.") Finally, the young man realizes how far below Utamaro he is in talent.

Later, Utamaro finds Takasode. The tattoo artist is in despair. He does not have a design worthy of the courtesan. If I paint a suitable one on her back, will you etch it?, Utamaro asks. The tattooist agrees and Utamaro draws a wondrous image. The plot takes a dramatic turn when Seinosuke abandons the Kanô School and Yukie to become a woodcut artist in order to learn from Utamaro. He deliberately leaves the world of high art in favor of popular art.

FIGURE 9 Utamaro (Minosuke Bandô) concentrates as he draws on the back of Takasode (Toshiko Izuka). The image on the lady's back is of Sakata no Kurando and her son, Kintarô, often referred to as the "Golden Boy". Utamaro made several prints of this mother and son.

Shortly afterwards, Okita learns that Shozaburo has eloped with Takasode. In retaliation, Okita seduces Seinosuke. Then Utamaro's friends take him to gaze secretly at a feudal lord's bizarre rite of sending a large group of young women to swim in the ocean in order to retrieve an object. The winner, Oran, enraptures Utamaro.

Utamaro is arrested. Okita leaves Edo to find Takasode and her lover. Seinosuke runs away with Oran. Then, Okita murders

Takadsode and Shozaburo. Overcome—but not ashamed—by what she has done, Okita declares:

> To be true to myself, to put an end to a genuine love, I had to do it...It's not a mistake. I don't want to be fooled by a half-hearted and selfish love. Utamaro, isn't it the same with your drawings? Doesn't the woodcut portraying me express the same idea? All my life I acted exactly as I felt.... I loved him so much. I had to be punished. Utamaro, is it love? It's love, isn't it?[9]

Utamaro's immediate response is perhaps surprising: "I want to draw!" In the next sequence, the manacles are removed. His friends congratulate the artist and then begin to celebrate. However, the artist has no interest in such trivialities. He tells Take to prepare his paints and begins once again to draw beautiful women.

Mizoguchi creates a narrative about the essential loneliness of the artist. Although attracted to women, he is never the object of their attention. The five women are besotted with other men, and he is a witness to their erotic pursuits. He may suffer regrets about this situation, but his true dedication is to render the "life" of these women into "art." Okita dies because of her "true" love for Shozaburo: she has given up playing her life as a lie. In his turn, Utamaro pays a price for the gift of bring able to make women into art: he never lives a fully flesh-and-blood existence.

Mizoguchi's scriptwriter, Yoda, was certain that Mizoguchi drew a self-portrait in his rendering of Utamaro. Both men worked in mediums run by cutthroat businessmen; both were subject to censorship; both achieved their fame for portraits of women. In the bathing scene, Utamaro is a very willing peeping-tom because only in that way will his eyes be fed the raw material that he can transform into great art. During his entire career, Mizoguchi focused sympathetically on women: he looked at them and then filmed them in order to demonstrate their struggles.

From a handful of facts, Mizoguchi creates a convincing portrait of Utamaro. Sometimes, such reticence becomes a biographer's greatest tribute to his subject. Such is the approach of Shunji Iwai in telling the story of Kon Ichikawa.

A PORTRAIT OF THE ARTIST AS FILMMAKER: *THE KON ICHIKAWA STORY*

Shunji Iwai's *The Kon Ichikawa Story (Ichikawa Kon monogatari;* 2006) is actually about his personal obsession with the great director, although he never uses voice-over. Instead, he employs calligraphy with inserts showing photographs and clips from Ichikawa's films.

Ichikawa's father died when he was young, and he was raised in a very maternal household consisting of his mother, aunts and sisters. Films dominated his childhood, especially those of Lloyd, Keaton and Chaplin; however, he preferred Japanese "sword play" films. However, he was taken with Disney's *Silly Symphony*. When he was found unfit for war service, he became an animator. He marveled at *Fantasia*: like Ozu, he felt that Japan could never defeat a nation that produced such a wonder.

Ichikawa's transition to live action films was assisted by his collaboration with the screenwriter Yumiko Moji, whose pen name was Natto Wada, whom he married. They called each other Master, and they collaborated on each of Ichikawa's films until *Tokyo Olympiad* (1965). After that, she retired from the film industry. However, when she was dying, she offered suggestions as to how her husband should end *The Makioka Sisters* (1983). As was often the case in their relationship, he demurred and then followed her counsel.

Rather than allowing many personal details into his narrative, Ichima finally brings the movie to the point where he, the adoring younger man, meets his mentor and collaborates with him. For Ichima, Ichikawa lived up to expectations, and the film ends on that note. By concentrating on Ichikawa's early obsession with cinema and his marriage but by also deliberately refusing to intrude into his subject's personal life, the film becomes a moving testimony to Ickikawa's greatness. Such idealization may work well for Ichima, but it seriously disrupts the credibility of Sokurov's *The Sun*.

A PORTRAIT OF THE EMPEROR AS ACTOR: *THE SUN*

Biographies are often self-reflective texts. This is obviously true about Mizoguchi's *Utamaro* and Ichima's *Ikchikawa*. Schrader was straightforward in acknowledging that Mishima's narcissism fascinated him and that while making *Mishima* he wrestled with some of his own inner demons. Sokurov's deeply sympathetic portrait of Hirohito speaks to the Russian director's abiding interest in how power can corrupt, but his real fascination is with the internal world of an adult who has been forced to live as a child.

If Paul Schrader's *Mishima* invests its subject with a great deal of irony, the same claim cannot be voiced about Sokurov's portrait of Hirohito. The film borders on the blasphemous because it insists on seeing the Emperor as in many ways an ordinary person and because it spends much screen time displaying the daily events that consumed Hirohito's existence. Moreover, there is another controversial edge to this film: despite the abundance of evidence that was available by 2004 indicating the Emperor's full complicity in the war machine, Sokurov chose to ignore the published research. The director may have committed a taboo in depicting the Emperor, but, at the same time, he went out of his way to whitewash him.[10] Why Sokurov would have felt compelled to do this is problematic. He is fascinated with imperial life, nationalism and fallen aristo-crats. Moreover, his anti-Communist sentiments (particularly given that Hirohito was Stalin's enemy) might have led him to present Hirohito in the way he does.

The mise en scène is both gothic and claustrophobic: the Emperor (Issey Ogata) lives in an underground bunker. He has servants to wait upon him, but his only real companion is the radio, which he asks to be turned on, then off. The day's schedule is read to him, and it immediately becomes apparent that he is the prisoner of those who serve him. When one of the servants points out to him that the Emperor is directly descended from the

FIGURE 10 A very conflicted Hirohito (Issei Ogata) conducting a meeting of the War Cabinet in *The Sun*.

Sun Goddess, Hirohito calmly replies, "But my body is the same as yours. I have no distinguishing marks." When the downcast Emperor states that no one loves him, the servant coolly assures him that he is beloved by the people. The Emperor counters: "Because of this love, I couldn't stop the war." In these opening scenes, Sokurov shows the Emperor as both the hapless and helpless captive of fate. At a meeting of the War Cabinet, he observes that he wants peace but not at any price. After this encounter, Hirohito's Chamberlain (Shirô Sano) reminds the

Emperor that he is scheduled to be at his marine biology laboratory.

In his laboratory—where he is treated as much as possible as an ordinary person—the Emperor examines the *Dorippe granulata*, a crab, the carapace of which resembles the face of a Samurai warrior. The allusion is to the fact that the defeated samurai after the Battle of Dannoura in 1185 continued to haunt the ocean in this form. More specifically, Antoku, the seven-year-old Emperor, chose to drown himself rather than be captured; in some ways, Hirohito has reached a similar turning point.

After this sequence, the Emperor returns to his bedroom, tries to put himself to sleep but cannot and the film fast forwards— using a frenetic, surreal dream sequence involving planes and monster-like flying fish—past Hirsohima, Nagasaki, the Emperor's radio broadcast announcing the surrender of Japan, and MacArthur's arrival in Tokyo.

Rising from his bed, the Emperor sits at his desk. First, he examines his family album that includes pictures of himself as a young man and a photograph of his son, the Crown Prince, with his mother, the Empress; he kisses that photograph. Then, he looks at a smaller album containing photographs of a number of film luminaries, including Humphrey Bogart, Charlie Chaplin, Tyrone Power, Gene Tierney, Myrna Loy, Marlene Dietrich, and Greer Garson. Loosely inserted into that album are two photographs showing Hitler (with von Hindenburg). At this point, the Emperor gets ready to meet MacArthur (Robert Dawson).

When the Emperor emerges to be driven to that meeting, two American soldiers are trying to round up one of the imperial cranes. When the men see Hirohito, they perfunctorily instruct him "to get in the car." After a drive through the devastated landscape of Tokyo and arrival at MacArthur's headquarters, the Emperor, unused to the experience, has difficulty opening the door to the audience chamber. The interpreter—a Japanese-

American Warrant Officer (Georgi Pitskhelauri)—is overcome with awe at seeing Hirohito. He asks if Hirohito will accept the will of the American Supreme Command, a proposition to which the Emperor assents. However, the translator tells MacArthur that the Emperor does not seek mercy.

When MacArthur makes some negative remarks about persons such as Hirohito sending people to their deaths, the interpreter refuses to translate such sentiments. Then, the General asks why the Emperor is wearing Western-style clothing rather than a kimono. At this point, Hirohito responds in English. He only wears traditional Japanese clothes on ceremonial occasions; moreover, this day is one of disgrace for him and his nation. The translator interrupts again: the Emperor will lower himself by speaking in any other language than Japanese. MacArthur becomes furious with the Warrant Officer and sends him away.

The conversation between Emperor and General consists of a further exchange of trivialities before MacArthur tells Hirohito he can return to the palace. Throughout the sequence, MacArthur is bumptious; the taking of the famous photograph (of the somewhat informal general looming over the Emperor) is not dramatized; the Emperor has trouble yet again opening a door on his own. If Hirohito has been the victim of too much respect (in the form of intrusion by his servants) in the first portion of the film, he receives little respect at the hands of the Americans.

Back in the bunker at his desk—with busts of Darwin, Lincoln and Napoleon facing him—the Emperor removes the one of Napoleon and places it in a drawer. He then examines closely a Dürer engraving on a side table. When two boxes of Hershey chocolate bars arrive from SCAP (the office of the Supreme Commander for the Allied Powers), there is much consternation before the Emperor's Chamberlain takes a bite from one to ensure it is not poisoned. Then a scientist (Tajirô Tamura) summoned by Hirohito is announced.

As a child, Hirohito observes to his visitor, his father told him that his grandfather, the Meiji Emperor, had once seen the Northern Lights on the palace grounds. Tremulously but firmly, the scientist informs the Emperor that this is impossible and that perhaps his grandfather, a poet of considerable skill, was speaking poetically? "Perhaps you are correct," the Emperor, obviously relieved, assures the scientist: Hirohito has been given further evidence that diminishes his divine status. As soon as that interview is concluded, Hirohito tells his Chamberlain that he accepts MacArthur's suggestion that he appear and pose before photographers.

The soldiers are again rude and overbearing and do not obey the protocols of not getting too close to Hirohito. "That's an Emperor?" one of them asks. In fact, the Emperor mugs for the camera and, in turn, the photographers comment on how much he resembles Charlie Chaplin. The comparison is obviously not displeasing to Hirohito.

At their second meeting, the General and the Emperor have dinner at SCAP using china from a "defeated Germany." MacArthur asks Hirohito about his "friend," Hitler, and the Emperor states that he never met him. MacArthur refers to the fact that his father once worked as a military attaché at the American Embassy in Tokyo, but MacArthur is really talking in a churlish way *at* the Emperor, whose "fate is unresolved." MacArthur advises the Emperor that agreeing to have photographs taken will make him appear more human and that, as a consequence, it will be "easier for people to be more charitable towards" him.[11] The Emperor then confesses that he has always wanted to smoke a Havana cigar:

"What's it like being a living God?" asks the General.
"I don't know what to tell you. An Emperor's life is not easy."

MacArthur excuses himself. The Emperor looks out the window

and begins to dance in the solitary splendor of the large room. MacArthur secretly observes him, smirks, returns to the room, and then observes that Americans can buy anything they want. As in his first conversation with the Emperor, the General asks about the Emperor's children. Hirohito mentions that they were removed from Tokyo after the American atrocities. "What atrocities?" inquires MacArthur.

"After you dropped the bomb on Hiroshima, we expected to be attacked by beasts," the Emperor replies. MacArthur points out that he did not give that order and then asks: "Weren't those who attacked Pearl Harbor beasts?" The Emperor responds: "It was ordered without me. I did not give that order." Everything now depends, the General observes, on Hirohito. "I won't make you do anything, and I won't insist on anything." In both of his extended appearances in the film, MacArthur is both churlish and self-aggrandizing, very much an ugly American in contrast to the childlike Emperor.

The Emperor reaches the decision to speak to the nation and to renounce his divinity in the name of tranquility, prosperity and peace. After that broadcast (not shown), the Empress (Kaori Momoi), who has apparently not listened to it, requests an audience with her husband. "It's so long since we've seen each other," he observes. He embraces her: "Now I have done it. We are free."

"What have you done?" she inquires. He replies: "I am no longer a god. I have renounced such a fate."

"I thought so."
"What, I shouldn't have done it?"
"What was the problem?"
"Basically I feel uneasy. Not good at all."

Then in a wonderful domestic touch, Hirohito helps his wife remove her hat.

"So, what will be next, now that the Emperor is merely a common person?" he asks. The couple laughs, somewhat shyly. He wants to see their children, who are waiting for them in the main hall. As he prepares to leave, the Emperor asks his Chamberlain about the young man who taped his speech? He is told:

"He committed hara-kiri."
"Did you try to stop him?"

"No," answers the Chamberlain, obviously sympathetic to the sound engineer.

Somewhat embarrassed, the Emperor and Empress leave. The Chamberlain closes the door behind them.

Even more than Mizoguchi's recreation of Utamaro, Sokurov's account of Hirohito is almost entirely fictional except for the well-known fact that the Emperor was a marine biologist. Sokurov ignores what has been carefully recorded as too obvious. For example, as mentioned above, he does not recreate the taking of the famous photograph of the two men where the American towers over the Japanese.

In fact, Sokurov does everything in his power to create a character who has finally, and with considerable relief, come to terms with himself as an ordinary person. His Hirohito is a family man obsessed with film celebrities; he seems exhilarated when the American soldiers think he resembles Chaplin, and he then shamelessly poses for them; the incident with the Warrant Officer did no take place; well before his first meeting with Hirohito, MacArthur (and Washington) had more than likely decided that the Emperor would not be treated as a war criminal.

When he peers at the images in his photo album, Hirohito takes on several personalities in turn. He becomes the devoted family man who dotes on his wife and son. The images of Hitler remove him from the domestic into that of international power politics, where he became associated with the German Chancellor. Although he is a man who has wielded considerable military power, Hirohito's collection of portrait stills of famous actors reduces him to the level of the fan, someone who collects iconic images of his favorite stars. And yet he himself is the subject of iconic imagery. However, he wants to escape his celebrity status.

Why embroider history to such an extent with obvious fictions? Sokurov's film is about a man whose entire life has been centered on public events. Except in his laboratory, he has had no time for himself. Suddenly, in the wake of Japan's defeat, he has an opportunity to become humdrum, and he enthusiastically seizes the opportunity. Sokurov's film may be a deeply sympathetic exploration of a side of the Emperor never before seen, but it remains a fiction.

The question then becomes: does a biographer have the right to re-script the life of a subject to such an extent that it bears no resemblance to the evidence of the lived life? What purpose is served if history is so completely distorted? It is almost as if Sokurov has turned the whole question of the biopic inside out. Previously, many such films were accused of being grossly inaccurate: one scholar has observed, "Hollywood biography is to history what Caesar's Palace [in Los Vegas] is to architectural history: an enormous, engaging distortion, which after a time convinces us of its own kind of authenticity."[12] Yet, most biographers would accept the fact that biography is really a form of fiction: Barthes called biography "the fiction that dares not speak its name." Carolyn Heilbrun once asked, "Who can write a biography without inventing a life? A biographer, like a writer of fiction, imposes a pattern upon events, invents a protagonist, and discovers the pattern of his or her life."[13]

There is invention but there is also deliberate distortion. Not content with ignoring history, Sokurov invents a self-serving account by the Emperor to explain Japanese military aggression—and the Emperor's defense of it —by reference to the Johnson-Reed Act of 1924:

Migration...migration...yes, it never leaves its shores. Migration...Settled. Settled. Distant migration...migration of species...migration. Emigration! Discrimination! Unfair immigration laws! I remember...Wake up! I remember about the causes that brought about the Great Asian War...When the American government forbade Japanese immigration, that discrimination became a serious cause of anger and indignation among our people, and the military rode this wave of protest.

There is no evidence that the Emperor felt such sentiments on this particular subject.

Surely the biographer has to be guided by some rules? Sokurov did not feel the necessity of being so led. In fact, he went out of his way to stomp on any accepted regulations. In a masterstroke, he invited one of Japan's great comedians to inhabit the role, which Issey Ogata does masterfully (he is especially deft in recreating Hirohito's labial tics). In his hands, Hirohito becomes a stunted, infantile personality, who has never before had the opportunity to lead his own life.

Like Chaplin, Hirohito has lived his life as a performer, a mimic wrapped up in perpetual performances. His desire to resemble the man who played the Everyman Little Tramp implies a desire to be to be at one with humanity. Of course, in *The Great Dictator* (1940), Chaplin plays both Hitler and a Jew. Chaplin's exchanging of roles humanizes Hitler—which is, after all, what the Emperor appears to desire for himself and what Sokurov aims to accomplish in this film. Chaplin's Hitler and Sokurov's Hirohito are cinematic twins. In the context of this film, Hirohito ultimately exchanges one form of divinity for another. Movie stars are, after all, often worshipped as the new gods.

In putting together a kaleidoscope film narrative in which refracted pieces of Mishima are seen in a variety of ways, Paul Schrader attempted to keep within the lines of truth (for example, the known events of Mishima's last day are scrupulously recreated). Sokurov felt no similar obligation. He set out to create a fictional account of Hirohito. For Schrader, authenticity means creating his Mishima by playfully pushing but working within the boundaries of known truths; Sokurov's authenticity consists of creating a fiction in order to elicit a moving portrait of a limited, damaged person who spent much of his life chained to the claim of divinity.

Unlike their Japanese counterparts (Mizoguchi and Iwai), Schrader and Sokurov intrude into the subjectivities of their subjects. In the West, this is considered to be an obligation imposed upon the biographer; in Japan, the situation remains markedly different.

CHAPTER FOUR

AMERICANIZING JAPAN: THE OCCUPATION

WHITE MEN'S BURDENS

Released in 1949, seven years after *Casablanca*, Humphrey Bogart as Joe Barrett in *Tokyo Joe* is very much a run-down version of Rick Blaine from the earlier film. Barrett, who left Japan after Pearl Harbor and served during the War as a pilot in the American Air Force, returns during the Occupation to find that his bar, "Tokyo Joe's," is off-limits to Americans, civilian and military. He is reunited with his Japanese friend, Ito (Teru Shimada), who now runs the "joint," but Joe is taken completely aback when he hears a woman singing "These Foolish Things" in an upstairs room. The sultry voice, he soon discovers, is emanating from a phonograph. Joe desolately wanders around the room. Why has Ito put on a recording of his late wife, Trina, a White Russian exile who stayed behind and was imprisoned? Joe is both aghast and overjoyed when Ito tells him Trina (Florence Marly) is alive and well. Before Ito can tell him anything more, Joe rushes out to find Trina.

The residence he arrives at is a stunning modernist house that blends European Art Deco with traditional Japanese decor. Joe boyishly greets Trina, "Hello, Kid!," but is quickly dismayed to find out that his wife—whom he walked out on seven years earlier—has divorced him and married Mark Landis (Alexander Knox), a suave businessman. Despite his wife's new spouse, Joe is quite clear: "She belongs to me." Alone, the married couple discuss the situation: she makes it clear that she was once "weak" with desire for Joe. Now, however, under Mark's tutelage, she has learned "more" about the real nature of love.

FIGURE 11 In this poster of *Tokyo Joe*, Trina (Florence Marly) on the left by herself appears much more seductive than she ever does in the film and the villainous Baron (Sessue Hayakawa) on the right looks positively saintly.

Anxious to remain in Japan after his sixty-day visitor's pass expires, Joe begins negotiations with shady Baron Kimura (Sessue Hayakawa); he will operate (i.e., "front") a freight airline owned by the Baron, who, as a Japanese citizen, would not be granted a license to run such a firm. The bureaucracy of the Occupation will likely hinder Joe—"the paperwork could take months." One way to circumvent the process, the Baron tells Joe, is to threaten Trina and thus secure her new, well-connected husband's co-operation.

The documentation provided by the Baron provides evidence that Trina worked for the Japanese during the War broadcasting anti-American propaganda. A tearful Trina informs Joe that her baby, born in prison, was taken away from her when she was two weeks old: the survival of her daughter depended upon her compliance. "What mother would not try to save her daughter's life?" Joe threatens to blackmail Trina if she does not come away with him, whereupon she asks her maid to bring her daughter downstairs. The little girl bonds with the stranger quickly and asks him to attend her birthday party. Slowly, it dawns on Joe that he is Anya's father.

Joe now decides that he no longer wants to be the Baron's business partner, but the Baron is obdurate. Joe then approaches Landis, who quickly secures the co-operation of a friend. Soon Nippon-American Air Freight is in operation. At the birthday party, Joe's attempt to embrace Trina is interrupted by an urgent summons from the Baron to pick up freight in Seoul. Then Landis learns that the freight being carried is contraband. Having eavesdropped on her husband, Trina rushes to tell Joe he is about to be arrested: "You got yourself into trouble because of me." Landis then confronts Joe and Trina. She confesses her past as an operative to her distressed husband.

Ever resourceful, Landis arranges for Joe to be interviewed by some high-placed American military officers, who inform him that on the next day he will be picking up three Japanese war criminals in Korea and returning them to Japan. These men will be reviving the "Black Dragon Society" and fomenting "Communist" dissent against the Occupation. Barrett then agrees to deliver the men to the Americans.

Meanwhile, the Baron, aware that his plans may about to be foiled, arranges for Anya's maid to deliver the child to two of his thugs. Through an elaborate series of twists and turns, Joe, pretending to co-operate with the Baron, rescues Anya but dies from a gun wound inflicted by him. "See you later, kid," are his dying words to Trina.

The Tokyo seen in this film may be desolate, but the Japanese residing there are characterized as devious, ungrateful opponents of the American hierarchy. The Baron is trying to import dangerous war criminals; the nursemaid betrays her employers and the child she is looking after; even Ito, who seems to be Joe's buddy, turns out to be secretly working for the Baron. Deeply ashamed, he commits seppuku but, before dying, reveals where the child is being held. Joe gives the dying man a pious lecture before saying, "Sayonara, pal."

Why did you have to do it?

Don't you understand what guys like that have done to you? For a thousand years they've made suckers out of you. All they wanted was the gravy. Guys like you on your hands and knees to hand it up to them. You think we're the real enemies because we're occupying Japan. You know why we're doing it? To help the Japanese people stand up on their hind legs, like men and women have a right to in this world. And you still don't get it.

Joe's history lesson, filled with rage and resentment, addresses the issue of the white man's burden and voices American superiority over a conquered nation. The Westernized Landis house—which is prominently featured—is obviously much more inviting than any other interior shown in the film. *Tokyo Joe*, released in the third year of the Occupation, ultimately plays to widespread distrust of the Japanese and displays residual anger at the country that staged Pearl Harbor and caused the loss of life to many American servicemen in the subsequent war. In the film's mise en scène, the glamorous Landis house reflects safe, Western values as opposed to the scruffy sets used in other parts of the film.

To play the role of the menacing Baron, Bogart implored Hayakawa to return to Hollywood (the film was shot there and in Tokyo). The Baron has much charm on display, but in reality he is a ruthless profiteer who embodies "Oriental Menace." In the United States, Hayakawa himself was a bit of a dubious figure: on January 9, 1949 the *New York Times* claimed that his "activity during the German occupation of Paris came into question" when a visa was applied for. There was even the possibility, Robert Lord, the producer of *Tokyo Joe*, felt, that Hayakawa was too old and feeble for the part. During an interview in Paris with Lord's representative, Hayakawa commanded his visitor to attack him: "At first he wouldn't, but finally he swung at my chin. I grabbed his arm and twisted his wrist until he cried" out. After that encounter Hayakawa's salary was negotiated and a contract signed. For the film's success to be ensured, Hayakawa had to be a particularly underhanded figure.[1]

This necessity has to be placed into the context of the Korean War then being waged. American forces were again fighting in Asia, this time backing South Korea against the North Korean forces supported by Mao's China. On the home front, many Americans felt they had been forced in to yet another conflict in Asia. Baron Kimura is associated with the Communist menace in Korea; he is, after all, supposed to be importing Japanese war criminals to advance such a cause. Significantly, this film was the first time after the Pacific War that an American film cleared rights with army authorities for filming in Japan. The burden of the Korean War looms even larger in *Tokyo File 212*.

Released two years after *Tokyo Joe*, *Tokyo File 212* also stars the

Czechoslovakian-born Florence Marly, who in this film plays opposite Robert Peyton (also known as Lee Frederick). Marly is now Steffi Novak, a flirtatious free-lance translator, assisting Jim Carter, a U.S. secret agent posing as a reporter. The elderly Mr Matsudo (Tasuo Saito) joins them in the film's opening sequence: they have been asked to meet at noon by an unnamed person. There is an enormous explosion, and the film then goes into flashback.

Two weeks before, Carter arrived in Tokyo. His "spot job" was to investigate Japanese Communists assisting the North Koreans. He was selected for this task because his college roommate Taro Matsudo (Katsuhiko Haida) had been observed at Communist rallies and other "rats' nests". Carter's assignment is to accidentally bump into his old friend and, through that connection, gather information.

When Carter arrives at his hotel room, the alluring Steffi is there, reclining on the bed, supposedly sleeping. Unlike her role in *Tokyo Joe* where she is remote and austerely beautiful, Marly in this film is a vamp, very much in the noir tradition. Her "business" is to act as a sort of a personal assistant to Carter, who is, she points out, "a babe in the woods" in Tokyo.

Taro flees when he spots Carter, who learns from his friend's father, a high-level government official in Occupied Japan, that Taro was trained to become a kamikaze pilot who would willingly sacrifice his life for his country. (At this point, the film recreates episodes from that training.) "Self-destruction became the only real glory," the father sadly recalls. However, just as he completed his course, Japan surrendered, a distraught Taro disappeared and surfaced again as a Communist supporter.

Carter finally has a secret meeting with Taro but when he returns to his hotel room, he is roughed up. He also meets a strange, loomingly tall English journalist, Mr Jeffrey (Byron Michie), and is summoned to the home of an exporter, Mr Oyama (Tetsu Nakamura). He receives a typewritten note that Namiko

(Reiko Otami), Taro's ex-fiancé, is working as a dancer at the Tarkarazuka Review (see below and Chapter Seven). He meets her there, but she is soon kidnapped and thrown out of a car. At the hospital, a distraught Taro visits her, where Carter is waiting for him. Namiko speaks glowingly of the changes introduced into Japan by the Occupation:

> Please, Taro, you think we are blind, but it is you who cannot see. In the old Japan, did the farmer ever own his land? Could the worker demand fair treatment? Was the voice of the lowest as strong as that of the highest? These [changes] are good, Taro. Why would you destroy them?

Moved but silent, Taro leaves.

Returning to his room, Carter handcuffs Steffi, who finally confesses that she has been acting as an operative for Oyama in order to save her sister, who is being held prisoner in North Korea. When Carter reveals to her that her sister has been murdered, she vows revenge and, of course, switches sides.

Taro is ordered by Oyama to lead a general strike to disrupt Japan. At a rally, his father confronts him and his lackeys, who throw the elderly man to the ground. Taro, distraught, attempts to assist his father. Then Taro, having decided to reform himself, visits Namiko in hospital. Finding her dead, he phones Carter to pledge his allegiance to the Allied cause.

Oyama, displeased by Taro's loyalty to his father, calls him to his office, where he reveals that forged letters from Taro have been used to summon his father, Novak and Carter to their doom. There is another document: a letter from Taro confessing to the bombing. The film then switches back to the opening scene. To save his comrades, Taro jumps to his death, which causes the three to rush away before the explosion can cause them harm. In the following scene, Oyama, who like the "bamboo bends with the wind," is about to save himself when an underling stabs him to death. At the airport to send Carter off, Mr Matsuto regrets his son's death but is of the conviction that it is better "to die honorably than to live dishonorably."

Unlike *Tokyo Joe*, Tokyo and its environs are used throughout *Tokyo File*: nightlife, street festivals, and outdoor scenes are incorporated into the story line. Although Korea and the Communist menace are underscored, the Japanese characters are shown to be persons, like the Western-born protagonists, of conflicting emotions. Matsudo is a fervent supporter of the Occupation; Namiko has remained steadfast to Taro, although he has abandoned her; Taro is deeply conflicted about the fate of Japan, but when he learns how evil Oyama really is, he courageously sacrifices his life for his father and friends.

The film's scenario, nevertheless, recreates the notion that the Japanese have to be rescued from themselves—once again. Despite American efforts during the Occupation seen in *Tokyo File*, there are still some Japanese who persist in thinking of the *gaijin* as their enemy. Some, like Oyama, are inflexible in their belief system, but there are those like Taro who ultimately can be made to see the truth. A similar consortium of director, producer, cinematographer and editor made *Oriental Evil*.

There is another curious link between *Tokyo File* and *Oriental Evil* (1950): Byron Michie, who has a small role in *File*, is central to this film as Roger Mansfield, who turns out to be the mysterious Thomas Putnam, whom Cheryl Banning (Martha Hyer) has come to Tokyo to meet. Putnam was her brother's business partner, and she is certain by locating him she will discover who killed her brother, although, according to the Tokyo police, he committed suicide. Roger Mansfield and Thomas Putnam are one and the same person, and he did indeed kill the brother.

The film begins with an elaborate portrayal of the supernatural Unmei, a form of Japanese fate who oversees bad deeds, knows the sources of evil in the human heart and only appears to those who are villainous. Roger, who has impregnated his

Japanese girlfriend, weds her in an elaborate ceremony at the outset of the film's narrative action. The bride's brother (Tetsu Nakamura) gives him a home in exchange for marrying his sister.

When Cheryl arrives, she meets the churlish Mansfield, to whom she takes an "instinctive dislike." She then becomes friendly with him and is then visited by her brother's Japanese partner, Mr Yoshida, who has never met Putnam. An additional complication is a stash of missing opium.

After a series of misadventures, Cheryl, who has decided not to play detective any longer, begins to fall in love with Roger. In turn, Roger, who is being hounded for debts, tells Yoshida that he wants to set a trap to lure Putnam from hiding. In a fit of peak, he assaults his pregnant wife, who miscarries. In another plot twist, Roger arranges to unload stolen black market goods with the assistance of his brother-in-law, but the person being burgled turns out to be the owner of the warehouse from which the goods were taken.

Then O'Brien, a shady character from "Tom's" past, sends Cheryl a note asking for five thousand dollars in exchange for information about her brother. Putnam meets with and assaults him. Under increasing pressure from other debtors and O'Brien, Roger becomes frantic. He marries Cheryl, but she soon overhears a conversation in which he as addressed as Tom. Roger provides a weak excuse, and Cheryl returns to her hotel room.

The truth of the increasingly complex situation gradually dawns on Cheryl when Mr Yoshida and Roger's Japanese bride visit her. They inform her that Roger married Mr Yoshida's sister in a fake ceremony. The Japanese woman confronts her husband, who admits the truth. She then quickly commits seppuku, whereupon he burns their house down. Roger is chased but arrives back at Cheryl's place. His brother-in-law attempts to kill Roger, who is, however, impaled on a statue.

Japanese elements are incorporated into the story line. The

black market is shown to be fully operational, and Roger/Tom's Japanese partners are crooks. However, the Japanese woman in the film is victimized; Mr Yoshida remains a stalwart champion of justice.

The strange thing about *Oriental Evil* resides in its title because the evil is completely that of Roger/Tom, who at one point haplessly seems to blame his place of residence for his behavior: "strange things happen in the Orient." (In this way, the East can be said to be the source—and cause—of Evil.) The film may be book-ended by the mysterious Unmei, but the blackness in this film ultimately resides in the heart of a Westerner.

In Samuel Fuller's *House of Bamboo* (1955) rough-speaking and acting Eddie Kenner—also known as Spanier (Robert Stack)— arrives in 1954 Tokyo as a secret operative, very much in the same manner of Jim Carter in *Tokyo File*.

The film opens with a flashback sequence in which a military train guarded by American servicemen and Japanese police is ambushed between Tokyo and Kyoto. Carried out with crack precision, the cargo of guns and ammunition is taken; an American sergeant is killed. Five weeks later, an armed robber, an American named Webber, is riddled with bullets used in the train heist. Webber, who was shot and left for dead by his own gang, refuses to implicate his buddies. In his dying moments, however, he reveals that he was secretly married to a woman named Mariko. On his person is a letter from one Eddie Spanier, who is eager to join Webber in Japan after his release from prison.

Three weeks later, Spanier's ship docks in Yokohama, and he immediately heads for Tokyo in search of Mariko (Shirley Yamaguchi). When he locates her, she is certain he is a member of her husband's gang sent to exterminate her. Eddie, after showing her a photo of himself with Webber, warns her to keep quiet about her marriage to ensure her safety.

FIGURE 12 Although Sandy (Robert Ryan) is the villain in *House of Bamboo*, his countenance is the center of attention in this poster.

Eddie then visits *pachinko* parlors, where he attempts to sell protection. In the second one, he is apprehended, beaten and warned by Sandy Dawson (Robert Ryan) and his henchmen to keep his nose out of their business. Intrigued, however, by Eddie, Sandy arranges for him to be arrested on a trumped-up charge and his "rap sheet" obtained. Now convinced that Eddie is a genuine thug, Sandy invites him to join his gang, very much against the instincts of Griff (Cameron Mitchell), his chief assistant. Sandy's crew is comprised of American enlisted men, all of whom have been dishonorably discharged.

Eddie meets secretly with Army intelligence and the police, and it is at this point that it becomes obvious that his surname is Kenner, and he is an operative attempting to bring Dawson and his crew to justice. (Sessue Hayakawa plays the role of efficient, kindly Inspector Kito). Meanwhile, Sandy is disturbed when

Eddie mentions that he has "kimono business" and soon Sandy and Riff hunt down Mariko. Convinced that Eddy's relationship with Mariko is on the level, Sandy backs down. Quite soon afterwards, Eddie and Mariko become lovers; she even agrees to act as his "kimono," although she does not know he is a police investigator. Although ostracized by her neighbors for her fraternization with an American, she remains loyal to Eddie.

FIGURE 13 Sandy (Robert Ryan) kills Griff (Cameron Mitchell) in *House of Bamboo.*

Sandy is a meticulous organizer with exacting rules. If a member of the gang is shot, the wounded man is immediately killed so that no one can squeal. "You're only good if you don't take a bullet," he sardonically observes. During the ensuing heist, Griff kills a wounded gang member but Sandy makes an exception to his rule by allowing Eddie, also wounded, to live. "Why," he wonders, "did I contradict my own order? It'll never happen again."

Eddie now reveals to Mariko that he is really Sergeant Kenner and that he is investigating Sandy and the gang. Griff becomes increasingly jealous of Eddie's hold over Sandy. Mariko, under Eddie's orders, meets the chief American officer at the Imperial Hotel, where they are spotted by one of Sandy's men. Sandy assumes Mariko is cheating on Eddie and warns Mariko—calling her a "cheap little tramp"—of the consequences of two-timing.

Griff has been "pitching too hard" according to Sandy, who tells his former *ichiban* (number one assistant) that he will not be allowed to participate in the next heist. Meanwhile, Sandy's informant warns him that the police have set a trap, whereupon that operation is aborted. Certain that he has been betrayed by Griff, Sandy kills him. Subsequently, an informant reveals to him that he killed the wrong man. Sandy retaliates by setting up Kenner to be killed by the Japanese police during a robbery of a pearl broker. When that goes awry, Sandy is chased by the police to a rooftop amusement park where Kenner shoots and kills him.

Japan seems to have further liberated Fuller's flair for experimentation in gangster films. For example, *House of Bamboo* contains a fascinating homoerotic sub-text first revealed when Sandy betrays his own rule and allows the wounded Eddie to live. When Sandy lashes out at Mariko, Robert Ryan infuses the part with strong sexual undertones, as if to imply he is attracted to Eddie and is furious at someone who would betray him. Griff, of course, is jealous that Sandy had replaced him with Eddie. On the surface, the gang members all have "kimono girls" but, in its handling of Sandy and Griff, the film seethes with unresolved and buried issues about male bonding. The reference to "pitching too hard" can be read as a reference to Griff's jealousy over Sandy's interest in Eddie.

The gay elements in the film were, surprisingly, green-lighted by Daryl Zanuck, the film's producer, as Fuller recalled: "In the fifties, homosexuality was taboo. No studio would go anywhere near it. Zanuck allowed me to use that scene [where Sandy shoots a nude Griff while he is bathing] because it was dressed up like a gangster vendetta."[2]

Fuller, who often worked with minimal budgets, was given the opportunity by his producers to produce a high-quality film, as Keith Uhlich has observed: "Quite simply, *House of Bamboo* has some of the most stunning examples of widescreen photography in the history of cinema. Travelling to Japan on 20th Century Fox's dime, Fuller captured a country divided, trapped between past traditions and progressive attitudes while lingering in the devastating after-effects of an all-too-recent World War. His visual tableaus, a succession of silhouettes, screens, and stylized color photography melds the heady insanity of a Douglas Sirk melodrama...with the philosophical inquiry of the best noirs."[3]

Indeed, the real star of *House of Bamboo* is the exceptional use of cinemascope to show the cityscapes and landscapes of Japan. The tableau shots seem to have been inspired in part by the flat planes used in Ukiyo-e woodcuts, particularly in the triptych format.

The film may have an angry violence, but Japan itself is rendered as "the politest nation in the world"—and its great physical beauty is emphasized. In retrospect, Fuller considered his life "richer" for having made a film there "The light there is unique and wonderful. Colors come out looking postcard crisp. Even their blacks and whites are different, sharper and purer."[4]

These four films set out to depict a Japan that had been off-limits for a number of years. All four directly or indirectly comment on the "Communist menace," on the obvious fact that Japan's co-operation was vital if the interests of the USSR and Mao's China were to be kept at bay in the Far East. In such a context, World War II in the Pacific was fought to ward off the Japanese threat but now danger lurks if Japan were to slip out of America's hands or if Japan was to be used as a pawn by the Communists to prevail in the Korean War.

In addition to exploiting this prevailing zeitgeist, *Oriental Evil* and *House of Bamboo* imply that Japan is a seductive place, where a Westerner's latent evil can come to the fore. Neither film makes such an overt statement, but both are indicating that the lack of strong, prevailing codes of good and evil might be the undoing of the white man.

Four months after the surrender of Japan, the *Saturday Evening Post* printed an article entitled, "The GI Is Civilizing the Jap."[5] The job of the soldiers during the Occupation was described, as John Dower has pointed out, "simply to be themselves" and by an osmosis-like process reform the Japanese.[6] A pamphlet called *Our Job in Japan* argued that the occupiers could "prove that what we like to call the American way, or democracy, or just plain Golden Rule common sense, is a pretty good way to live."[7]

The burden of the white man is that he is, by definition, superior to the Japanese whom he must exploit. In the contexts of these films, might is right. If the Japanese were willing to be charmed into submission, so much the better. In any event, Japan must be Americanized; in effect, it must become a smaller scale-model of the United States. These films were able to obtain financing in large part because Americans wanted to see the landscape of the nation they had vanquished and because such films could be made into excellent propaganda pieces. The reality is that the grim plight of the Japanese during the Occupation is rarely highlighted in either Western or, for that matter, Japanese films. Suzuki's *Gate of Hell* is a notable exception.

POSTWAR JAPAN AS SURREALIST NIGHTMARE

The cinematography and the color values in Seijun Suzuki's 1964 *Gate of Flesh* (*Nikutai no mon*) are as outstanding as those in *House of Bamboo*, but the sets and costumes are deliberately glaring and surreal. In addition, the entire look of the film is theatrical in order to heighten the fact that what the viewer is seeing is a deliberate amplification of reality. Rather than recording something in a quasi-documentary way, Suzuki wanted to make the viewer aware of the true horrors of Occupied Tokyo. This is the subject matter of very few Japanese films.[8]

Maya (Yumiko Nogawa), an eighteen-year-old orphan, steals a sweet potato from a street vendor and soon encounters Sen (Satoko Kasai), a prostitute who lives in the black market area with a group of women following the same profession: Roku (Tamiko Ishii), Mino (Kayo Matsuo) and Machiko (Misako Tominaga). This sisterhood has a strict code: no pimps, no GIs and no free services.

A local yakuza gang protects the women. If a girl breaks a rule, she is punished by being tortured by her confederates. Although one of the women feels: "A woman's happiest when married," she would never espouse that to the other members of her sorority. As a group, they are trying to get on with their lives by rejecting the "victim mentality," and "spitting" on society. They are heartily sick of the "new democracy" and "the brotherhood of man." At one point, Sen tells a client that Japanese men are pathetic: "You lost the war!"

The costuming of the women is simple but effective: Sen in Red, Roku in yellow, Mino in purple, and Maya in green. Although some critics described the four primary colors as deliberately symbolic, Suzuki scoffed at this: each of the women was clothed in a single color to differentiate her from the other prostitutes. Machiko wears a kimono and sandals because she represents Japan's destroyed past; she often speaks of the values of hearth and home in contrast to the much harsher sentiments expressed by the other women. One of her colleagues cautions her, "A whore shouldn't try to play housewife."

The trajectory of the plot begins when a returnee soldier Shintaro Ibuki (Jo Shishido) takes refuge with the women: he has stabbed a GI to death and the Americans are pursuing him. He makes the point to a friend: Japan "is hardly a country worth coming home for." Shin quickly becomes the center of the world of the five women, although they do not willingly divulge their changes of heart to him—or each other.

Machiko is severely punished when she gives herself to a man without charging: "When I'm with you, I feel like I'm your wife," she confesses to the client. When she is stripped in preparation for being beaten, Shin makes the situation worse for her by exclaiming at the beauty of her body; she is expelled from the group after being tortured. Venturing from the women's den, Shin sets off on a series of muggings.

There are additional episodes of violent behavior. A black American Catholic priest, who attended Maya when she was raped, intervenes when a GI propositions her; under the shadow of his church he then has sex with her. Meanwhile, Machiko is seduced by Shin, who attaches value only to that which he can touch: he does not believe in any abstract concepts. In a gruesome scene, he captures a water buffalo and dismembers it. A celebratory feast follows in which Shin wraps himself in the Japanese flag as if it commemorates his disgrace—and Japan's.

Sen is outraged when Shin rejects her. Maya, in mourning for her brother who died in Borneo, confuses him in her mind with Shin. Recalling the consequences involved in having an affair with Shin, Maya resolves to murder him and then kill herself. He prevents her from doing this and begins an affair with her. Falling in love with Shin is filled with consequences, Maya realizes: "The moment I become a real woman, I become an outcast." She asks Shin: "Does feeling human mean you can't go on living?"

In the context of this film the answer is, of course, yes. The three other women plot their revenge against both Maya and Shin. First, they subject Maya to a severe beating. Then the women tell a yakuza that Shin is making off with a stash of penicillin: when Shin is shot by MPs, the gangsters discover he was, for sentimental reasons, carrying the papers of a fellow soldier slain in the war. When Maya returns to her enclave, she spies a Japanese flag sunk in muddy water. In the closing sequence, Sen, Toku and Mino return to work, and the camera pans to provide a view of the entire black market area. In the distance the American flag waves, signifying that this terrain is under foreign domination.

Suzuki was confronted with a wide array of problems in making this film. Nikkatsu would only provide the funds for making a B movie, and that studio wanted the movie to use some of the conventions of the new Pink (*Pinku eiga*) soft-core pornography. Casting the five women was a problem because the mainstay Nikkatsu actresses refused to be in the film: four outsiders had to be recruited.

Takeo Kimura, the production designer, had worked with Suzuki and had an excellent understanding of the fact that his boss welcomed innovation and daringness. Kimura decided to construct a deliberately theatrical looking series of sets in order to re-create war-torn Tokyo. Bombed-out ruins were not readily available in 1963, and so he constructed one on the cheap on the Shikkatsu back lot. He threw bright color washes against hastily made, often broken pieces of architectural elements. His garish, highly saturated designs perfectly match the over-the-top performances the director deliberately elicited from the cast.

Suzuki was well aware that he was expanding the stated objectives to which he had contracted himself. However, he not only kept his end of the bargain but he also allowed his own sense of Japanese postwar humiliation and despair to become his true subject matter. He did not like Americans, and he allowed his film to show how the American flag had taken pride of place over the Japanese one. In startling contrast to the American-made films about the Occupation, Suzuki tried to demonstrate how the Japanese felt in defeat, of how their worldview had been completely overturned. Suzuki's film is rooted in the psychological reality that still confronted many Japanese in 1964, a decade after the Occupation had ended.

THE OCCUPATION AS COMEDY

Comedy's ability to employ irony and, thus, introduce and play with the idea of self-ridicule surfaces in another group of Occupation films. The White Man's Burden is still very much in evidence, but it is possible, especially in the case of *The Teahouse of the August Moon*, to poke fun at this notion—even satirize it. In the case of *Back at the Front* and *Cry for Happy*, condescension towards the Japanese prevails.

Back at the Front (1952) is a sequel to *Up Front* from the previous year and features rascally, bumptious infantry soldiers Willie (Tom Ewell) and Joe (Harvey Lembeck) as reincarnations of characters made famous by the cartoonist Bill Maudlin. Having returned to the States from active duty, the two have joined the reserves and are astounded to be called back to active service. At training camp in the States, they do their best to suffer from various illnesses but are found out. At the base in Japan, they volunteer to undertake an unknown mission, which turns out to be a series of experiments in which they are being used as guinea pigs to test army gear. On furlough in Tokyo, and anxious to get rid their army fatigues, they abscond with a MP jeep, are chased and then leap into a taxi, where they meet Nina (Mari Blanchard), the accomplice of Johnny Redondo (Russell Johnson), a smuggler. Joe, who always is full of "bright ideas," is smitten with Nina whereas she reminds Willie of a "Black Widow spider, always ready to bite."

Contrary to their expectations, the MPs they encounter are sympathetic to their tattered appearances and urge them to go to a service club. However, Joe prefers another establishment: "EXCELLENT TYPE YOUNG LADIES IN ATTENDANCE ... BATHING IN MILK A SPECIALTY." The two do not notice, however, that this place is off limits to enlisted men and thus available only to officers. Their American-educated rickshaw boy, however, shows them the back entrance. The two are furious when their bath attendants turn out to be young men, and a brawl ensues. MPs are summoned, but the two, attempting to escape dressed as geisha, are about to be captured when they mention the name Nina. Immediately, they are brought to a backroom where they encounter Johnny.

Johnny offers to take them to his house, where they can get "some action." Nina is there, sake is served, and the lady attempts to pump them for information about the equipment they have been testing. In these encounters, Joe and Willie are uncomfortable with the strange food they are being served and with the absence of chairs. Completely drunk, they seize a geisha's samisen and attempt to sing "Home on the Range." As his butler shows the drunken twosome out, Johnny informs Nina: "These boys will work out fine. Just fine."

Joe and Willie are about to be taken into custody once again when they express regret at not being able to meet up with Johnny. An alert General Dixon, who has long been attempting to arrest Redondo, immediately offers the two GIs anything they want if they agree to assist him. Back at Redondo's house, the smuggler inveigles the two to carry contraband in an army truck. The set-up would have worked perfectly, but Willie gets hungry and decides to open a can of crabmeat, which turns out to be an explosive. Further mayhem ensues. Eventually, when Willie throws a can at the escaping plane of the thieves, the villains are brought to justice.

In the final scene of the film, the two hapless heroes are being returned to the States. General Dixon informs them: "We are trying to maintain friendly relations with Japan and so if you two ever come back to Tokyo, I'll have you boiled in oil."

Generically, *Cry for Happy* (1961) may be an Occupation movie, but its steady concentration on geisha as sexual objects becomes a strong sub-text. In the first sequence, Admiral Bennett (Howard St. John) asks a Japanese government minister about geisha. Are they, in fact, women of easy virtue? He is assured this is not the case. What is true is that in Japan, the minister claims, women place men on a pedestal.

Boastingly and mendaciously, CPO (Chief Petty Officer) Andy Cyphers (Glenn Ford) tells a press conference that he and his navy buddies, Murray Prince (Donald O'Connor), Suzuki (James Shigeta) and Lank (Chet Douglas) have opened an orphanage for Japanese children. Meanwhile, Cyphers lends photographic equipment to Mr Endo, a Japanese film director, who offers in exchange his cousin's home for a vacation, but the place turns out to be unexpectedly inhabited by four Japanese women. Cyphers think that the four females are provided with the house, but he and his buddies then learn that one of them is the cousin, who has returned home unexpectedly. Then, the four men learn that this residence is a geisha house.

Of course, living in a geisha house is "off limits" to service personnel, but, if Suzuki becomes CPO Suzuki, Cyphers argues, his Japanese ancestry will make the matter acceptable in the eyes of the geisha. Chiyiko (Miiko Taka) is the owner of the geisha house, and one of her employees is Harue (Miyoshi Umeki). The four women are romantically interested in the four Navy men, but they are much more subdued than the men in expressing their feelings. Chiyiko tells Cyphers that there will be "no hanky-panky" and that she believes in democracy: "Nothing for Everybody." To the other women, she laments that American men like instant coffee, instant tea and instant girls.

The two plot lines converge at the premiere of Endo's "The Rice Rustlers of Yokohama Gulch," at which the Americans in the audience laugh loudly, much to the director's displeasure. The four Americans, accompanied by their geisha, are in attendance as are the two members of the press sniffing out the whereabouts of the mysterious orphanage, the existence of which they reveal to an astonished Admiral and Mrs. Bennett (Harriet E. MacGibbon). Shortly afterwards, Cyphers and his men have to transform the geisha house into an orphanage because Mrs. Bennett, overjoyed by what they have done, wishes to visit.

Eventually, two of the men marry their geisha, and the geisha house becomes an orphanage. On the way to this resolution, Murray learns that Harue's father is not the successful industrialist she claims. In fact, Izumi was a captain in the Japanese navy, his ship was sunk and he now works as an elevator operator at a department store. Moreover, he has just "sold" his daughter to an elderly suitor, whom his daughter has never met. When Murray and Cyphers meet Izumi, he tells them flatly that he wants his daughter to marry a Japanese man but that he has rejected the elderly suitor's attempt to buy Harue. Although the "price of defeat" may be high, he is no barbarian.

Quick-thinking Cyphers comes up with a solution: if Izumi is made a "consultant" to the Navy, he might be willing to reconsider the matter of the nationality of a son-in-law. The ploy works. After his wedding, Murray exclaims, "geisha are not hard to get—you just marry them!" Like everyone else, he is so filled with joy that he "cries for happy." In this film the fascination with geisha has been brought into line with American norms. The foreign Other has been domesticated.

John Patrick adapted the screenplay of Daniel Mann's *The Teahouse of the August Moon* (1956) from his Pulitzer and Tony award winning Broadway play (1953), which was derived from Vern Sneider's novel of the same name published in 1951. One of the bloodiest battles of the Pacific War was fought on the island of Okinawa, an irony of which Sneider, Patrick and Mann would have been well aware.[9] This film comically shows two American officers rejecting their native traditions in favor of Japanese ones, but the assimilation goes so far that it becomes outrageously far-fetched and unbelievable.

Captain Fisby (Glenn Ford), a misfit in the psychological warfare division, is sent to "Americanize" the village of Tobiki on Okinawa. Pompous Colonel Wainwright Purdy III (Paul Ford), his commanding officer, assigns a mischievous, wily local, Sakini (Marlon Brando) to act as his assistant/interpreter.

Fisby desperately tries to implement the military's plan: he encourages the locals to build a school in the shape of a pentagon but they want to build a teahouse. Rather than "Americanizing" the natives, Fisby becomes completely assimilated to local customs. To revive the local economy, he decides that the Okinawans manufacture souvenirs, which nobody wants to purchase. Then Fisby discovers a potent local beverage, which soon finds a very willing market among the American soldiers. With the influx of capital, the teahouse is quickly constructed.

A worried Purdy sends a psychiatrist Captain McLean (Eddie Albert) to check up on Fisby's mental status, but the newcomer goes native in the same way as Fisby. When Purdy does not hear from either officer, he travels to the village where he finds his two subordinates have been assimilated into the ways of Okinawa. Purdy orders the teahouse destroyed, but, instead, the villagers merely dismantle it. Later, the village is chosen by SCAP (MacArthur's office: the Office of the Supreme Commander of the Allied Forces) as an example of successful democratization. The teahouse is then reassembled.

The American occupiers in the film are shown as often well meaning but almost always befuddled. They might have techno-logical know-how, but they lack insight, a quality possessed in abundance by Sakini, who manipulates the colonizers consis-tently.

Marlon Brando chose to play Sakini because by this time he had complete freedom to choose his roles, and he was playing "out some fantasy of championing the oppressed citizens of the Third World." He also had the right to pick Daniel Mann as director. What he did not have any power over was the selection of Glenn Ford to play Fisby, an actor of a completely different temperament from his own.

FIGURE 14 Sakini (Marlon Brando) is the embodiment of charm and chicanery in *The Teahouse of the August Moon*.

The first of many difficulties in filming began in April 1956 just as production was under way. The Americans felt that the Japanese members of the crew were too slow moving. Louis

Calhern, who was to play Purdy, died suddenly, and Paul Ford, who had performed the role on Broadway, was rushed over to Japan. Some scenes had to be re-shot. Mann refused to molly-coddle Brando, but the biggest problem was the acerbity between Brando and Ford. Brando's left-wing opinions angered Ford, who was essentially a middle-of-the-road liberal. At press conferences, Brando became an expert on the East: "Of all the countries in the world that suffer from backwardness, America is first. 'Orientals' don't strive for success the way we do. They consider the moral development of the inner man equally important."

> Americans don't even begin to understand the people of Asia.... Our understanding of Asians will never improve until we get out of the habit of thinking of [these] people as short, spindly-legged, buck-teethed little people with strange customs.[10]

The film itself supports many of Brando's arguments since the American are mercilessly satirized. When Americans attempt to become Japanese-like, they behave ridiculously. *Teahouse of the August Moon* may lampoon American militarism and conde-scension and be at pains to puncture some stereotypes of the Japanese, but it concludes that Japan will always remain an exotic, ultimately inscrutable locale, a place that will remain closed to the West.

All three Occupation comedies construct postwar Japan in humorous terms with almost no reference to the fact that the Japanese had endured a crushing and humiliating defeat in the Pacific War. Neither the Korean War nor the Communist threat is mentioned. What is emphasized is that Japan is a place filled with "strange customs" that can be poked fun at (for example, shoes are removed when one enters a house and the women often wear "strange" clothing).

The other side of the coin is evident in the ways in which Americans are shown to have rigid ideas about the customs of others. The lascivious intentions of the Navy men in *Cry for Happy* are countered by the quick-witted Japanese women, who have no intention of prostituting themselves.

The American eagerness to dominate, to decide what is good and bad, and to establish a new moral code for the Japanese is broadly satirized in *Teahouse of the August Moon*. Sakini continually emphasizes how his American superiors have views of the world that are outlandish, self-aggrandizing and, quite often, wildly misguided. That film ends with a sense of accord, although the colonial spirit of the American enterprise in Occupied Japan is ridiculed. Nevertheless, as Ian Littlewood, has observed, the film ends with a trade-off: "The villagers need American help to get the local economy going, but when it comes to taste and sensibility the balance is heavily on the side of Japan."[11] What none of these films emphasizes is the vastly changed world of the Japanese during the Occupation. In part, *Sayonara* attempted to remedy that deficiency.

MADAME BUTTERFLY ALL OVER AGAIN?

Joshua Logan, the director of *Sayonara* (1957) called on Samuel Fuller before leaving for Japan: he was worried about directing Michener's inter-racial love story (1954), which, at that point, had what might be called a tragic ending. "Josh told me," Fuller recalled, "he'd considered making the picture's ending more upbeat. The white man, played by Marlon Brando, would show up just in time to prevent the suicide of his Japanese lover, played by Miiko Taka. Brisk competition among the studios pushed creative people to consider changing a story line, even that of a classic tragedy, to make a box-office hit. Thankfully, Logan ended up sticking to the original."[12]

FIGURE 15 The sexual chemistry between Gruver (Marlon Brando) and Hana Ogi (Miiko Taka) is much more evident in this poster from *Sayonara* than it is in the film.

Fuller's recollection is filled with factual errors, but it demonstrates clearly that the ending of the film, an issue that took a long time to resolve, was a major concern well before production commenced. During filming, Brando, who was frequently at odds with Logan, wanted to be the film's *auteur* as well as star; the disagreements between the two were made public by Truman Capote in "The Duke in His Domain," a profile of Brando in the November 9, 1957 issue of *The New Yorker*.

The film begins in Korea in 1951. A disgruntled, melancholic Major Lloyd Gruver, an ace pilot, has just returned from a combat flight in which he downed two planes (to his dismay, he glimpsed a face in one of the planes he shot down) and is informed he is being sent to Kobe, Japan at the request of General Webster.

For a while, Gruver has been worried about one of his men. Joe Kelly (Red Buttons) has been toying, to his superior's disdain, with the idea of marrying a Japanese woman, Katsumi (Miyoshi Umeki, who appears in *Cry for Happy*). In an attempt to turn the tables on his commanding officer, Kelly informs Gruver that he is being summoned to a desk job in Japan so that the Major can, at long last, cement his relationship with Webster's daughter, Eileen (Patricia Owens), to whom he has been loosely engaged for an inordinately long time.

Kelly cynically informs the Major that the General is arranging one marriage while Kelly's Congressman, with considerable difficulty, has been assisting him to obtain permission to marry Katsumi. Rank has its privileges, he insinuates. Gruver then informs Kelly that he should look at a photograph of Eileen, a true American girl. Gruver says Katsumi looks "bright," but he assures him he is taking a risk in marrying the Japanese woman, whom he refers to as a "slant-eyed runt." Gruver apologizes for the remark, but he tells Kelly he is insane to give up his American citizenship to enter a mixed marriage. Kelly, after agreeing that he is crazy, then asks a deeply relevant question: "Perhaps you don't feel as strong about your girl as I do mine?" Reluctantly, Gruver agrees to be Kelly's best man.

In every possible way, Kelly is the opposite of his superior. He is a trouble-maker, goes AWOL, and is obviously not of the same social class of Gruver, the son of a General. When he first appears in the film, Kelly has embraced the Other in the form of a Japanese woman. Gruver is adamant that this is a terrible idea.

Of course, Eileen is waiting with her parents (Kent Smith and Martha Scott) at the airport when Gruver arrives in Kobe. In a major confrontation, Eileen asks Lloyd what their relationship means to him. She tells him directly that she does not want the kind of frigid, distant relationship his parents have endured. In addition, Eileen rejects the idea of a traditional, old-fashioned marriage. Gruver remonstrates with her: she has been thinking and talking a lot of "nonsense." He wants a girl *like* her. She is affronted; she wants to be liked for herself. Moreover, has he never thought of dragging her away to a shack somewhere, an obvious reference to their non-existent sex life. Yes, he agrees. "What's holding you back?" she asks. He tells her to grow up and realize that there's a "right" time and a "wrong" time for everything. He defends himself "like a fort," Eileen counters. The scene ends with the couple at loggerheads.

When the couple attends a Kabuki performance, Eileen is very taken with lithe, muscular Nakamura (Ricardo Montalban), who sometimes plays *onnagata* (female) roles. At this performance, however, he plays a man who is transformed into a lion. These actors, Eileen informs her fiancé, are trained to have the grace of women and the power of men. He is duly impressed, although he thinks a real "woman" — a Marilyn Monroe — would spice up the performance.

The next sequence shifts to the marriage ceremony of Kelly and Katsumi. Although he does not wish to be, Gruver is moved. When Gruver meets with the Websters at their request, they remonstrate with him for serving as a witness — they are adamantly opposed to all kinds of "fraternization." Then Mrs. Webster broaches the real reason for the encounter. What is

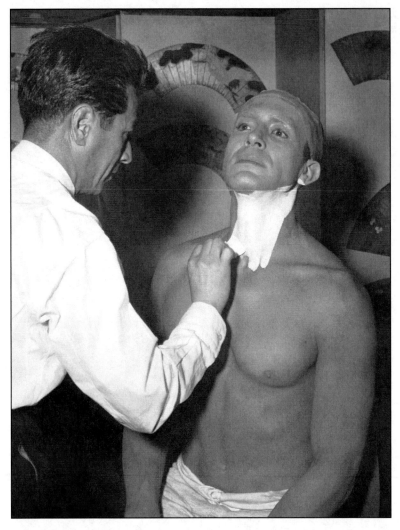

FIGURE 16 Okamura (Ricardo Montalban) being prepared by a make-up artist. Okamura's masculinity is the most self-assured of the men in the film.

going on with Eileen? When Eileen arrives, she rebuffs two invitations from Lloyd.

A depressed Gruver then begins to get in touch with some inclinations that have been suppressed. As a teen-ager, he had acted in a play by Molnar and had thought of becoming some sort of artist and not going to West Point. However, his father had talked him out of such sentiments.

Outside the Matsubashi Theatre (the Shochiku Kagekidan Girls Review, where male roles are obviously played by women; in reality The Takarazuka[13]), Gruver sees the star, Hana Ogi (Miiko Taka, who appears in *Cry for Happy*) dressed in a white sweater and blouse. During the show (this scene is meant to be read directly against the earlier Kabuki sequence), she appears in a variety of costumes—male and female. Gruver is smitten: "She is the greatest thing I ever saw." Matsubashi performers are forbidden to date anyone, but Gruver asks Katsumi to intervene. At first, her efforts are not successful. Hana Ogi will not speak to any American: her "father was killed by one of their bombs."

For Gruver, persistence eventually brings success after he pesters Hana Ogi. In addition, Kelly and Katsumi act as go-betweens. Despite language barriers, Gruver and Hana Ogi agree to forget that their countries were at war; in fact, she asks forgiveness for her hostile thoughts in thinking he was from a race of "savages." She has never been in love before, but she reminds him that they both are dedicated to their careers and that such "fraternization" could be dangerous. She assures him: "I will love you if that is your desire." Meanwhile, Okamura and Eileen, contrary to Mrs. Webster's wishes, are attempting to "fraternize." In addition, Eileen overhears a conversation in which she learns that Gruver is seeing Hana Ogi and realizes that his affair with the Japanese woman is allowing him to come to a fuller, more satisfying understanding of himself.

This tranquility is disrupted when Kelly is ordered back to the States—without Katsumi. The Websters refuse to interfere, despite the pleas of both Eileen and Gruver. In this scene, it becomes obvious that the General and his wife are engineering the return to the States of many soldiers married to Japanese women. Mrs. Webster is affronted when Gruver announces that he intends to marry a Japanese. Eileen very reluctantly accepts the situation and realizes that Lloyd has finally dragged someone else off to a shack. She then storms off to see someone. "In fact, he's Japanese" (an obvious reference to Okamura). Gruver, meanwhile, has decided—without bothering to consult Hana Ogi—to marry her.

"We've never spoken before about marriage," she points out.
"Well. Now we are," he somewhat sternly replies.

She is obligated to stay with the troupe, she informs him. If she forfeits her word, she will lose honor. In fact, she was sold into the Yoshiwara (the licensed quarter in Tokyo) by her destitute father but was eventually rescued by a close friend (although many members of the audience might not be aware of it, Hana Ogi is stating that she was once a prostitute). In turn, the theatrical company has been a genuine home to her where she has been treated kindly; her success there has restored the good name of her family.

This conversation is interrupted when Kelly storms in; he is furious because his wife has just been about to have her eyes "Westernized" by a quack doctor. Kelly insists he wants Katsumi the way she is. That evening, the four attend a puppet theatre performance in which two runaway lovers kill themselves. Kelly is appalled by the suicide, but his wife reminds him that the two lovers are taking the only way that will allow them to be together forever. When Katsumi and Kelly arrive at their home, it has been sealed off by the military. General Webster takes it upon himself to re-assign Gruver and to make certain Hana Ogi leaves for Tokyo.

Kelly and Katsumi steal back to their home and commit suicide. Separately, Gruver and Hana Ogi see the dead bodies. Japanese locals, aware of what has occurred, attack Gruver and a colleague. Gruver searches unsuccessfully for his beloved. General Webster tells him that a law is just about to be passed by the US Congress to allow US Servicemen to return home with their Japanese brides.

Gruver leaves for Tokyo and arrives at the theatre where Hana Ogi is now performing, costumed in a Japanese bridal dress. He makes one final plea. He and she will have trouble in their subsequent lives unless they are completely honest with each other. "Do you love me or not?" he asks. He tells her to answer with the "deepest part" of herself. "We must do the right thing," she asserts. He replies that their first obligation to each other is to become man and wife. She pleads the disadvantages. "Will you come?" he asks again. In the following scene, Gruver emerges outside the theatre. A bit later, Hana Ogi, dressed (significantly) in a kimono, appears. In response to military reporters, she announces that she and Gruver will marry. What is Gruver's response? He simply says, "Sayonara."

When *Sayonara* was released in 1957, the *New York Times* pointed out that the film followed Michener's novel ("porously obvious modern rewrite of the old 'Madame Butterfly' tale") but that the film "fixed everything up with a happy ending."

At the conclusion of the novel, the two lovers go their separate ways. The novel is told from the first-person perspective of Gruver; his pursuit of Hana Ogi is more aggressive; there are a great many details about the unhappy married life of General and Mrs. Gruver; Gruver's father suddenly appears in Japan to talk things over with his son; Gruver and Hana Ogi have heated debates about the nature of art.

Alongside the "happy" ending, there is another crucial difference between the novel and film. Michener's Gruver began to write short stories when he was at prep school. This was an avocation of his mother's, and she encouraged her son. He abandoned this pursuit when he went to West Point and then the Air Force; through his relationship with Hana Ogi, this side of Gruver is partially restored. In the film, he alludes to his part in a school play and a possible flirtation with becoming a writer.

The book accentuates his artistic propensities much more fully than the film.

Obviously aware of having eliminated a crucial aspect of the novel, Joshua Logan and his screenwriter, Paul Osborn, made a daring adaptation of their source. Rather than emphasizing Gruver the alienated would-be artist of the novel, in the film Gruver is a man caught between conflicting gender identities. In addition, he is heterosexual, but he is deeply confused about who he is and what he wants. The implication is that Gruver has lost touch with the creative side of himself—which he associates with the feminine—and been forced to live an enforced masculinity with which he is uncomfortable.

In the film's use of Kabuki and the Revue, gender identity is shown to be flexible. A man can be trained to play female roles; women can perform male roles. The rigidity in Gruver's early life and military career has not allowed him any mobility in such matters. In Kobe he witnesses some theatrical conventions that contradict his previous mindset. He begins to breathe more freely.

As the film progresses and he falls in love with Hana Ogi — a woman whose stage career demands she display a prominent masculine side — Gruver begins to balance the masculine and feminine sides of himself. Having shown this process, the film's happy ending does not seem overly forced.[14]

That conclusion, however, was one engineered by Brando, who had originally turned down the role of Gruver. He told William Goetz, the producer:

I don't like the ending where the major leaves Japan and the dancer goes back to the theater.

But if he marries, her, then it becomes a typical Hollywood happy ending. There's no truth to the story.

Why not? People of different races are marrying all the time. Why avoid the issue? Face the fact that an American could marry a Japanese girl.[15]

Faced with Brando's somewhat conflicted intransigence, Logan and Osborn quickly agreed to the change: "The original ending was Madame Butterfly all over again. Marlon's suggestion is a wonderful idea."[16]

Nevertheless, Sayonara's original ending was not really "Madame Butterfly all over again." In the novel by Loti and in Puccini's opera, Butterfly is a courtesan who has an affair with an American naval officer; they marry; he abandons her; she has a baby, and her subsequent existence is infused with the hope that Pinkerton will return. When he does come back, his American wife accompanies him; they wish to adopt and raise the child. Butterfly agrees and then commits suicide.[17]

Michener's novel embraced the possibility that a man and woman from different races could fall in love but then decide not to live together. The film concludes with the marriage that had evaded Butterfly, and it is in many ways "a typical Hollywood happy ending," which was what Brando claimed he wanted to avoid.[18]

"Face the fact that an American could marry a Japanese girl," Brando asserted, and that is exactly how the film concludes. What is strong about the film remains its insistence in dramatizing gender identity as a complex issue. Gruver is restored because he comes to terms with the masculine and feminine sides of himself, and it is in a specific Japanese context that he makes this discovery. The film, nevertheless, contains many unresolved jarring moments. Kelly is brutal to Katsumi and even threatens to kill her when she seeks to "improve" her eyes. Gruver is taking Hana Ogi to the United States at the film's conclusion, the implication being that the West is a far "safer" place than Japan. The film thus validates the United States in preference to Japan. If an American male leads the way, in this context, the result is satisfactory. However, when Kelly discards his soldier's uniform for a kimono, this signals that he is abandoning American normative rules of conduct and will come to a bad end. Despite Brando's wish to enshrine progressive attitudes in *Sayonara*, the film privileges American values over foreign, Japanese ones. The East remains a dangerous place.

In an article published in *Holiday* in August 1952 four months after the official end of the Occupation, Michener contributed a report that the editor claimed provided an "intimate, colorful and surprising" vista on a recent enemy country. It reads in part:

> If you are one of the lucky ones [fortunate enough to visit Japan], you will find in Japan a land of exquisite beauty and a people dedicated to its cultivation.... In the cities, where the ways and comforts of the West are at your disposal, you will be captivated by the gaudy colors and the sensitive artistry with which the Japanese dress up their lives.... One thing is certain, however; no other nation is so profoundly dedicated to art.... Japanese books are the most artistically printed in the world. Japanese gardens are things of rare beauty and even the most ordinary implements of living are apt to be as lovely as Grecian urns.

Like Barthes, Michener perceives Japan as a land of the senses. Like Wilde, he found the art of Japan exquisite. Although he had witnessed the Occupation first hand and wrote about many of its problems in *Sayonara* in 1954, Michener in this essay elevates the status of Japan to a place of "rare beauty," a nation that facilitates Westerners in their quest for inner transformation. The film version of *Sayonara* falters in its attempt to embrace that beauty.

CHAPTER FIVE

"A GEISHA'S LIES ARE NOT LIKE THE LIES OF OTHERS"

GEISHA AND HYPER-FEMININITY

The word geisha derives from two kanji: gei meaning art and sha referring to a person. An accurate translation into English would be "performing artist." Although geisha first appeared in the pleasure quarters of places like Edo (Tokyo) and Kyoto, they were entertainers, not courtesans or prostitutes. They were trained rigorously from an early age in music, dance, and the tea ceremony. Apprentice geisha are maiko ("dance children"). These young women wear white make-up, and their hairstyle and kimono are frequently more elaborate than that of full-fledged geisha. This occurs, in part, because maiko at the outset of their careers have to establish themselves in particularly memorable or remarkable ways in order to attract attention.

The world of the geisha is sometimes called the *karyukai* ("the flower and willow world") because their profession demands that they establish a retreat or sanctuary for their male clients away from the everyday world. Now and in the past, the profession of geisha is a serious one for a woman. The celebrated geisha Mineko Iwasaki, one of Kyoto's foremost geishas in the 1960s and 1970s, puts the matter well: "The geisha system was founded, actually, to promote the independence and economic self-sufficiency of women. And that was its stated purpose, and it actually accomplished that quite admirably in Japanese society, when there were very few routes for women to achieve that source of independence."[1]

Japanese films about geisha tend to concentrate on two issues. A director such as Mizoguchi emphasizes how the so-called independence offered by the profession of geisha actually becomes a way of controlling women economically by imprisoning them in a system where they are completely dependent on male approval for survival.

Second, geisha are often portrayed in Japanese cinema as the embodiment of a mode of hyper-femininity. As children and apprentices, these women learn the skills needed to captivate men. As such they are ur-women, who embody a fantasy of the perfectly accommodating, compliant, sexually desirable woman whose every desire is to please men. There is also sometimes a great deal of confusion about the difference between a geisha and a prostitute.

Japanese filmmakers often investigate the limits of this system (in the case of Mizoguchi showing that there is a fine line between geisha and sex workers) whereas Western filmmakers concentrate on the fetishistic codes associated with these women: their costumes, their compliance, and their "foreignness" to American and European standards of womanhood. Ian Littlewood explicates the significance of these differences:

> For many westerners the image of the Japanese woman starts and finishes with the geisha. She is demure, remote, artistic, but she also holds out the promise of sexual pleasure. Her elaborate hair, rich kimono, and otherworldly make-up proclaim both her strangeness and, according to popular belief, her availability. In a single exotic figure she unifies the principal qualities by which the west has chosen to define the Japanese woman.[2]

In the West, therefore, ideas about Japanese womanhood are commonly centered on a fetishistic response to geisha, and this assumption is examined in the films studied in this chapter.

In *Teahouse of the August Moon*, Fisby is ordered to establish a chapter of the Ladies' League for Democratic Action (not a real organization in Occupied Japan). Soon afterwards, a geisha, Lotus Blossom, is presented to him as a gift. At the same time Fisby is putting American democracy into action, she insists he put on Japanese culture. Soon afterwards, when Lotus Blossom is apparently shown favoritism by Fisby, the other Japanese women in the village insist she be removed if Western ideals of democracy are to prevail. Fisby, who had initially seen Lotus Blossom as someone trained in "hanky-panky business," then begins to perceive her as a victim who has been "hired out" by unscrupulous men. Of course, neither view is correct, as the ever-wily Sakini points out in his definition of geisha:

> Poor man like to feel rich. Rich man like to feel wise. Sad man like to feel happy, so all go to Geisha house and tell trouble to Geisha girl. Now she listen very politely....She makes tea, she sings, and she dance. Pretty soon troubles go away.

Despite the multiplicity of interpretations of what constitutes a geisha's existence, such women have become one of the predominant images of Japanese Otherness, and this helps explain in large part the lure of Arthur Golden's *Memoirs of a Geisha* (1997).

A GEISHA'S LIFE AS FAIRY-TALE

When Golden was researching his novel, he interviewed the celebrated geisha, Mineko Iwasaki. As he recalled, she

> opened her Kyoto home to me during May 1992, and corrected my every misconception about the life of a geisha— even though everyone I knew who had lived in Kyoto, or who lived there still, told me not to expect such candor.... I wondered that Mineko, whom I had not yet met, might talk with me for an hour about the weather and call it an interview. Instead, she took me on an insider's tour of Gion, and together with her husband, Jin...patiently answered all

my questions about the ritual of a geisha's life in intimate detail. She became, and remains, a good friend.[3]

The form of Golden's novel seems in some ways to mirror this friendship: in this scenario, he is the translator figure who makes available a geisha's life history in English. However, that friendship between the novelist and Iwasaki came to an abrupt close once the former geisha read Golden's book. She took particular exception to that portion of the book devoted to the *mizuage* (taking of virginity), a ritual she claims never existed in the geisha world. (Liza Dalby, the first non-Japanese trained as a geisha, is of the opinion that the *mizuage* tradition has always been a constituent part of the geisha world.) This is what Iwasaki says:

This [issue] goes back to the separation between the pleasure quarter and the entertainment quarter. *Mizuage* is really a coming-of-age ceremony, and apparently there was some selling of the virginity that went on in association with that ritual ceremony in the pleasure district a long time ago. However, that has never been true for the geisha. For the geisha, it was simply when they were becoming a young woman, similar to a sweet 16 in the West, and it was symbolized by the change in hairstyle, into a more womanly, grown-up hairstyle. And also certain subtle changes in the ensembles. There are a lot of rites of passage, but for some reason this one has been really latched on by people....

There is one other potential source of confusion, and that is with the word "*mizuage*" itself. In the Gion, the geisha district, and in many areas of the entertainment industry, "*mizuage*" is also a term that directly means "gross earnings," because it's an old fishing term; as you may know, Japan was dependent on fishing for one of its main economic bases for many years. "*Mizuage*" means "to take out of the water." It stood for the catch. "What was your catch?" — "How much money did you make from the water?" So when I refer to *mizuage*, I'm actually referring to my earnings, rather than the ceremony itself.[4]

However, Iwasaki's anger with Golden went far beyond his emphasis on *mizuage*. According to her, she spoke to Golden on the condition of anonymity whereas he warmly thanked her in his Acknowledgements. In so doing, she felt that many readers were left with the impression that the novel was a thinly disguised biography of her. As a result, she was accused of betraying the secrets of her profession and claimed that she received death threats. She also felt that the novel might, by implication, associate her with the sex trade. Iwasaki's lawsuit against Golden was settled out of court.

Golden's novel is told is in the form of the recollections of the geisha, Sayuri, who lives in Manhattan in the Waldorf Towers; she is being tape recorded by one Jakob Haarhuiss, a translator; the film uses a similar device, the voice-over of Sayuri, as its basic organizing principle. Both the film and novel are divided into three parts.[5]

In the first section of the film, a young girl, Chiyo (as a child, Suzuka Ohgo; as an adult, Ziyi Zhang), and her sister, Satsu, were taken away from the fishing village where they are born; the elder sister becomes a prostitute, but the younger one has such an unusual beauty that she is taken in by Mother (Kaori Momoi), the proprietor of a geisha house (*okiya*) in the Gion district of Kyoto and there is befriended by another apprentice geisha, Pumpkin (as an adult, Youki Kudoh). The two youngsters draw the jealous ire of the house's star attraction, Hatsumomo (Gong Li), although the geisha's rage is reserved for Chiyo, whom she sees as a potential threat. For instance, she forces Chiyo to destroy an expensive kimono owned by Mameha

(Michelle Yeoh), Hatsumomo's rival. She also accuses Chiyo of stealing an obi brooch, and Mother, taking Hatsumomo's word over Chiyo's, adds the cost of the brooch to the already elaborate debt Chiyo owes her.

Then, Chiyo finds Satsu, and the two work out a plan to run away together. Chiyo falls off a roof and is injured, while Satsu manages to escape, never to be heard from again. Mother adds Chiyo's doctor bills to her debt and halts her geisha training, since investing in a girl who will run away does not make sense. Chiyo is henceforth destined for a life of servitude to the *okiya* as a maid.

FIGURE 17 The Chairman (Ken Watanabe) befriends Chiyo (Suzuka Ohgo) in *Memoirs of a Geisha.*

Feeling particularly sad one day, Chiyo encounters a handsome middle-aged man, The Chairman (Ken Watanabe), who bestows kindness upon her. She is immediately taken with him—for her he is both a father figure and a potential lover—and resolves to become a geisha worthy of him and his class. Mahema pays an unexpected visit to the *okiya* and convinces Mother to resume Chiyo's training. She becomes Mahema's "little sister," and Chiyo's name is changed to Sayuri. The rigorous training to be a geisha is shown in painstaking detail throughout this portion of the film.

As a child and young woman, Chiyo/Sayuri is schooled in one basic principle: everything in the *okiya* exists at the pleasure of men. If a geisha becomes popular, she is a success. Popularity is achieved only by satisfying what are deemed male needs. So immersed does Sayuri become in this world's narrowly focused regulations that she becomes stuck in a fantasy existence wherein the Chairman's approval and love become her only goals. She never displays a force of personality of her own— through fantasy she merges her existence with that of the Chairman.

In the second part of the narrative, Mahema devises a plan to sell Sayuri's *mizuage* by auction. If successful, the proceeds will liberate Sayuri from her debt to Mother. Mahema's plan is to arouse the interest of Nobu Toshikazu (Kôji Yakusho), a close friend of the Chairman, who will not, to Sayuri's dismay, bid against his business partner. However, the two men willing to pay the exorbitant price are the Baron (Cary-Hiroyuki Tagawa) and Doctor Crab (Randall Duk Kim); the latter wins. Mother adopts Sayuri as the *okiya*'s daughter. This means that her debts are cleared and her future is secure. An outraged Hatsumomo acts so outlandishly that Mother dismisses her. Sex is a commodity in this version of the geisha world. When the right to her virginity is successfully sold, Sayuri obtains acclaim never before envisioned by the likes of Hatsumomo.

In the remaining part of the film, Sayuri's successful career is cut short by the outbreak of the War. However, her safety is ensured by the Chairman, who sends her to a place of sanctuary, where she nevertheless endures a life of hard labor. After the end of the war, Nobu visits her and asks that she return to Gion to help entertain Colonel Derricks (Ted Levine), who can help to restart the Chairman and Nobu's company that was all but destroyed during the war.

Once returned to the Gion, Sayuri enlists the help of Mameha and Pumpkin to entertain Colonel Derricks. The three women become geisha once more, and Sayuri reunites with the Chairman through the resulting gatherings. She tells Derricks she will not have sex with him at any price. Nobu declares his love and wants to become her *danna* (patron). Mahema tells her she must accept Nobu's offer, but Sayuri's heart is set on the Chairman.

Sayuri then devises a plan to have sex with Colonel Derricks and to be "discovered" by Nobu, thereby ending any affections Nobu has for her and freeing herself to be with the Chairman: she arranges for Pumpkin to bring Nobu to an abandoned place at a predetermined time, and "stumble" upon Sayuri and the American. Pumpkin, still harboring resentment towards Sayuri's success and adoption, brings the Chairman instead of Nobu. Humiliated, Sayuri believes that her dream of being with the Chairman is lost forever. In a dramatic scene at the top of a mountain, she throws a long-treasured handkerchief given to her by the Chairman into the sea. Her voice-over reflects that the geisha's life is essentially one of sorrow and shadows.

However, Sayuri is soon summoned to a teahouse encounter with Nobu, but the person who shows up is the Chairman, who tells her Nobu finds her conduct unacceptable. However, the Chairman understands. He explains that it was he who engaged Mameya to assist Sayuri. Having been deeply attracted to her since he encountered her as a little girl, he has been secretly acting as her protector (fairy godfather) ever since. The Chairman then kisses her, the first true "kiss" she has ever received. Her long-cherished ambition to be loved by the man of her dreams becomes reality. The kiss may be erotic, but it is most certainly imbued with a sense of incest.

The film follows the novel closely, although there are some important divergences. In the novel, Nobu's face is disfigured, and this helps explain both his haughtiness and Sayuri's lack of interest in him. The Baron's sexual overtures to Sayuri are more graphically rendered in the film. A crucial turning point in Sayuri's ascendancy is staged according to the conventions of film musicals. The book is more successful in implying that Sayuri's early childhood losses contributed to her fixation on the Chairman: she has never fully recovered from being a cast-away; her attraction towards the Chairman can be explained in large part because he is a father figure. The person whom Nobu asks in the novel to assist him after the War is a powerful Japanese businessman.

In both book and film, Sayuri does not have a well-developed sexuality. This is especially evident in her post-*mizuage* life with her *danna*, a military officer. In fact, Sayuri's erotic thoughts are vested solely in the Chairman: she never moves beyond that experience.

Book and film are Cinderella stories, suitably populated with an evil step-mother, an evil step-sister, and a fairy godmother, about a young outcast who is kissed back to life by Prince Charming. Although Arthur Golden's research is thorough and the film's costumes and setting accurate, both book and film are Western-style fairy-tales masquerading as Japanese narratives. The setting may be Japanese, but the values are Western. When all is said and done, women remain in the service of men, whose attention they crave and thus privilege. No notion of a woman as an independent entity is valorized.

"WHY DO THERE HAVE TO BE SUCH THINGS AS GEISHA?"

Kenji Mizoguchi's *Gion Bayashi* (*Gion Music Festival*) from 1953 contains many elements in common with *Memoirs of a Geisha*, but he recounts the events in the lives of two geisha to infer that they are pawns in an oppressive patriarchal system. Moreover, both women in that film have staunchly-held convictions about their rights within the system. Mizoguchi does not deal with *mizuage*, but his film shows that many Japanese men associate geisha with the acquisition and use of sexual favors. He never implies that a patron could be a Prince Charming about to kiss a Sleeping Beauty back to life.

In the postwar Gion district of Kyoto, the geisha Miyoharu (Michiyo Kaguke) agrees to apprentice the 16 year-old Eiko (Ayako Wakao), whose mother was a former geisha who has just died. Eiko informs Miyoharu that her father is both ill and destitute; in addition, her uncle, with whom she is living, insists that she sleep with him. Although a bit reluctant to take on the ensuing emotional and financial obligations, Miyoharu decides to do so in memory of her close friendship with the dead girl's mother.

After a year of training the two have to find a large sum of money before Eiko can debut. Miyoharu borrows the money from a teahouse Mother, Okimi (Cheiko Naniwa), who in turn obtains the money from the businessman Kusuda (Seizaburô Kawazu). However, Kusuda fancies Eiko himself and wants to give Miyoharu to Kanzaki, a government bureaucrat, in order to cement a business deal.

The film opens with Eiko arriving unexpectedly at Miyoharu's *okiya*, where she overhears the geisha rejecting a marriage offer from a young dandy. Outraged at her refusal, the man claims that she misled him. She counters: "A geisha's lie is not like others' lies." In an extremely hard-boiled way, she is reminding the client that a geisha often allows clients to think what they want: that is part of the process of entertainment to which a geisha's existence is consecrated.

What soon becomes apparent is that Eiko, to whom the professional name of Miyoei is assigned, is a young woman of strongly held opinions. She is not willing to sleep with men to further her career. She seems to be of the postwar generation that conceives of the role of the geisha differently from her predecessors. She sees a future when "men will come to serve us." When Okimi confronts her, she realizes that they are not on the same "wavelength."

Meanwhile, Kusada invites Miyoharu and Miyoei to attend, at his expense, a dance festival in Tokyo. This invitation turns out to be a ruse, an excuse for sexual exploitation. Kanzaki, much younger than Miyoharu, has fallen in love with her, but she refuses his overtures. In order to cement an important business deal, Kusada pleads with Miyoharu to have sex with Kanzaki. She reluctantly agrees to this but, meanwhile, Kusada attempts to rape Miyoei, who inflicts a severe wound on her attacker. This event disrupts everything. Miyoharu rushes to Miyoei's assistance; Kusada winds up in hospital; Kusada is furious that Miyoharu will not listen to Kanzaki's further overtures.

FIGURE 18 Kusada (Seizaburô Kawazu) forces himself on Miyoei (Ayako Wakao) in *Gion Music Festival*.

Kusada insists Okimi intervene, which she does by taking Miyoei captive. In order for Okimi to return the young woman,

Miyoharu has to attend the Nakanishi house and sleep with Kanazki, which she does. When Miyoharu returns home, she is upbraided by a furious Miyoei, who informs her that she should never have done this for her sake. In fact, she sees Miyoharu's actions as a betrayal. The older woman responds: "I have been broken by the dark side of this profession, but I want to protect you so that you remain pure." At the end, it is obvious that Kanzaki has become her *danna*. Business is back to normal, and the two women walk out to fulfill their obligations that evening at a number of teahouses.

Mizoguchi is particularly adept at directing Koguke in the role of Miyoharu. She is a cynical, world-weary creature at the outset of the film and plays her part both comically and teasingly. As the film progresses, her countenance takes on an increasingly weary look and, at the end, her face is considerably softened. Miyoei remains essentially the same throughout the film: she is steadfast in her refusal to compromise. Okimi is a hard-core businesswoman who serves the needs of men. At the end of the film, Miyoei and Miyoharu are bonded as sisters (the young woman has replaced her dead mother as Miyoharu's closest friend), but the two women recognize, however, that they can only survive by following the codes and conventions of a geisha's existence.

Although the two siblings in the same director's *Sisters of Gion* (*Gion no shimai*) are geisha, this film from 1936 only deals peripherally with their work world. However, it emphasizes that such women are economic outcasts completely dependent on male whims. This fact of life has made the younger Omocha (Isuzu Yamada) bitter and cynical in contrast to the more naïve Umekichi (Yôko Umemura).

Women should use men, Omocha instructs her sister. She is certain that women can outwit their male foes. In an early sequence filmed outdoors, the two sisters discuss their plight with the more harsh Omocha dressed in Western style and her sister in kimono. This differentiation in dress between the two sisters is maintained throughout most of the film.

Omocha is disgusted by the kindness that Umekichi bestows on the bankrupt Furusawa. Very adept at manipulation, she secures, without paying for it, a kimono from Kimura, a store clerk, so that her sister can obtain suitable work as a geisha; she also tries to arrange for Jurakudo, an antiques dealer, to become her sister's patron; she then arranges for Furusawa to leave their home where he has been free-loading by paying him off from money borrowed from Jurakudo.

Having set these various plans in motion, Omocha is visited by the clerk's irate boss, Kudo, who accuses her of acting duplicitously. After claiming rather improbably that the kimono was a gift, she skillfully leads the conversation to the point where she beseeches Kudo to become her patron.

Jurakado's affections for Umekichi are shattered when she rushes off to see Furusawa, whose whereabouts she has not known. Kudo is outraged when, returning to Omocha's home with her in tow, he finds Kimura there. The chastised clerk responds by pointing out that Kudo is doing what he warned Kimura against: keeping company with a geisha. After he is fired, Kimura calls Omocha a "tramp." She replies: "I am a geisha. If I always told the truth, I'd be out of business. Sometimes I have to lie."

It is Umekichi's turn to be furious when she learns from Furusawa that Omacha engineered his abrupt departure. Umekichi accepts her lover's invitation to move in with him: "I don't want to live with a sister who'd do such a thing." Meanwhile, Kimura telephones Kudo's wife to reveal her husband's involvement with Omacha.

Unexpectedly, a young taxi driver arrives, on Kudo's orders, to pick up Omacha, who is dressed in an elaborate kimono. As they drive along, the young man berates her: "As beautiful as you are, you still have to hustle for a patron. I feel sorry for you."

He offers to get her a "filthy rich playboy" patron: "If you'd prefer a younger man, how about me? I'd like that." Deeply insulted, she expresses her anger. Then she becomes aware that there is another man in the car sitting in darkness next to the driver: it is Kimura. "You're going to get what you deserve," he menacingly informs her. She obviously wants to get out of the car but is told to come along quietly. In the next scene, a messenger arrives at Umekichi's new residence with the news that Omacha has been badly hurt. (She has been thrown out of the speeding car.)

Umekichi lectures her badly injured sister: "This is what happens when you treat men like that. Terrible things happen." Omacha is unrepentant: "Something like this won't make me give in to men. Any man who does this to a geisha simply because she refuses him is a coward. I'll make him pay." If Omacha had listened, her sister responds, this incident would not have happened. Omacha replies: "No, your way means giving in to men. I refuse to do that! Why would anyone give in to them?" When Umekichi returns home, she is told that Furusawa has returned to his hometown, where he will manage a factory. He leaves a message for his mistress: she should find a better patron. Umekichi accepts her plight and is upbraided by her sister. Her voice breaking as she speaks, Omacha proclaims:

You meekly did what you were told and got nothing in return. If we do our jobs well, they call us immoral. So what can we do? What are we supposed to do? Why do we have to suffer like this? Why do there even have to be such things as geisha?

The film begins and ends with the two women in conversation. Umekichi remains the same and so does Omacha. At the outset, the younger sister was outraged by the plight of the geisha, and she remains even more convinced of her low opinion of her profession and of the men they serve. To a certain extent, she has set in motion her own unhappiness, but it is the profession of geisha—one in which women are sexual objects—that forced her to act as she did.

In a fairly brief sequence halfway through the film, Jurakado is selling a scroll painting to a man who is presumably a fellow dealer. They both agree that it is fake that can easily pass as authentic. Jurakado names the sum of 170 yen as his asking price; the man demurs but then Jurakado informs him the price is really 270. The man haggles but accepts the high price. In the Mizoguchi world, the surface of things is always delusory. For that auteur, the geisha existence is a simulacrum of authentic feelings. Geisha ply their trade in order to survive, but that survival is fraught. These women learn how to lie, he observes, but they are caught in a vicious trap where men are more mendacious and self-serving than women could ever be.[6]

Despite its English-language title, Juzo Itami's 1990 *Tales of a Golden Geisha* (*Ageman*) focuses on geisha only in the film's opening sequences. Nayoko (Nobuko Miyamoto), a foundling, is sent to geisha school by her adopted parents. At the age of eighteen, she acquires a patron, a sixty-two year old Buddhist bishop. The Bishop's mother handles all the details for her son ("don't act like a drudge; remember you're not his wife; send him home at midnight; don't allow perfume to get on his clothes.") The fumbling, sexually unfulfilling bishop even agrees to send his geisha to secretarial school. When he dies three years later, he has risen in the Buddhist hierarchy. His mother congratulates Nayoko on being an *ageman* (a person who brings good luck). A decade later, she has achieved a good position as the administrative assistant to the president of a bank but is unhappy because unmarried.

Her skills in her job are due to her ability to manage men the way a geisha does. She compliments men, says the right things, and lies when necessary, again like a member of her former profession. When she becomes friends with Mondo Suzuki (Mosahiko Tsugawa), a philandering bank manager, who has broken up with his rich girl friend, she attempts to steer him in the right directions to advance his career. When her affair with him falters, she helps a wealthy client set up a geisha house, where she resumes her career. Through a series of convoluted and dubious financial transactions, Nayoko, clad as a geisha, saves Suzuki from certain ruin. As the film ends, they seem to have established some sort of relationship, although his roving eyes still wander. In the moral vacuum that constitutes this film, one thing remains certain: once a geisha always a geisha.

Itami (1933-97) had a much more satirical eye than Mizoguchi. He established his reputation with films such as *The Funeral* (*Ososhiki*; 1984), *Tampopo* (1987), and *A Taxing Woman* (*Marusa no onna;* 1987). All of these films castigate the rigid rituals, customs and practices that he felt dominated Japanese society, and he tried to show how often Japan was out of step with the contemporary world. In 1992, he was stabbed, gangland-style, in his home allegedly in retaliation for his depiction of yakuza in *Mimbo no Onna* (*The Gentle Art of Japanese Extortion*).

According to Itami's perspective in *Ageman*, the profession of geisha may be declining rapidly, but society's attitude towards women remains the same. Women who choose to become geisha are forcing themselves to fit into patterns of subordination that are centuries old.

Like Mizoguchi's films centered on fallen women, Fukasaku's *The Geisha House* (*Omocha*; 1999) is one with a conscience, concerned with social and moral repression. The screenwriter of *Geisha House*, Kaneto Shindô, directed and wrote *Kenji Mizoguchi: The Life Of A Film Director* (*Arueiga-kantoku no shoga*) in 1974, and Mizoguchi's influence is evident.

Geisha House is set in 1958, when the Japanese Government was set to introduce and enforce the anti-prostitution act curbing and repressing the centuries-old tradition of geisha. There is the external challenge of changing law; there are internal conflicts represented by the different geisha employed in the Fujinoya Geisha House, one still run in the traditional manner.

Madame Sato (Junko Fuji), owner of the House, has been underwritten for the last decade by her longstanding relationship with a businessman-sponsor. This is now ending. One of her youngest workers is Tokiko (Mai Katajima) who aspires to become a *maiko* in order to support her poor family. At the outset of the film there is a long sequence showing Tokiko preparing the Fujinoya for another day. This she does quietly, without a grudge, accepting her lowly position in the establishment with loyalty and patience. At the end of the film there is a similar quiet sequence when she becomes a *maiko*. The parallel is drawn between her readying the geisha house and then her readying herself for service as a geisha.

There is an unspoken desperation in her sacrifice. Tokiko does what she does for her family in order to help send her younger sister to school and support her ailing father in his loom business. Her out-of-work elder brother decries the geisha world as a "feudalistic system," but he does nothing to assist the family. Tokiko has a crush on a boy of her own age, but she knows that such feelings must be pushed aside.

Another young man in the film—the son of Sato's estranged sponsor—seduces one of the geisha so that he can claim that she is a sex worker and thus dishonor her. This is his way of having sex, expressing filial piety, and ingratiating himself with his mother, a wealthy heiress, who is being revenged for her husband's waywardness. In order to launch Tokiko, Sato must borrow heavily. She accepts money from a wealthy moneylender on condition that she becomes, at long last, his mistress.

Fukasaku's vision is very similar to Mizoguchi's, and it would be fair to say that it is an updated one, although the sexual desires of men still control everything in the geisha world.

However, unlike Mizoguchi, Fukasaku clearly demonstrates that the inhabitants of the geisha house have a strong sense of community. "We're expensive living toys for gentlemen," one says shrewdly but jokingly. "I don't like pretense," Sato says, but she has lived her life according to its regimen.

At the end of the film, Tohiko's name is changed to Omacha, and the rite of *mizuage* is performed by a wealthy seventy-eight year old. When she smells her patron's expensive incense, she remarks that the scent reminds her of the sound of her father's loom. He replies that she is being poetic. She simply answers: '"To us kids, it indicated poverty and loneliness." Disrobed and about to have sex with her patron, her face is suffused with an enigmatic smile revealing that she is fully aware that her life has come full circle. At that moment, the elderly man asks the reason for the smile. She replies: "I am intoxicated by the odor of incense. Please be kind to me." Such reflective moments are absent from the three American films versions of geisha that conclude this chapter.

GEISHA AMERICAN-STYLE

Geisha Girl (1952) is a film that uses the word *geisha* merely as a code word to refer to Japan and the exotic. It was intended to be a B movie, and it is faithful in its acting and execution to that distinction. Two bumbling G.I.s, Rocky Wilson (Steve Forrest) and Archie McGregor (Archer MacDonald) serving in the Korean War are on leave in Tokyo. Wishing to ditch their uniforms so that they can enter bars and nightclubs off limits to soldiers, they attempt to purchase civilian clothing in a black market shop recommended to them. They change into their new clothing; the suit jacket selected by Archie contains in its breast pocket, to the clerk's dismay, pills, each of which is more powerful than an atom bomb; the clerk tries to prevent the sale, but he is interrupted by two MPs who wander into his establishment. Rockie and Archie are trailed to a bar, where Mr Nakano (Tetsu Nakamura), the ringleader of the gangsters, encounters them and invites them to his home. They are not very interested in his proposal until he mentions that his house contains a school for geisha.

Rocky and Steve are accompanied by Peggy Barnes (Martha Hyer), a stewardess who is actually a spy trying to locate the whereabouts of the mysterious pills. At his home, Mr Nakano shows the geisha arranging flowers and learning English. However, they are also learning Russian in case the "dominant" language of the world should change. He also informs the soldiers and the stewardess that Americans have the wrong impression of geisha: they are cultivated women who are trained as entertainers.

Mr Nakano—assisted by various henchmen, including some geisha—does not manage to wrest the pills from Archie. In fact, Michiko (Michiyo Naori), one of the geisha, attempts to foil her boss's plan by providing information to Peggy, who rushes to a police captain; he decides that the only way to prevail is to enlist the assistance of Zoro, a conjuror-hypnotist (Dekao Yoko), with a criminal record. Forced into service, he manages—somewhat ineptly—to hypnotize himself.

Meanwhile, an accomplice of Mr Nakano takes the two G.I.s and Peggy on a tour so they can be mugged and the pills recovered. At the very moment Archie attempts to demonstrate kissing to Michiko, he and she are struck on their heads by thugs; he is convinced that his powerful kiss rendered them unconscious. Then, Rocky and Archie don Japanese clothing in the dressing room of a Kabuki theatre to avoid capture, but they wind up, much to the amusement of the audience, on stage in the middle of a performance.

Back at the geisha house, Mr Nakano's employer, the Professor (Tatsuo Saito) takes charge, but Archie awakens the slumbering Zoro, who eventually subdues the villains. The two G.I.s are put in the custody of Peggy.

Despite the fact that the film inserts clips showing a genuine

Kabuki performance and a visit to the shrine at Asakusa, the Japanese in the film are presented as stock characters or buffoons. Despite its title, *The Geisha Boy* (1958), made as a vehicle for Jerry Lewis's version of screwball comedy, has, like *Geisha Girl*, almost nothing to do with geisha, who are shown briefly in one scene. In fact, their longest appearance is as a series of decorations to the opening credits. In the film, Gilbert Wooley (Lewis), an unemployed magician, is hired to be part of a USO tour. In Japan, he meets a young boy, Mitsuo Watanabe (Robert Hirano), who has been in a deep depression since he "lost his parents in a terrible accident." Delighted at witnessing Gilbert involved in a particularly madcap incident, the boy laughs and subsequently bonds with the magician. In fact, Mistuo wants Gilbert to become his father. In turn, Gilbert is moved by the boy's devotion.

Sessue Hayakawa plays Mr Sikita, Mitsuo's grandfather. When Gilbert visits his home, Sikita is busy building a bridge in his garden for the amusement of Mitsuo. At that moment, the film briefly cuts to Hayakawa's celebrated performance as the sadistic Colonel Saito in *The Bridge on the River Quai* (1957); a shot of Alec Guinness as Colonel Nicholson from the same film is also inserted.[7] This is the only attempt at highbrow humor in the movie, although there are scenic shorts of Japan, a visit to an exhibition baseball game in which the Los Angles Dodgers are defeated by the home team, and a sequence at a bathing house (*onsen*) at which men and women bathe together in the nude. At one point, Sergeant Pearson (Suzanne Pleshette) makes a slighting remark about Americans becoming involved with Japanese, but she later withdraws the remark by explaining that her American boyfriend left her for a Japanese woman.

Reluctantly, Gilbert leaves Japan and tells the boy, untruthfully, that he does not love him. The boy stows away on Gilbert's plane, is discovered and returned to Japan. On the return flight, Gilbert sneaks aboard and is reunited with Matsuo, Mr Sikita and Mr Sikita's daughter. In Tokyo, the four join forces to build a geisha house cum magic show.

In *Geisha Boy* and *Geisha Girl*, the word "geisha" is used almost as a word synonymous with exotic Japan; it is also employed to imply teasingly that the sexual connotations often associated with the term might be present in these two films.

False advertising is not on the agenda of Jack Cardiff's *My Geisha* (1962), which begins in Hollywood where the film director Paul Robaix (Yves Montand) is secretly planning a new film. His wife, Lucy Dell (Shirley MacLaine), has been the star of a string of successful films he has directed. However, Robaix announces to his producer Sam Lewis (Edward G. Robinson), his leading man Bob Moore (Robert Cummings) and to Lucy that he is heading to Japan to make a film version of Puccini's *Madama Butterfly*. He wants to use authentic sets and a real Japanese woman must obviously play the role of Butterfly. Lucy objects but appears to be submissive to this change in her husband's career plans.

Paul and Bob leave for Tokyo, and immediately Sam and Lucy secretly follow them. Soon after she arrives, Lucy stealthily peeks at her husband with some geisha. She opines that she has heard "conflicting stories" about geisha, i.e., she knows that they are supposed to be entertainers but wonders if they might also act as prostitutes. Lucy decides to transform herself into a geisha named Yoko Mori to see if she can in that disguise win the part of Butterfly from her reluctant husband. In that masquerade, she goes undetected by Paul.

Paul is intent on capturing the spirit of Japan "while it still exists" because he is convinced that Japan is becoming too Americanized. He decides to interview the "real" Japanese woman, the geisha, whom he met the night before. Somehow, he remarks, she reminds him of Lucy. When Yoko appears for her screen test, he is taken with her story about having been "sold" into the profession.

FIGURE 19 Lucy Dell as Yoko (Shirley MacLaine) is much more self assured in this publicity still for *My Geisha* than she is in the film.

In order to appear as "authentic" as possible, Lucy engages the services of a real geisha, Kazumi Ito (Yoko Tani) to assist her. On set Paul feels Yoko takes directions too easily, but he decides that the geisha's commitment to pleasing men explains her remarkable professionalism. There is a farcical scene in which

Bob attempts to seduce her. She refuses to be dishonored, even threatening to commit hara-kiri. The would-be suitor rushes off, but is now resolved to marry Yoko (this would be his fifth marriage). He asks Paul if he, following Japanese tradition, will act as his go-between?

During the ensuing sequence, Yoko informs Paul that she will make love with Rob if he so desires. She makes it clear that she has slept with her patron and his friends because it would be impolite to refuse. Then, Paul, who is shocked by this information, reveals to Yoko that he is making *Madama Butterfly* without his wife because he has become known in the States as "Mr Dell." He needs to achieve success apart from his wife. He is refreshed by this encounter and tells Yoko that geisha are "analysts without couches."

Paul refuses to assist Bob. Then, he is summoned to inspect some color negative film and looking at a close-up realizes that Lucy is Yoko. He wishes that she had not acted so deviously. She is far "too clever" for him. In order to teach his wife a lesson, he visits Yoko in her hotel room and kisses her passionately. She is aghast. "What's the matter, Yoko? Need a little more romance?" When she rebuffs him, he informs her that he does not chase women; he expects to be met half-way: "Sayonara, Yoko, you'll never know what you missed."

After Paul informs Sam that he knows what has been transpiring, the producer tells him that he would never have had the huge budget without Lucy being in the picture. He also says that he should be a "big enough man" to understand. Paul rejoins: "I was almost a big man." Paul asks Sam not to inform Lucy of the discovery, especially since the final scene (when Butterfly gives the child to Pinkerton and then commits suicide) will be shot the following day. In all this turmoil, Paul has discovered that Lucy has "another lover"—her career.

A very chastened Lucy-Yoko appears on set the next day and enacts the famous sequence from the opera. Her performance is assisted by her sorrow at her husband's attempted seduction of her the previous day. When, shortly afterwards, Lucy supposedly arrives from the States for the film's premiere, their reunion is subdued. Yuko is scheduled to reveal her identity at the conclusion of the showing of the film: the plan concocted by her and Sam is that she is to remove her wig and identify herself as the famous star.

Instead, she appears at the premiere as Lucy Dell and informs the audience that Yoko will not be there that evening. She has made her first and last performance as Madame Butterfly; the geisha intends to retire to a convent. Paul, realizing the concession his wife has made, tells her: "Don't be sympathetic to anyone but me, my geisha." She is overjoyed to realize that Paul knew all along he was attempting to seduce his own wife, albeit in disguise.

My Geisha begins as a farce to compliment the Lucy-Yoko binary. At the time the film was made, red-haired Lucille Ball and her husband Desi Arnaz had completed the 181 episodes of *I Love Lucy* (1951-7) in which Lucy Ricardo is frequently trying to put things over on her husband, the irascible but good-natured Ricky. To get her own way, she frequently resorts to disguises. The premise of *My Geisha* is based on the audience's recognition that they are watching a parody of one of television's most celebrated programs. Many viewers would also have been aware of the extremely successful *Bob Cummings Show* (1955-9) in which Cummings played playboy photographer Bob Collins. These two intertexts are then conjoined to Puccini's operatic melodrama. In this way farce gives way to potential tragedy in the plot development.

Like *Memoirs of a Geisha*, *My Geisha* argues that there is a *stated* behavior of women from that profession, but that those women are often associated with prostitution. In *My Geisha*, Paul's esteem has been wounded because his success is attributable to his wife. Her concession—to comfort him and allow him to feel fully masculine—is to place herself in a subordinate role. In this context, Lucy takes on the geisha-like role of listening to what a man desires and then complying with the request. Like Gruver in *Sayonara*, the male protagonist's wounded masculinity is restored.

The American-made films about (or referring to) geisha present that world in various simple-minded, fetishized ways, or, as in *Memoirs of a Geisha*, it depicts a world-view where some women, for economic or romantic reasons, choose to idealize men and live their lives accordingly. These films do not touch upon the bedrock issues of sexual domination and manipulation that is the foundation of that institution. Japanese directors are quite willing to confront the underlying issues directly and, in the case of Mizoguchi, condemn it wholeheartedly.

CHAPTER SIX

PUSHING LIMITS TOO HONORABLY

YAKUZA FILMS AND HYPER-MASCULINITY

Like their Western counterparts, Japanese gangster (yakuza) films allow their audiences vicarious, voyeuristic participation in illegal, anti-societal activities. Criminal transgressions are witnessed, and the viewer sees how the various mechanisms and strategies of the underworld operate. Often, these criminals are punished but, sometimes, the films have an amoral sensibility because this is how this part of the world manifestly functions.

In yakuza films, crossovers from other genres are frequently incorporated into the plot line. In Kabuki, the great theme is that of revenge: the protagonists find a way of paying back those who have done something awful to them or their families. "Wrongs" are constantly being righted in yakuza films. One gang can transgress the boundaries of the other, and this situation has to be put right. Or a gangster has to avenge the slaying of a member of his gang. If he does not do that, he and his associates will be dishonored.

Also, there is a connection between yakuza and samurai films. In the latter genre, there is often the theme of the samurai who has lost his master or who seeks to avenge a wrong inflicted upon his master. Such samurai (*rônin*) usually operate outside the law and are genuine anti-heroes.

Just as portrayals of geisha push the limits of what it is to be feminine, gangster films in Japan and the West perform a similar function about masculinity.

They often portray men as testosterone-filled creatures who find meaning in violent and forbidden acts. If geisha films are about fantasies of ultra femininity, yakuza films encompass a form of ultra masculinity. In both instances, gender identification and gender roles are defined through institutions or professions that are illegal (yakuza) or give the distinct impression of crossing forbidden boundaries (geisha).

How does a man operate in a corrupt world?, the gangster films ask. The answers are varied but go something like this: a man must be brave at all times and be ready to fight for what he believes in; such a man may (or appear) to act in a corrupt way, but he is really living his life realistically according to the way of the world as he perceives it. For example, he might prove his masculinity by revenging wrongs committed against himself, his family and those to whom he has strong filial ties. He must be resolute in accomplishing his aims *outside* the boundaries imposed on society; in this way, the audience is given the opportunity to live the fantasy of living outside the law. As we have seen, Mishima, whose sense of being truly masculine evaded him, played a yakuza with identity problems in *Afraid to Die*.

Initially, Hollywood gangster films heavily influenced yakuza cinema. Later, yakuza films had an impact on Hollywood, but a film such as *The Godfather* (1972) later left its mark on a new generation of Japanese gangster films. In general, there has been a strong cross-fertilization between Hollywood and Japan in the development of this genre. However, there are relatively few Western-made films using the yakuza: the gangster genre in Western films is a well-developed enterprise with many sub-divisions. Only occasionally have Western filmmakers chosen to look at interactions between Western visitors to Japan and the yakuza.

There is, however, a more fundamental problem in understanding why yakuza films have never made a successful adaptation to American cinema. David E. Kaplan and Alec Dubro claim that the yakuza genre, "descendants of the old samurai epics, bear little resemblance to American or European gangster movies; they are closer to the Western, in which cowboy and outlaw clearly define a code of morality. From the samurai, the yakuza has inherited the role of the last defender against the decadence and corruption ushered in by modernization and contact with the West."[1] In other words, yakuza films are often coded within Japanese culture as attacks upon government and corporate authority. A bit paradoxically, perhaps, American yakuza films tend to valorize the straightforward conduct of the Japanese in contrast to the villainous conduct of some American characters.

BLACKMAIL, MURDER, REVENGE AND EXTORTION ARE MY LIFE

The yakuza film has a long and distinguished pedigree.[2] The four films discussed here contain many of the formulaic ingredients of the genre, but I have chosen to highlight at the outset, among many other possible titles, *Tokyo Drifter* and *Blackmail Is My Life* because of their pyrotechnical virtuosities, which show just how avant-garde and stylistically extravagant yakuza films can be. I shall then examine *Lady Snowbird*, a period piece quasi-yakuza film, because it directly influenced Quentin Tarantino's take on the Japanese gangster film. Then I shall turn to *Minbo*, Juzo Itami's quasi-satirical look at the yakuza, a film that almost cost the director his life.

Seijun Suzuki's *Tokyo Drifter* (*Tôkyô nagaremono*; 1966) relates what happens when Tetsu (Tetsuya Watari) and his boss Kurata (Ryuji Kita) decide to quit crime. The mobster family led by Otsuka (Hideaki Esumi) threatens Kurata when he attempts to pay off the mortgage on an office building used for legitimate business dealings. Tetsu does his best to go straight, even when members of a rival gang beat him up in order to coerce him into joining them. When there are further complications, Tetsu decides to take to the road. He leaves Tokyo dressed in a powder blue suit and white shoes to disguise himself from the hit men in pursuit. He has a face-off on railroad tracks with one hired killer. In the countryside another crime boss friend of Kurata's protects him. Eventually, though, he is betrayed by his old boss and continues his new life as a drifter. While doing so, he croons the film's theme song. Eventually, there is a showdown in Tokyo, where Tetsu in a choreographed ballet-like manner vanquishes his enemies. In the final scene, the hero sadly informs his loyal girlfriend, club singer Chiharu (Chieko Matsubara), that he must continue to exist as a drifter and that he has no room for a permanent relationship.

FIGURE 20 Tetsu (Tetsuya Watari), on the left, displays the lean handsomeness Nikkatsu Studios hoped would make him a major star.

Evidently, Nikkatsu asked Suzuki to accomplish one goal: to make Tetsuya Watari a major star. That is one reason the director was especially lax in imposing plot coherence; this is replaced by sequences in which the lead actor's baby-faced good looks, his ability to quip, and his singing and dancing abilities are foregrounded. Of course, Watari's appearance goes completely against the grain of what a gangster should look like. Suzuki also pokes fun at samurai films in a sequence where the hero bests dozens of ineffectual swordsmen. A riotous color palette and deliberately over-designed but arresting sets contribute to the deliberate surrealism of the film.

Blackmail is My Life (*Kyokatsu koso Waga Jinsei;* 1968) is an extremely stylized, deliberately French New Wave-looking film. Told through the voice-over of Muraki (Hiroki Matsukata), the film demonstrates how he and three confederates (two men, one woman) take up blackmailing as an occupation. Once a waiter and a cleaner of lavatories, this young, self-admitted "punk" overhears two men plotting a scheme to water down the liquor one is selling the other. When the two realize their conversation has been overheard, they try to bribe him. Muraki rejects the offer and is then brutalized by the two gangsters and their lackeys. When he confides his disgrace to his three friends, he and they decide to blackmail both men. Thus begins their lives as blackmailers.

The film explicitly shows how the gang of four are outsiders to Japan's economic growth; they are completely separated from the salary men and the others enjoying the new postwar prosperity of the Sixties. At the very same time as Fukasaku shows the quartet's various schemes, he is careful to emphasize that they are joined together by strong emotional bonds—they take great pleasure in each other's company. There is also an erotic bond between Muraki and the woman.

At about halfway through the film, the mood darkens when one of the young men's fathers is murdered. Revenge begins to take precedence over blackmail, although the two are intertwined. "We're strictly blackmailers," Muraki claims, but he is the one who pushes the revenge plot forward. Quickly, they are, they realize, "over their heads." One man is killed, another decides to leave the gang, and, at the very end, Muraki is murdered: "What a stupid way to go," are his dying words. This scene is done in such an over-staged way so as to remind the viewer that this film is a deliberately melodramatic, self-conscious examination of a variety of forces at work in the Japan of the 1960s.

Fukasaku tells his story in vivid colors, but the narrative is frequently interrupted by black and white still shots from the past. As the film progresses, sequences once in color are turned into black and white snapshots. The film is filled with references to film-making: Muraki is blackmailing a film actress who is trying (successfully) to become a *pinku* star; the gang steals clandestinely-made scenes of persons having sex and then blackmails the participants; in order to get a pornographic film venture off the ground, one of the gang members allows himself to become the "star" of one of these films.

In addition to showing how film can be made to exploit, Fukasaku also emphasizes the power of texts. The undoing of the gang occurs when they try to get their hands on a politically sensitive document, the Otagaru Memorandum. In a masterly stroke, Fukasaku also displays how the media—which desperately wants to gets its hands on and publish this material—is undone when the authentic document is labeled a counterfeit by the sinister political forces that control Japan. The punks realize too late that the politicians and the yakuza are working hand in hand: the gang of four undoes itself because its chicanery is no match for that of far wealthier and better placed persons in government, finance and organized crime.

Blackmail is My Life belongs in the yakuza genre, but it deftly allows all kinds of layering to invade that basic story concept. The narrative is about the bonding that takes place among a small group of social misfits; about how the "reality" shown in films can undo lives; about how potentially powerful media forces can be tamed; about the various levels of deceit and illusion that are at the heart of Japan's new prosperity. Rather than being a film that can be assigned a generic identity, it is a film that uses some yakuza conventions as a launching pad to discuss alienated youth (the genre called *sheishun-eiga*) and the various forms of fakery at the centre of Japanese society.

In comparison to *Tokyo Drifter* and *Blackmail is My Life*, Toshia Fujita's *Lady Snowbird* (*Shurayukimi*; 1973) seems a much milder affair. In 1874, a baby girl is born in prison to a dying mother. From the moment of her birth, Yuki (Meiko Kaji) is a creature of the netherworld whose life is devoted to the hunting down and killing of the four criminals who killed her father and brutalized her mother. In fact, the heroine is conceived in order to be an instrument of revenge. Despite the fact that some uneasy feelings, such as of compassion and empathy, get in her way, the heroine remains purpose-directed. As a child, she endures a rigorous training as a samurai and assassin. She then hunts down and kills the four persons (three men and one woman) responsible for her parents' misfortunes.

At a crucial turning point, Yuki allows a journalist Ryurei Asio (Toshio Kurasawa) to tell her story in a supposedly fictional context in order to lure one of her prey out of hiding. The ruse works, but the heroine develops a strong emotional attachment to the writer, who is murdered at the same time victim number four is dispatched. At the end of the film, the daughter of one of her victims kills the heroine.

Although not rendered in the broad, comic tone of *Tokyo Drifter*, Toshia Fujita obviously enjoyed telling his story in vigorous strokes. In her first appearance, Yuki, demurely costumed in a white kimono with umbrella in hand, stops a heavily guarded rickshaw and kills its occupant and all his attendants. Since, as the title indicates, the snow that cleanses the netherworld is red rather than white, the director fills his canvas with plenty of arterial bloodletting against white landscapes. There is a constant use of slow motion in the action sequences, as is common in this genre. There is also the skillful use of manga-like graphics that are used mainly to tell the heroine's back-story and to place the narrative in the Meiji period.

Minbo—Or the Gentle Art of Japanese Extortion (*Minbo no Onna*,

1992) updates many of the features found in *Blackmail is My Life* and, like the other films discussed above, is extremely self-referential to its genre of origins. Hotel Europa is trying to get a prestigious contract as the site of a summit meeting of important foreign officials. Unfortunately, this hotel is quite popular with the yakuza and is a favorite target of theirs for extortion.

The Manager (Kôichi Ueda) appoints two of his employees— Suzuki (Yasuo Daichi), an accountant, and Wakasugi (Takehiro Murata), a bellhop—to solve the problem, but they are ineffectual. The manager finally begins to fight back effectively by hiring a woman lawyer, Mahiru Inoue (Nobuko Miyamoto), who is an expert at dealing with extortion tactics. She soon teaches her underlings her distinct brand of aggressive charm. "If you stand up to the yakuza, they become cowards." She also assures them that they only enact violence against each other because "Violence can land them in jail." And she reminds them, prison is expensive for gangsters because it is lost work time.

The movie's tone now darkens into melodrama. While Inoue is doing her best to neutralize her enemies, the same opponents inveigle the Manager into a situation where he becomes an easy target for blackmail. When she tries to extract him from this situation, her opponent cynically informs her that all that matters is "ethics" in a "law-abiding country" like Japan. However, Inoue *apparently* blackmails her chief enemy into submission. However, her opponent and his cronies change tactics by raising the stakes. The hotel's proposed new extension is an environmental hazard, the gangsters claim, and they organize a noisy protest that upsets the hotel's guests. The movie's atmosphere then veers into farce with a series of events involving the hapless Manager.

Inoue comes back on to the scene as a ruthless crusader against injustice, who refuses to give in to yakuza tyranny. Her courage derives from her childhood when a wounded gang boss showed up at her father's dental surgery. Assassins followed him there, but Inoue's father refused to hand his patient over. Inoue's father was shot and later died; the wounded gangster was buried alive. Her dying father told Inoue that it was better to die for your beliefs than live like a coward.

Having made this declaration, Inoue is critically stabbed by a henchman. Further inspired by her courage, Suzuki manipulates the gangsters to make self-incriminating remarks recorded for the benefit of the police. Unlike her father, Inoue survives. The film concludes with a new group of yakuza being sternly rebuffed as they try to enter the hotel.

Some yakuza were angered by their portrayal in *Minbo* as common thugs and bullies. Three knife-wielding members of the Goto-gumi gang attacked Itami near his home on May 22, 1992, six days after the movie opened. The director was beaten and his face slashed, and he nearly died as a result. The brutality of the attack, combined with Itami's popularity and the success of *Minbo*, led to a public outcry.

REPAIRING HONOR

Western films about the yakuza, as already argued, are not as stylized or as daring as some of their Japanese counterparts. They tend to concentrate in an unnuanced way on what they conceive is the Japanese code of the *bushido* and, especially, the central importance of honor. For many Westerners, *bushido* is best translated as chivalry.

In Sydney Pollack's *The Yakuza* (1974), at the instigation of his war buddy, George Tanner (Brian Keith), world-weary, stoic Harry Kilmer (Robert Mitchum) returns reluctantly to Osaka to rescue Tanner's daughter from the yakuza, who have kidnapped her in retaliation for her father's failure to deliver a shipment of firearms. The honor of the yakuza demands that a business agreement be kept; Kilmer's honor is at stake because he feels an obligation to Tanner for past favors.

After the war, Harry had fallen in love with Eiko (Keiko

Kishi). She refused to marry him and, in 1951, when her brother Tanaken Ken (Ken Takakura) returned belatedly from the war (he had been living for six years in jungle caves in the Philippines), their relationship ended; she became estranged from her brother when he informed her that she had placed him forever in the debt of his enemy, an American. Eiko then told Harry that she could no longer live with him, much less marry him. Subsequently, Ken became a successful member of the yakuza.

FIGURE 21 Harry Kilmer (Robert Mitchum) and Eiko (Keiko Kishi) are reunited in Tokyo in *The Yakuza*.

This is Harry's background story. In present-day Osaka he meets up again with Eiko and, in Kyoto, Ken, who has switched professions and become a swordsman instructor. Reluctantly, he agrees to assist Harry because of the *giri* (obligation) he owes him. The two rescue Tanner's daughter but two gangsters are killed in the fight; Tono (Eiji Okada), the boss, places a price on Ken's head.

Harry visits Goro (James Shigeta), a senior obuyan who is Ken's brother. Goro does not wish to interfere to save his brother because his own role as a counselor to his fellow gangsters will be compromised. He insists that it is Harry's *giri* to assist Ken. Meanwhile, Tono interviews Tanner and learns that the guns were never acquired. He informs Tanner that he will take care of Ken but that he must deal with Harry. At this point, it becomes clear that Tanner is villainous.

After an independent yakuza, hired by Tanner, attempts to kill Harry and does murder others, including Eiko's daughter, Ken and Harry resolve to break into and secure Tono's compound. Before that, Goro informs Harry that Ken is not Eiko's brother but her husband. When he returned from the war, he was enraged to learn his wife was living with a foreigner but grateful to the foreigner for saving his wife. Goro then offers this reflection: "In any case, Ken is a tormented man. It is [his difficulties with] Eiko, of course, but it's also Japan. Ken is a relic, a leftover from another age and another country."

Before taking on Tono, Harry kills Tanner. In the ensuing melee at the compound, Ken inadvertently kills Goro's eldest son. To make amends, Ken cuts off his small finger. Harry leaves for the airport, but he instructs the driver to turn back. When he arrives at Ken's, Harry cuts off one of his small fingers, places it in a handkerchief, and offers it to an emotionless Ken. Harry tells him: " I brought great pain into your life, both in the past in the present. Please accept a token of my apology." He then continues: "If you can forgive me, surely you can forgive Eiko?"

The screenplay by Paul Schrader—his first for a feature film—was completed more than a decade before *Mishima*: there may be a very tortured hero in *The Yakuza*, but it took Schrader over a decade to re-define this concept in a Japanese context, layer it and thus give it the complexity it deserved. As in *Mishima*, however, Schrader is at pains to point of that a strong code of honor prevails in Japan in contrast to the American Tanner's double-dealing.

In John Frankenheimer's *The Challenge* (1982), down-and-out boxer Rick Murphy (Scott Glenn) is approached by wheelchair-bound Toshio and his sister, Aiko, to smuggle a sword into Japan. When he arrives in Tokyo with the sword concealed among his golf clubs, Rick is kidnapped and soon learns that he has been used as a decoy: he does not have the sword, one of two called The Equals, in his possession.

Toshio and Akio are the son and daughter of Toru Yoshida (Tôshiro Mifune), the eldest of two brothers. Toru, who lives according to Japanese traditional values, operates a martial arts academy. The other brother, Hideo Yoshida (Atsuo Nakamura), is an industrialist who owns a huge multinational company. Years before the present day story commences, Hideo stole one of the swords; the other has been restored to the possession of Toru.

After attempting unsuccessfully to be paid by Toru for his services, Rick accepts a lucrative offer from Hideo to become a student at Toru's academy, ingratiate himself and, in the process, steal the sword. Hideo will then have both weapons.

This scheme goes askew when Rick comes to admire Toru and his values. In fact, he returns the sword to him after having the perfect opportunity to escape with it. Then, it turns out, one of Toru's followers betrays him and steals the sword. Rick leaves Toru's compound and has a brief affair with Akiko. She is kidnapped. In the final sequences, Toru goes to Hideo's industrial complex where he is shot by Hideo's chief henchman, Ando (Calvin Jung). Ando is slain by Hideo for this transgression, and Murphy, who has decided to resume his relationship with Toru, arrives on the scene and fights Hideo in order to defend his *sensei*. In Japan, Murphy discovers, and accepts, a culture in which a strong moral code prevails.

Osaka in Ridley Scott's *Black Rain* (1989) is a dark, futuristic metropolis reminiscent of the Tokyo-looking Los Angeles in the same director's earlier *Blade Runner*. Despite the deliberately Japanese-like setting of the earlier film, Scott found Japan "difficult visually, awkward visually." To his taste, Tokyo and Kyoto were "squeaky-clean New Town. Everything is well-kept, with gigantic freeways and a gigantic scale of architecture....But this architecture is really not definitely Japanese, except in pockets and pieces and bits." This problem was only resolved when Alan Poul, the film's resident Japanologist and associate producer, took the director to Osaka, which Scott was pleased to find was "big, but provincial, [with a] European feel because of a lot of parks and also a gentility." On screen, it was rendered as "an industrial center whose streets are dense with pedestrian and motorized traffic and whose skies are dense with pollution."[3]

In fact, Osaka looks much more austere and forbidding than the Manhattan cityscape where the film opens. There, two New York policemen, Nick Conklin (Michael Douglas) and Charlie Vincent (Andy Garcia), witness a gruesome double murder performed by Sato (Yusaku Matsuda). The two Americans capture the Japanese mobster and accompany him back to Osaka, where they inadvertently hand him over to members of his own gang masquerading as policemen.

In order to restore his sense of tarnished honor, Nick is especially anxious to assist the Japanese police in finding Sato. Reluctantly, the authorities in Osaka allow the two Americans to accompany Matsu (Ken Takakura). When he hears Nick telling Charlie that they can find a "Nip" who speaks English, Matsu interjects: "I speak fucking English." When Nick acts impetuously and removes crime evidence, Matsu confronts him: "I will have no more to do with you....You have dishonored me. You are a thief." Nick later explains that he removed the evidence—American one hundred dollar bills—in order to prove they were counterfeit. The relationship between the two is restored but remains rocky. Charlie's eager camaraderie keeps the three together, but then Sato murders him. Matsu takes responsibility because he should have been more actively overseeing the two Americans.

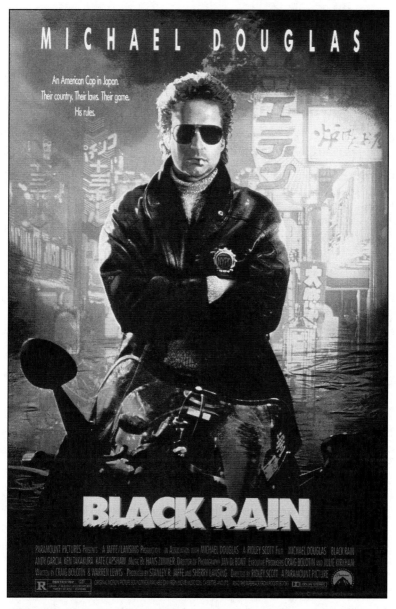

FIGURE 22 Nick Conklin (Michael Douglas) is featured in this *Black Rain* poster because the film was conceived of as a star vehicle for Douglas.

The focus of the film now turns on the relationships between

Sato and the much older Sugai (Tomisaburo Wakayama) and between Matsu and Nick. According to Sugai, an *oyabon* (head boss), Sato has acted disrespectfully by not following the established protocols within the gang hierarchy. Matsu does things by the rulebook whereas Nick's philosophy is: sometimes "forget your head and use your balls." When Nick breaks too many rules, Matsu is suspended because of the American's bad conduct. He is outspoken in his resentment: "I am not like you. For a moment I thought I could be. I belong to a group." Nick's reply is predictable: "Sometimes you have to go for it." In another scene, Matsu asks if the reports are true that Nick is a cop on the take back home. Nick tells him that this is the case. "If you steal," Matsu replies, "you disgrace [Charlie] and me and yourself."

Without Matsu, Nick approaches Sugai, who reveals that he was in Hiroshima on the day the bomb was dropped. He and his family were underground and were unscathed physically by the black rain. However, in the intervening years, he has come to see Japan as ruined by the American invaders. In fact, it is the U.S.A. that "created Sato," whereas Sugai, by implication, is a true Japanese "bound by duty and honor." Reluctantly, Sugai makes a deal with Nick: he tells him the location of a meeting where Sato will be on a certain day and, in exchange, Nick will capture or kill Sugai's rival.

Acting very much like a lone wolf, Nick stalks his prey, but he is finally assisted, very much to his surprise, by Matsu, who observes: "Sometimes you have to go for it." The result is a slaughter from which only the two policemen emerge intact. At the airport when Nick is leaving Japan, the two men exchange gifts. Underneath the shirt Nick has left for Matsu are the "missing" counterfeit plates. The implication is that Nick will no longer act as a counterfeit cop. He will not behave like Sato. Perhaps his venomous dislike of Sato has in part been fuelled by his realization that in looking at him, he was looking in the mirror?

Michael Douglas chose to star in *Black Rain* because he felt "there was something between us [Americans] and Japan that was unresolved, that was a mixture of hostility and admiration on both sides—really confused. It involves Japan's cultural imitation of the United States, followed by its economic supremacy over the United States, all of which is colored by lingering memories of World War II."[4] He meant the latter reference to signify the bombing of Hiroshima and Nagasaki. He thought this "particular picture, as a cop-action picture, could explore some of the differences in culture and behavior – explore some of the hostilities that our two cultures have for each other."[5]

According to Ridley Scott, Nick,

re-establishes some lost values in himself—traditional values, which somewhere along the line have been lost in the West but which I think still exist in Japan, such as a sense of honor and a sense of family—through his experience with this Japanese character. And Ken—who plays a kind of Japanese Everyman, the salaried man, the bourgeois, what we think of as the automaton—loses his rigidity, and opens up through his contact with Michael and Andy Garcia.[6]

Douglas emphasizes cultural differences, which the film certainly stresses. In contrast, Scott sees Japan as a place, which embodies values abandoned by the West. In his opinion, Nick and Matsu get in touch with diminished or lost aspects of themselves and, in the process, are enhanced. As Paul M. Sammon has argued, "a strong undercurrent of spiritual enrichment flows through the supposedly formulaic crime thriller *Black Rain*, as Japan's ethics-and-community oriented culture transforms Michael Douglas's selfish, abrasive New York copy into a humbled, morally-aware team player."[7]

At the outset of the film, there is the implication that Matsu acts in a robotic manner as opposed to the two Americans. However, this aspect of the Japanese detective vanishes as the film progresses. Nick finds redemption in emulating his Japanese colleague. American values of right and wrong are further challenged when Sugai points out that his fellow criminal, Sato, has learned his methodology from Americans. Sugai belongs to the pure Japanese strain (he is a genuine, made-in-Japan yakuza) whereas Sato is a hybrid gangster, who does not play by the rules. The black rain to which Sugai was subjected was caused by the Americans and, moreover, Sato uses American-based gangster methods. The film's moral drift implies that American values are inferior to Japanese ones. Yet, it can be argued that Nick has always been—and remains—a sterling example of American manhood. He maintains his air of superiority even when he becomes a vigilante; he may experience some inner change and no longer be a crooked cop, but he remains a rugged individual. In this sense, American superiority reigns supreme.

The Pollack and Frankenheimer films deal with the themes of honor and loyalty in rigidly straightforward ways that do not take advantage of the complexities that can be readily found in some yakuza cinema. These two films might be best deemed yakuza-style or yakuza-like because they are not infused with the shadings Japanese directors have perfected in this genre. *Black Rain* presents the American-Japanese binary in a more convincing manner, suggesting as it does that the West's values are sometimes corrupt next to Japanese ones. In his *Kill Bill* films, Quentin Tarantino explores similar complexities.

YAKUZA-STYLE PASTICHE

Tarantino's *Kill Bill Volume I* (2003) and *Kill Bill Volume 2* (2004) are deliberate mish-mashes of a wide variety of genres, only a few strands of which are in the yakuza tradition. Moreover, more crucially for my purposes, only three episodes in *Volume I* are actually set in Japan: a sequence in Okinawa where The Bride

(Uma Thurman) commissions a sword and, immediately following, two scenes in Tokyo where first of all an obdurate, unflinching O-Ren-Ishii (Lucy Liu) becomes the head of the yakuza gangs in Japan and, subsequently, an epic confrontation in which The Bride revenges herself on O-Ren. Other than those three scenes, the remainder of *Volume 1* and all of *Volume 2* takes place in the United States.

The event that propels the quest for revenge occurred in El Paso, Texas, where The Bride, a former member of the DiVAS (Deadly Viper Assassination Squad) and pregnant by her former boss (David Carradine), had renounced her previous life. She was engaged to marry the owner of a used record store but is rudely surprised when Bill and the other DiVAS arrive, massacre the groom and all the members of the wedding party, beat her senseless and leave her for dead. Four years latter, she emerges from a coma and begins her search for Bill and his confederates.

In *Volume I*, The Bride murders Vernita Green in her suburban Pasadena, California home; although Vernita's young daughter does not witness the actual killing, she is in the house when her mother is killed. The Bride apologizes for the inconvenience and tells the girl she is welcome to pursue her for revenge in the future. In Okinawa, The Bride looks up the retired ninja Hattori Hanzo (Sunny Chiba), who reluctantly makes a sword for her. The Bride then travels to Tokyo to take on O-Ren.

O-Ren's background story is told in an anime sequence of spectacular violence: as a young girl, she witnessed the murder of her parents. As an adult, O-Ren's pedigree as a young woman of Chinese-Japanese parents born on an American Air Force base is used by a yakuza rival to invalidate her claim to be supreme leader. She deals with her opponent by chopping off his head; in this sequence Liu deliberately overacts in an attempt to demonstrate the bottomless pit of rage that consumes her. Then, in parallel sequences, The Bride flies from Okinawa to Tokyo and O-Ren and various members of her retinue are shown at a nightclub, The House of Blue Leaves. After The Bride confronts and defeats various members of O-Ren's entourage, she then faces her nemesis. That scene is shot in falling snow that quickly becomes red.

FIGURE 23 The Bride (Uma Thurman) and O-Ren (Lucy Liu) in their epic confrontation from *Kill Bill Volume I*.

Like all of Tarantino's films, *Volume I* is filled with all kinds of cinematic references: it is a carefully wrought vessel of phrases, quotes, parodies, ironic glances and imitations. The most obvious references are to the various kinds of martial art films produced by the Hong Kong-based Shaw Brothers Studio. There are many references to Japanese films, however. For example, the influence of both Fukasaku and Suzuki is obvious in the use of color and black and white sequences and the penchant for clashing, bright colors. The casting of Sunny Chiba against type (he was usually an anti-hero figure in Japanese action films) adds another note of Japanese authenticity to *Volume I*. The frequently sarcastic, comic voice-over of The Bride may be derived in part from *Blackmail is My Life*.

However, Tarantino is directly indebted to *Lady Snowbird* for many details: the song "Flower of Carnage" in *Volume I* is taken directly from *Lady Snowbird*; the early life of O-Ren resembles that of Yuki; the duel between The Bride and O-Ren in a snow covered garden is filmed exactly like a sequence in *Lady Snowbird*; both films are divided into chapters; in both films, Yuki and The Bride undergo rigorous training by demanding masters; both films use animated sequences.

Tarantino's strength as a director emerges in large part from his mastery of film history and his willingness to take all the risks associated with making a pastiche-laden film. The complex and intricate set for The House of the Blue Leaves was filmed in China at the Beijing Film Studio, and this is an important clue for evaluating the concept of Japan in *Volume I*. For Tarantino, China and Japan are almost synonymous places in their fascination with martial art and gangster films. As a director, Tarantino picks and chooses elements that he can thread into whole cloth, but he is not the least bit concerned with any kind of authentic cultural or geographical landscape. Rather, he is an orchestrator, who brings seemingly conflicting material together. Tarantino's extremely limited use of yakuza elements is, nevertheless, the most imaginative use of the tradition by a Western director: his alignment of violence with gang crime is accurate and suggests the blood-filled landscapes that such films freely inhabit. In a masterful stroke, he produces in the character of the ultra-feminine O-Ren a gloriously perverse example of an ultra-masculine-acting yakuza. In his rendering, no rigid binary is constructed between East or West: both the Bride and O-Ren are strong women, who just happen to be on opposite sides.

CHAPTER SEVEN

MYSTERIOUS (NON-FICTION) TRUTHS

Documentaries made by Westerners view Japan in a variety of ways. Sometimes it is a place so removed from the West that it allows entirely new perspectives on a wide variety of issues. In addition, it can inspire new personal and artistic liberties, very much in the way Barthes described it. In contrast, some Japanese filmmakers envision their native land in less than ideal terms. Some Western filmmakers follow this lead and treat Japan as a contemporary society engulfed—and often overwhelmed—in complexities that are symptomatic of life everywhere on the planet.

Documentaries follow exacting but often nebulous rules. They supposedly record truths as opposed to fiction's lies, but choice of subject matter and the decision of how to frame the chosen subject means that from the outset all documentaries consist of large fictional components; they (teasingly) arouse the viewer's expectation that the "truth" will be revealed and then thwart that expectation. These kinds of films are fictions with a series of regulations and rules about truth-telling sometimes carefully, sometimes carelessly applied. In all the films in this chapter, the directors have chosen to show a truth about Japan that fascinates them and that always means that the resulting narratives must be seen as extensions of their creators' sensibilities.

Wim Wenders' *Notebook on Cities and Clothes* (1989) is supposedly about the fashion designer Yohji Yamamoto, whom the filmmaker admires. This documentary, commissioned by the Centre Georges Pompidou in Paris, was shot in Paris and Tokyo. There are cityscapes, head-on interviews with the designer, interactions between Wenders and Yamamoto, preparations for a runway show in Paris. However, the film is never really about its stated subject. Rather, Wenders, at the outset, deconstructs the idea of identity: there is really no such entity. If this is the case, the idea of a film portrait disappears. As Homay King has argued, the genius of this film is to show Germany and Japan as interwoven cultures. Wenders bought a shirt and jacket designed by Yamamoto. He states:

> From the beginning they were new and old at the same time. In the mirror I saw me ... more me than before, and I had the strangest sensation I was wearing the shirt itself and the jacket itself, and in them, I was myself. Who was he, what secret had he discovered, this Yamamoto? It came from further away, from deeper. This jacket reminded me of my childhood, and of my father, as if the essence of this memory were tailored into it.

Wenders' search for his own past becomes embroidered in Yamamoto. The implication is that Wenders might learn *something* about his own identity if he makes a film about Yamamoto, although, from the outset, the whole issue of identity has been discarded:

> While the film continues to be structured by connections and parallels that Wenders finds between himself and Yamamoto, between filmmaking and clothing design, and between East and West, Wenders eventually abandons the questions he asks .... Rather than set off in hot pursuit of Yamamoto's secret, he explores the relations between self and others in a roving, sketch-like way.[1]

Yamamoto, it turns out, has been heavily influenced by German designs, and the link between West and East is established, if anything in the film can be said to be "firmly established." My point is that Wenders constructs a fiction even though his film belongs to the genre of documentary. A similar imposition of the filmmakers' sensibilities informs the documentaries considered in this chapter.

ACCIDENTAL BEAUTIES

Chris Marker's *The Koumiko Mystery* (1965) preserves a series of conversations of the director, who had previously collaborated with Resnais[2], with French-speaking, twenty-something Tokyo resident Koumiko Muraoka, at the time of the 1964 Tokyo Olympics, a critical milestone whereby Japan demonstrated to the international community that it had evolved into a modernized democratic society. Evidently, Marker was invited to make a documentary about the Olympics, but that project does not seem to have gotten off the ground, unlike Kon Ichikawa's *Tokyo Olympiad* (1965). In 1964, Muraoka was a student at the French-Japanese Institute in Tokyo. Although Japanese, she was born in Manchuria and did not arrive in Japan until she was ten years old. To a certain extent, she saw herself as an outsider within Japan. She also considered her face old-fashioned and aspired to have had a more in vogue, "funny face" (Audrey Hepburn) look.

Marker, who claimed to have met Muraoka by chance, allows her to be the fulcrum through which he is introduced to the disorder and simplicity he, as first-time visitor, envisions is Japan. Like Barthes, he appreciates the various surfaces of Japan and sees them as distinctly non-Western. It is a country where appearances refreshingly signify everything. As Catherine Lupton points out, however, Marker sees a difficulty wherein the Japanese are seen to be "completely Westernized and thoroughly" themselves. For Marker, Koumiko is the embodiment of the "mysterious, feminine Orient."[3] However, she considered her face too classically Japanese and wished to erase her Asiatic features in order to appear more Western.

The trajectory of the story line consists of Marker encountering Muraoka, filming her, inundating her with questions, and then returning to France but leaving her a questionnaire to which she sends tape-recorded responses. The film is thus divided into two parts: Muraoka tours Tokyo with Marker and then her voice is heard in the second part accompanied by visuals of her sitting on trains and restaurants, absorbed in her own world. The more the interviewer queries Muraoko, the more elusive and playful become her answers.

Although Marker is interested in the exotic East as incorporated into his female protagonist, he is also self-consciously working in the French New Wave tradition: the visuals of Tokyo in the rain are accompanied by the haunting, bittersweet music from Jacques Demy's *Les Parapluies de Cherbourg* (1963). In the late Fifties and early Sixties, Godard had created a series of entrancing but elusive screen heroines in Jean Seberg and Anna Karina: Muraoko is Marker's reinvention of Godard's preoccupation with women as engaging but often retreating muse figures.

Muraoka shares many traits with Marker: for example, she likes the writings of Jean Giradoux and she is partial to cats. The similarities help form a bond: the Frenchman is an outsider to Japan; she considers herself an outsider to Japan. The contrasts are also striking. She does not share the Frenchman's interest in global politics. In being someone Japanese but also a person who is non-Japanese in many ways, Muraoko is a true hybrid. For Marker, she is an excellent portal into a foreign culture.

Marker and Muraoko did not meet by chance at the Olympics, as the director implies. She was working for Marcel Giuglaris, a journalist at *France Soir*, at his office near the Yurakucho section of Tokyo, a kind of refuge for various intellectuals and artists. Giuglaris asked Muraoko to assist the filmmaker, who was using a silent 16 mm Bolex camera that had to be cranked up frequently. Her task was to remind him to perform this essential task. This was a ploy. Every time she reminded him, Marker said: "Then we'd better test to see if it works." This was how the film was constructed: she did not know that these "takes" were to form the basis for a film centered on her; she assumed that her new friend was actually making a documentary about the Olympics.

The resulting film is more autobiography than biography. Muraoka does not represent Japan as much as she signifies someone who exists in Japan, speaks the language but remains intrigued by foreign things. The subject is really Marker's entry into Japan and his willingness to look for the first time at a culture significantly different from his own. What does Marker see there, what will he see there in the future?: these are the queries posed. However, he never fully answers those questions, even in his next Japanese documentary, *Sans soleil*.

UNLIKELY BEAUTIES

At the conclusion of the deleted color sequence from Imamura's *Black Rain*, two women are hawking remnants of tiles salvaged from houses and buildings destroyed by the bomb. One sequence in Marker's *Sans soleil* (1983) highlights the story of Okinawa's desperate resistance for more than a month before falling to the American infantry in June 1945. The narrator reminds the viewer that Okinawa had a separate identity and was a matriarchal society. At the end of the battle, two hundred local girls used grenades to commit suicide rather than be taken alive. This event is memorialized, as Marker shows, by a tourist site where "souvenir lighters" in the shape of grenades are on offer.

Tiles from Hiroshima and imitation grenades from Okinawa become fodder for the tourist industry and, in the process, modern man removes himself from unendurable pain by sentimentalizing and enshrining such feelings. Humankind cannot bear much reality, T.S. Eliot claimed, and Marker agrees with that pronouncement. At one point, the narrating voice quotes the commonplace—"Time heals all wounds"—and reverses it: *Time heals everything but wounds.* This is, of course, one of the themes of *Hiroshima Mon Amour.*

An unseen woman called Alexandra Stewart, who is pulling together reflections from a series of letters to her from one Sandor Krasna, an obvious alter ego for Marker, voices the film. It is possible to suppress memory, he observes, but it also has the power to assert itself, often painfully. Memory also distorts. Once again, these are also the themes of *Hirsohima Mon Amour,* and those key concepts obsess Krasna/Marker. He adds his own spin on this topic by introducing into his documentary, Hayao Yamaneko, a computer technician, who generates synthesized

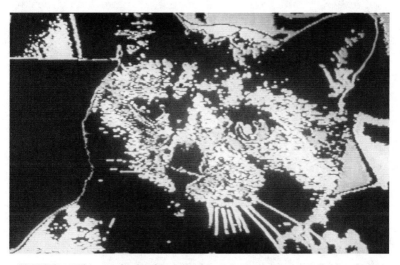

FIGURE 24 This synthesized image of a cat is one of many such visuals by Hayao Yamaneko seen in *Sans soleil.*

images in what he refers to as The Zone, based on the space of the same name in Tarkovsky's *Stalker* (1979).[4] Past events can be changed, Yamaneko claims, and the resulting images "are less deceptive than those you see on television. At least they proclaim themselves to be what they are: images, not the portable and compact form of an already inaccessible reality."[5] These images, removed from the appearance of reality, may allow both reflection and contemplation, but this is ultimately an illusion.

Krasna's attitude towards Japan is very similar to that of Barthes': Japan is a place where people are able to enter into things in a way from which the West has closed itself. There is recognition of both separateness and aloneness. It is a locale where the "unsaid" is more privileged than the "said": as such, it offers possibilities of positive change to a Westerner.

However, Krasna resists idealizing Japan: it is a place that has endured—and continues to endure—trauma. For example, the faces and bodies of the desolate burakumin are transformed into images of great beauty. They becomes art objects, but their social reality remains unchanged and, of course, unaffected by the clips made by Yamaneko and inserted into Krasna's letters (The burakumin are a class of ostracized persons whose existence is often denied in Japan; this Japanese social minority are descendants of outcast communities of the feudal era whose jobs were tainted with death or racial impurity (undertakers, workers in slaughter houses, butchers, tanners). In 1871, restrictions against this group were lifted, but prejudice against them is still widespread.)

In an extended passage, Krasna provides a way into the huge array of images he has been collecting. For him, Hitchcock's *Vertigo* becomes the supreme film about the vertigo of time (and not the vertigo of space to which the title of Hitchcock's film refers), and Krasna makes a pilgrimage to San Francisco to visit all the surviving locales filmed there by Hitchcock. What is that film about?, Krasna wonders. Did Scottie (Jimmy Stewart) rescue Madeleine (Kim Novak) from death in San Francisco Bay only to lead her to her death at the end of the film? Who is controlling whom? Scottie is manipulated in the first half of the film but becomes a manipulator in the second half when he constructs a false Madeleine. Is that male character ever really in control—or is he completely controlled by others and, especially, by his own memories? The Krasna figure is asking these questions about himself: is he trapped in the vertigo of time?

This reflection about indeterminacy makes Krasna melancholic and leads him to think that he might like to make a film *Sunless* named after the Mussorgsky's song cycle of the same name: verses filled with notions of unhappiness and memory. Mussorgsky was confronting the specter of death in his music and verse. Krasna may be making the same suggestion about himself in the images he is gathering. In their own time, the Mussorgsky song cycle was considered avant-garde, and Krasna may be making a similar claim about his documentary. These may be some of Krasna's intentions but they may not be the only (or real) reasons for the name of the film: Krasna's own memory, of course, he is aware, could be playing him false. Perhaps he is simply trapped in a sunless existence?

Another area of the mysterious Zone are clips from World War II, including Hirohito on horseback. This image—rendered in blue and orange—provides a completely different reality in that it reduces the Emperor to an abstract shape, rendering him an ethereal configuration. Memory is erased/reconfigured yet again.

Towards the end of the film, Krasna makes this observation: "I remember that month of January in Tokyo, or rather I remember the images I filmed of that January in Tokyo. They have substituted themselves for my memory, they *are* my memory." Another important literary intertext introduced by Krasna is a reference to Sei Shônagon, the author of the *Pillow Book*, a literary text reconfigured by Peter Greenaway (see Chapter Eight). Shônagon delighted in "the contemplation of the tiniest things" and "things that quicken the heart." The more trivial an image, the more delight it might bring. This becomes an additional metafictional commentary on the nature of the clips inserted into the film and of their subsequent electronic transformations. Shônagon—like Marker—also freely mixed various kinds of narratives into her text.

For Krasna, Japan is a place where appearances remain such. The cat temple of Gotokuji, the Bisai carnival, the copulating stuffed animals in the Josenkai sex museum, the Dondo-yakei Festival: for Krasna these places and events allow the public expression of feelings of loss, feelings of erotic bliss, and feelings of fleetingness to be validated.

In contrast, life can be full of tragic happenings. *Sans soleil* begins with what seems a happy moment: three Icelandic children walking. A black bar marks that segment; later, the viewer is told that the clip was made during a volcanic eruption that destroyed the town where the children lived. Were the lives of those children really carefree? Appearances are always deceiving, of course. The film is reminding the viewer of this grim fact constantly. Krasna, very much like Tarkovsky's stalker figure, is in search of a Zone, very much hoping that Hayao Yamaneko can assist him. However, does the Zone really exist? In addition, if it does, does it not also repress and deny memory?

In one scene Japanese children are shown depositing white chrysanthemums on a shrine dedicated to a dead panda. Over this sequence, we hear the voice of the narrator reading one of Krasna's letters:

I've heard this sentence [in Japan]: "The partition that separates life from death does not appear so thick to us as it does to a Westerner." What I have read most often in the eyes of people about to die is surprise. What I read right now in the eyes of Japanese children is curiosity, as if they were trying— in order to understand the death of an animal—to stare through the partition.

Immediately following this scene, the film cuts to a segment in which an unseen hunter shoots a giraffe. After the first shot, the giraffe falls to the ground. It then slowly lifts itself up and the unseen hunter sends another bullet through the giraffe's neck. In a scene that lasts for over a minute with no accompanying narration, the viewer watches the giraffe frantically running, spurting blood from its neck before it finally falls to the ground, exhausted. Revealing himself, the hunter enters the scene from the left and again shoots the already dying giraffe. The animal convulses and dies, and the camera cuts to the flight of an incoming vulture that, alongside another, begins to consume the corpse's eyes.

The Japanese children may "stare through the partition" between life and death, but no such mercy is accorded the giraffe or those looking at the animal's slaughter. There is, moreover, a critique of Japanese values in Krasna's response to his visit to the Hokkaido museum, which displays the taxidermically altered bodies of animals in various sex acts, one of which shows primates alongside a nude woman. As the film shows a series of images of primates, tigers, and zebras (among others) frozen in coitus, Stewart reads,

...one would like to believe in a world before the fall: inaccessible to the complications of a Puritanism whose phony shadow has been imposed on it by American occupation. The second part of the museum—with its couples of stuffed animals—would then be the earthly paradise as we have always dreamed it. Not so sure: animal innocence may be a trick for getting around censorship, but perhaps also the mirror of an impossible reconciliation. And even without original sin, this earthly paradise may be a paradise lost. In the glossy splendor of the gentle animals of Josenkai, I read the fundamental rift of Japanese society, the rift that separates men from women. In life, it seems to show itself in two ways only: violent slaughter, or a discreet melancholy, which the Japanese express in a single untranslatable word. So, this bringing down of man to the level of the beasts—against which the fathers of the church invade—becomes here the challenge of the beasts to the poignancy of things.

The end of this quotation echoes concepts of the animal prevalent in Western thought; the filmmaker interprets the museum as "bringing man down to the level of beasts," which echoes the classic dichotomy between man and the primitivized figure of the animal, the "beast." However, what does it mean that the "beasts" challenge the poignancy of things? In Krasna's epistle, Puritanism has been imposed upon Japan after the War. Certainly, the rift between Japanese men and women seems to be attributed in the commentary to Western-introduced Puritanism, but the interest in pornography and representations of fertility has a long history in Japanese culture.

Since Japan is a civilization that recognizes that appearances are everything, it offers a refuge from the West, where the appearance of things has always been distrusted and where everything must be labeled and endlessly categorized. Perhaps Japan will provide Krasna/Marker with his innermost desires? However, the West has corrupted Japanese sensibility. The film insists that here is no safe "Zone" in Japan or anywhere else. Memory always distorts. Japan certainly has, Krasna/Marker realizes, changed a great deal in the twenty years since he first visited it. For Marker the filmmaker, Kurosawa remains, nevertheless, an (idealized) still point on a turning wheel.

KUROSAWA AND OZU AS IDEALIZED FILMMAKERS

Chris Marker made *A.K.* (1986), his documentary homage to Akira Kurosawa in October and November 1984 during the filming of the Japanese director's *Ran* (*Chaos*), a Japanese version of *King Lear*. For Marker, Kurosawa is the consummate professional filmmaker, and the film becomes an exploration of various abstract personality characteristics of the director such as Patience and Faithfulness and of how he handles such issues as

Fire and Rain. In addition to being allowed with his crew on the various sets of *Ran*, Marker made use of audiocassettes of interviews with the director and videos of his films. Like *Koumiko* and *Sans soleil*, *A.K.* becomes by extension a film about Marker: here, he is paying a genuine tribute to Kurosawa, but he is also commenting indirectly on his own existence as a filmmaker.[6] At the outset, Kurosawa asserts: "Memory is what you create from." At first glance, Marker seems to take this proclamation at face value; he treats the observation as a given. In his voice-over, Marker the Acolyte is anxious to separate himself from Kurosawa the Master by assuring the viewer that he is trying to avoid "borrowed beauty": he knows that he will be filming while Kurosawa is filming, and he does not wish to take advantage of the other man's eye, especially as his own, he clearly implies, is second-rate in comparison. Marker certainly takes on the role of the naive follower, who dutifully records the great man's pronouncements such as "I make a film as I want it to be" and "What is *not* filmed is often the most beautiful." Kurosawa is shown in a variety of moods: most of the time, he simply acts his role of boss. At other times, he becomes mildly exasperated when technicians do not follow instructions; often, he is courtly and patient. He cautions the actors not to make the horses nervous: "They are upset because you are acting upset."

Marker observes that the Japanese director is in essence a sculptor imposing his will even on bad weather, which eventually capitulates in his favor. Gradually, however, Marker offers a biographical explanation of the source of Kurosawa's greatness as an artist.

In September 1923, at the age of thirteen, Kurosawa witnessed the great Kantô earthquake; on the following day, he wandered the streets of Tokyo with his elder brother and saw the devastation first-hand. In addition to the terrible destruction of buildings, he gazed upon the bodies of the many Koreans murdered because they had supposedly taken advantage of the destruction to loot. Kurosawa did not wish to look at this brutality, but his brother told him to keep his eyes open because only by doing so could he confront and deal with reality. The younger man followed his elder's advice.

In that traumatic moment from Kurosawa's adolescence, Marker implies, arose the determination and strength to look directly at reality and master it. "Showing what you want to see is the essence of filmmaking," Kurosawa proclaims: "The camera can go anywhere and is all powerful." Throughout his career, to his dismay, Kurosawa was often described as having a penchant for showing violence. "I hate violence. I am scared of it. I am haunted by it." These assertions may be true, Marker thinks, but he is also of the opinion that the early trauma made Kurosawa confront the specific visual reality of violence. Without ever making any kind of pedagogical explanation, Marker offers some telling observations on how a frightened teenager eventually became a director who saw into the heart of chaos.

Wim Wenders' *Tokyo Ga* (1985) is another Western film director's fan letter to another great Japanese director, Yasujirô Ozu. Like Marker, Wenders also plays the role of naïf. He celebrates modern Tokyo as seen in Ozu. This Tokyo is a city that no longer exists except in Ozu's celluloid versions, which are devoted to the Japanese family, an institution undergoing a slow deterioration. As such, nostalgia infuses his films.

At the outset of his journey to Japan, Wenders worries: will anything be left to find? Will there be people to interview? He also introduces another difficulty. If he records footage, won't his memory be affected to the extent that, without a camera, he would remember more precisely what he will see? When Wenders records a bullet train and cherry trees in full blossom, it is as if he has entered a dream world.

Seeing a rebellious little boy at a train station, Wenders remembers the mischievous, disobedient children who populate Ozu's films. In an instant, Tokyo becomes "familiar" because, of course, it is a place he knows through Ozu's eyes. However, the reality of present-day Tokyo immediately contradicts such sentimental reflections; it is a place filled with pachinko parlors and Japanese-made television sets broadcasting American-made movies.

The homage to Ozu is extended by bookending scenes from *Tokyo Story* so that examples of Ozu's genius directly confront the viewer at the outset and conclusion of the film. At the beginning appears Chishû Ryû, who played lead roles in many of the director's films and, at the end, Yuharu Atsuta, who served as second assistant cameraman, first assistant cameraman and, finally, cameraman for many of Ozu's films. Ryû remembers the director as someone who was rarely satisfied with two or three takes and sometimes rehearsed a given scene twenty times. Often, the actor felt that he was not quick enough in following the master's leads. He vividly recalled the day Ozu quipped: "Today is not one of your best days, is it?" For Ryû, Ozu was always the Teacher—everything on set was an extension of the director: camera positioning, the smallest detail of costuming. Nothing was left to chance. The actor felt that his career had been "made" by Ozu: he felt that he was the "chosen one," although he sometimes wondered why he had been given that honor. Unlike Marker, Wenders does not shy away from "borrowed beauty"; in fact, towards the end of the film, he imitates Ozu's much favored place-establishing static shots by shooting similar locales in highly-saturated color.

In an elaborate sequence, Wenders examines how the "examples" of food displayed in the shop fronts of various Tokyo restaurants are manufactured. These plastic sculptures begin with pieces of real food which are made into molds; the plastic results are painted and, as much as possible, resemble the items on offer at the restaurants. This is an example of the importance of verisimilitude—of paying attention to the surface. Although he never draws a direct connection with Ozu, the implication is that the great director sought as much as possible to recreate the visual reality of a vanishing Japan just as the appearance of the food is the overriding concern of the sculptors whom Wenders visits.

At one point, Wenders meets up with fellow countryman, film director Werner Herzog, who is en route to Australia. Herzog laments that there is so little left in the world that can be photographed in genuinely new and exciting ways. In fact, if he had the opportunity, Herzog would travel into space with NASA in order to record something new about the planet. Wenders understands his friend's lament, although he remains fixated on the world "below" and that means he searches within Ozu's films for inspiration. There is a chance meeting with the reclusive Chris Marker, who does not usually allow his face to be photographed: he does not wish his "appearance" to be captured, as if his identity would be robbed.

At the very end of the film, Atsuta is interviewed. He also felt that his life had been ennobled by the director's choice of him. However, the Master very infrequently bestowed praise but, when he did, it was a transforming moment. As he got older, Ozu tended to eliminate as much as possible traditional establishing, tracking and panning shots in favor of the camera being positioned close to the ground—on a camera support invented by the director. Before filming began, Ozu looked through the viewfinder and, once satisfied, no one was allowed to alter the angle of the camera. At the end of their collaboration, Ozu gave the cameraman one of his most prized possessions: his stopwatch.

As his interview with Wenders nears its end, Atsuta, overcome with emotion, orders Wenders to stop filming. The cameraman bursts into tears, so strong are his feelings of gratitude and love for Ozu.[7] At that point, Wenders shifts his film to the concluding sequences from *Tokyo Story*. Once on the train back to Tokyo, Noriko takes out and looks at the watch her father-in-law has given her. Wenders' film ends with the concluding credits to the film often considered Ozu's masterpiece.

In allowing some of Ozu's best work to conclude his own documentary, Wenders is acknowledging the greatness of the Japanese director: he is admitting that he himself has not found images that are in any way genuinely new or innovative. Just as *Tokyo Story* ends in a bittersweet way so does *Tokyo Ga*. Wenders has not discovered new images, but he has expressed his own love and admiration for Ozu. In so doing, he conducts himself very much like Ryû and Atsuta. Wenders, with Ryû, even visits the gravesite of Ozu, where a single Chinese character adorns the headstone: it means "emptiness." Ozu may have chosen this character to signify that his life no longer existed, but he may also have wanted it to signify that the old Japan was in the process of becoming "empty."

Kurosawa and Ozu were geniuses, men who expressed their inner lives in films of enduring value. Marker and Wenders are disciples: extremely talented filmmakers who have the grace and courage to bow down before those whom they consider more inherently blessed than themselves. They freely admit that their work is dross when placed alongside the gold of the two great Japanese directors. There is also the implication that Japan is a treasure house of yet unexplored images that can assist an Occidental filmmaker. Donald Richie, whose admiration for Ozu was boundless, also found in Japan a refuge from the Western world.

LANDSCAPES PASSING AWAY

About halfway through Donald Richie's *Inland Sea* (1991), the author-narrator arrives at the Kosanji Temple in the town of Setoda on Ikuchijima Island. Deeply alarmed at the prospect that his recently-deceased mother might not enter Buddhist paradise, Kanemoto Kozo (1891-1970), who retired early from his career as a steel tube magnate, changed his name to Kosanji Kozo, grew his hair long, and purchased a priesthood in the True Pure Land Sect, and began work on the temple complex which opened in 1936. For the next thirty years, he used large portions of his vast wealth to enlarge and improve the site. The resulting testimony to filial devotion contains many types of temples, shrines and other buildings, many of which are reproductions of famous sites such as the Yomeimon Gate at Nikko and the Phoenix Hall at Byôdôin Temple in Uji in Kyoto Prefecture. In addition to the architecture, there is the One Thousand Buddhas cave.

On close inspection, as Richie points out, a visitor will notice that Kosanji's fortune was not limitless: the Nikko gate is made out of plywood. Such an assembly of copies might be "kitsch," the commentator observes without malice, and he obviously feels that the bringing together of a series of famous buildings is deeply impressive—and moving. What the Western mind frequently fails to grasp about the Japanese mind-set is that outward show is central. And that is precisely what this temple complex is all about.

The buildings might be labeled replicas or even fakes, but that is beside the point because they are inspired by genuine feelings of devotion by the son for his mother. Richie's documentary is about the search for the "lost" Japan that can still be witnessed in the Inland Sea and its pine-filled islands (over 3000). In that remote area, far from Tokyo and other metropolises, Japan is a place where you can experience yourself as you wish. If you desire to be unhappy or lonely or exuberant, you have the freedom to access that emotion. That is something that Richie feels is key to the understanding of the Japanese personality: it is certainly the main reason he immigrated from the West to Japan, but he has noticed with sadness that city-dwellers in Japan now only sporadically have the ability to be themselves.

As a foreigner, Richie stands apart. He is obviously not Oriental. He has the freedom to be an outsider, which is a consid-erable advantage because it means he is not judged by the sometimes-harsh rules the Japanese apply to their fellow countrymen. In Japan, therefore, Richie has enjoyed considerable liberty, but he fears that the entire basis of his sense of the Japanese love of the form of things—of that faith they place in the beauty of the tangible world—is fast disappearing:

> These islands are extraordinarily beautiful, and a part of their beauty is that it is passing. Already the modern mainland is reaching out, converting each captured island into an industrial waste; already the fish, once so abundant, are leaving their annual paths, maintained over the centuries, and seeking clearer depths. When this paradise, this ideal sea garden—310 miles long, 40 miles at its widest and 4 at its narrowest—when it goes, devoured by the land, so will the people who inhabit it....[8]

This is the tragic dimension in what is essentially a celebratory exploration of Japan.

Described by Tom Wolfe as the Lafcadio Hearne of our time, Richie, who was born in Lima, Ohio in 1924, served aboard Liberty ships as a purser and medical officer during the Pacific War. He first visited Japan in 1947 as a member of the Occupation force. He became entranced by Japanese culture and began writing about it. He returned to the States to study at Columbia University and then returned to Japan in 1953 as a film critic. He has spent most of his subsequent life there and written widely about Japanese culture. His most widely recognized accomplishment is, with considerable justification, his writing on Japanese cinema.

Richie is also a filmmaker. He directed his first experimental film when he was seventeen-years-old in Ohio, and he pursued this avocation in Japan, in the process making a number of short features. These are coterie films, originally made for only Richie himself and a small circle of friends. They are lyrical, short film poems.

In practice, Richie is fascinated by how people conduct themselves in groups. In *Wargames* (1962), small boys act out ritual masculinity in a rigidly deterministic way reminiscent of Golding's *Lord of the Flies* (1954). *Cybele* (1968) tells of a Greek goddess who kills her lover and then leads her followers in an absurdist naked romp. She then kills them all and lies on top of their outstretched bodies.

Tatsumi Hijikata (1928-86), the choreographer who founded butoh, appears in *Gisei* (*Sacrifice*; 1959), the same year the dance form was introduced. The film shows the highly stylized, unorthodox manner of his artistry, but one performer, an extremely handsome, muscled truck-driver friend of Richie called Hatakeyama, was called upon to perform a traditional *matsuri* dance in contrast to the modernistic, writhing movements of the others. He pauses but when he attempts to rejoin the group, they torment and eventually kill him. In this instance, to be dissimilar is to be dangerous: the group is so threatened by difference that it murders the outsider. (See Chapter Eight for Dorris Dörrie's use of butoh in *Cherry Blossoms*). The same savagery inhabits *Five Philosophical Fables* (1967), which Yukio Mishima admired for its willingness to show how cannibalistic impulses may reside at the core of much ritualistic activity. As a unit, these films may be commenting on Japanese dependency upon group solidarity as a cornerstone of society.

The nude corpse of a young man lies at the edge of the ocean in *Dead Youth* (1967), and it is probably his lover who mourns him in the scenes shot in the interior near a graveyard. Other young men wander this area looking for men with whom to have sex, and several men visit the graves of dead lovers and then masturbate. Here Richie is encapsulating the loneliness and isolation of the gay man in contemporary Japan. Like *Dead Youth*, *Atami Blues* is a story of isolation and fragmentation within contemporary society. Very much influenced by Antonioni's

L'Avventura (1960), this narrative, centered on a young man and woman who flirt with the possibility of loving each other but remain disconnected, was originally forty minutes long, but Richie, under the influence of Ozu, reduced it to twenty. In the process, he feels, it became a much finer film.

Richie is particularly adept at incorporating Japanese landscapes into his films, but he does not attempt to be anyone but himself. He remains a Westerner who loves Japan, but, who, at the very same time, retains a critical distance from what he observes.

JAPAN AS MISTRESS

In contradistinction to Richie, Alan Berliner's *Intimate Stranger* (1991) is about the dangers of a foreigner loving Japan too much. This film is devoted to a grandson's attempt to come to terms with his maternal grandfather, Joseph Cassuto (1905-74). As the film unfolds, Cassuto's daughter and three sons comment on their enigmatic father: two of the sons despise him, one grudgingly admires him and his daughter, with reservations, respects and loves him. Although he was a Jew from a Spanish family, Cassuto was born in Palestine but as a youngster immigrated with his parents to Egypt. There, he began work for the Japanese Cotton Trading Company, which imported top-quality Egyptian cotton. As a young man, he saw Egypt as a paradise. In Alexandria, he married his wife, Rose. The couple's four children were born there. Life was good, even during the Depression and early years of World War II.

Then, Pearl Harbor intervened. Japan was seen as an outcast nation, and life became difficult. Cassuto decided that his wife and two youngest children should immigrate to the United States (the two eldest children were not eligible to leave Egypt). The Cassutos became two different families: father and children in Egypt were sophisticated and metropolitan whereas mother and children in America felt deprived and destitute.

Five years later, after the War, the family was re-united in the United States, but Cassuto felt out of place: "he had been a big fish in a little pond in Egypt." Having established many close business relationships in Japan before the War, Cassuto moved to Japan, where he spent eleven months of every year. Since Japan had little money with which to purchase goods, Cassuto became an expert in bartering Japanese manufactured goods for much-needed cotton.

The Japanese Cotton Trading Company changed its name to Nichiren, and, in some ways, Cassuto assisted the success of that firm. He felt at home in Japan; although he spoke little Japanese, he realized that Japan was his spiritual base. Moreover, he could be a person of real influence there. He was a "diplomat without credentials."

All four children felt that their mother, as well as themselves, had been abandoned. The household of an increasingly frail mother and four children became emotionally volatile, leading to Rose's nervous breakdown. Meanwhile, Cassuto lived a life very much resembling that of a Japanese salaryman, where business comes before family. He was also chameleon-like: if someone was pro-Zionist, he took on that stance; if someone was anti-semitic, he made sure that they did not realize he was Jewish. He had, as one of his sons observes, a survivor mentality. For his Japanese friends, he became more Japanese than most Japanese, who, in turn, felt he had a very feeling heart and a strong sense of duty.

Japan, according to his children, became Cassuto's mistress. Two of the sons feel he played it "safe" in Japan: he lived there at a time when the Japanese economy was exploding, yet he never became a wealthy man. If he "lacked courage," he replaced that virtue with kindness his Japanese friends assert.

When Cassuto returned from Japan permanently in 1956, he "came home to roost." He still worked for Nichiren, and visitors from Japan streamed in and out of his house. His home became a "little Japanese museum." As a father, he showed little interest in his children's abilities: he discouraged one from becoming a photographer, another from becoming an athlete. He determined that his daughter was to go to secretarial school rather than university. In the United States, he curbed the enthusiasms of his children while at the same time offering himself unstintingly and unreservedly to his Japanese colleagues: whatever they wanted to accomplish was completely acceptable to him. When his grandson Alan wanted to become a film director, his grandfather warned him against such a move, as one likely to end in failure.

Berliner, who dutifully acknowledges that his mother's attitude towards her father is balanced, attempts to come to grips with his enigma of a grandfather. At the end, he and his mother attend a ceremony in Tokyo honoring Cassuto. However, the film ends with a shot of Cassuto's gravestone and then his wife's: the voice-over of one of the sons praises his mother as the "real hero" of the family.

Cassuto's love affair with Japan consumed his existence. The viewer realizes that he was overcome by the kindness bestowed upon him there. He felt validated, but the film asks some significant questions. Did Cassuto escape to Japan because it allowed him to distance himself from his real life? Was his view of Japan simply based on half-baked notions of *giri* (sense of duty) or *ninjô* (kindness, tenderness)? Was there ever any genuine understanding of the Japanese on Cassuto's part? Alternatively, did he simply idealize that nation? Idealization is the core sentiment in Sokurov's Japanese documentaries.

DREAM LANDSCAPES

Aleksandr Sokurov made three documentaries set in Japan before embarking on *The Sun* (2005). The first, *Oriental Elegy* (1996), is in black and white, color and sepia. That film uses locations in and around St. Petersburg. For example, Vera Zelinskaya and her team built the scale model of the island village.

The narrating voice speaks directly in a tone of great intimacy. The speaker is first positioned in a dream-like fog. No one is around but then an island appears. The fog lifts. Suddenly he is on an island (he is seen on the shore looking at the island). He takes in deep breathes of jasmine. If he has reached paradise, why does he feel so sad? The houses he beholds look as if they have been turned into stone. The speaker cannot hear his own footsteps, and he feels a chill.

He beholds a light in a small window; there is the scent of a candle. He comes upon an old woman in a house. Her head is all that can be glimpsed, but it cannot be seen clearly. She is obviously a ghost, and the speaker has entered the spirit world. He is either dreaming, or he has just died: perhaps he is a spirit who has not yet learned his way about in this new form of existence. The woman tells him: "All my life I thought I could manage on my own." If there is anything worth asking for, it is good judgment, she counsels. Her own life, she admits, wearied her.

He leaves her and comes upon an old tobacco shop in what appears to be a traditional rustic Japanese village. He encounters yet another woman. As a small girl, she suffered from paralysis and from solitude but learned to live a solitary life. "What can one ask God for?," the speaker wonders. She also recommends good judgment. Has life wearied you?, he wants to know. She admits it has. Then the narrator arrives at a distinctly Western (perhaps Russian) house: "Yes. This is my home." The river is also his—and the old park. It is all like a dream, he informs us.

Then there is an abrupt shift to the night of a shipwreck when fishermen placed corpses on the shore. This information is provided while the Russian house is still visible, but then another ghost-like person appears: an old Japanese man. He tells of a madwoman from the village who came upon the bodies covered with mats: she screamed and then jumped on them. She grimaced while dancing. The old man remembers standing there and looking at this scene, but he then beheld bodies tossing in the waves. "Young faces with jet black hair." On a wave, he saw the most handsome man he ever beheld in his entire mortal life.

Finally, the dead sailor addresses the old man: "Don't be afraid of anything. Everything will be all right." The narrator then intervenes and has the impulse to ask the old man about his father, who turns out to have been an annoying, childish person. In response to another question from the narrator, the old man claims that men become tenderer after they die. In the dream-like, free association that characterizes their interaction, the narrator asks why there is such sadness in poetry. "Perhaps you know why?" The old man does not answer the question whereupon the narrator asks not to be abandoned: "No. It is quite enough. I do not want to [be part of human life anymore]. I am weary. If I had to live my life over again, I would like to be a great tree with red fruits."

The outline of the narrator is now seen framed in a doorway. He returns to the old woman he visited at the beginning. "I want to ask you only one thing . What is happiness?" There is a weary smile on her face as she informs her interrogator that she cannot possibly answer the question since she has never experienced that phenomenon. She talks about the company of dear ones, but then draws back: you must never thrust yourself upon others. At this point, she becomes more physically real, as if a veil has been drawn away from her countenance. She remarks that wars are unnecessary but does not answer the question posed to her.

The narrator looks out the doorway again, and the scene cuts to a cherry tree in the rain. "It seems I am welcome here. Moreover, this island is enough for all my dreams. I shall stay." Whether the landscape is of a dream or of death, the narrator feels welcomed.

The film has many long takes and slow dissolves from one sequence to another. The music, both stately and melancholic, is mainly by Tchaikovsky, Mahler and Wagner. There are poignant shots of cranes both in the air and on doorsteps. Where does the speaker feel welcome? In the context established by the film, he is an outsider to Japan but one fully engaged with its physical and spiritual beauty. (The brief allusion to Mother Russia in the center of the film signifies that he is a stranger.) The film's European resonances—particularly its soundtrack—enforces the subject position of the speaker as the outlander, one who does not know if he will be fully welcomed.

The dream vision convinces him that he has found a new home, a place where he finds acceptance. This kind of filmmaking is heavily indebted to Andrei Tarkovsky's use of "sculpting." Such cinema rejects many of the tenets established by Sergei Eisenstein in that it deliberately avoids creating cinematic truth through montage. Instead, this approach concentrates on simple shots and slowly realized and intense moments of reflection; such cinema does not attempt to capture everyday reality as much as it concentrates on how the subject sees connections between things according to the caprices of his or her individual sensibility. In other words, the logic of dailyness is abandoned in favor of the seemingly loose but ultimately logical world of dreams.

A Humble Life (1997) begins with a tribute by Sokurov to Hiroko Kojima, who became his companion in Japan. Her entire family was oriented towards Russia, which made her suggest to the director that she could assist him in making a "visual study" of Japanese life (*Elegy*). After speaking glowingly about Kojima, Sokurov arrives at a place in Japan in twilight. Then his mind goes back to war, the past and Russia. There are photographs of "somebody's mother" and of children frolicking in the sun. Only after these two passages are concluded does Umeno Matsuyoshi, the old lady of the mountain "place" appear. The sequencing may seem eccentric and illogical, but it is not so for Sokurov: Kojima helped cement Sokurov's bond with what he labels her nation of sadness; those reflections trigger some memories of the past, of his relationship with another woman, his dead mother; he then visits another woman from whom he can learn a great deal by observing (and capturing) the texture of her daily life. The old woman of the mountains may feel abandoned and disconnected, but she accepts her fate.

Slowly and precisely, the camera records a day in her life: she sews, she makes a fire, and she gives to mendicants who arrive at her doorstep. This is an intimate study of a life in which nothing apparently happens—but in which, paradoxically a great deal is taking place.

When work on the film was concluding, the old woman asked if she might recite some of her *haiku* before the camera. Those poems are about the beauties of the landscape in which she lives, although she stresses the fragilities of that environment. One of the poems is about her sadness at the death of her husband, another is about a married daughter who has no interest in visiting her mother in her rural retreat.

The documentary about Matsuyohi may have elements of a performance piece, but *Dolce* (1999) is essentially a one-woman play in which Miho Shimao performs her existence. Like the female ghost in *Elegy*, she has endured a great deal; like the woman in *A Humble Life*, she feels abandoned. The film opens with a fast-paced, seven-minute sequence (using photographs) telling of the life of the celebrated novelist, Toshio Shimao (1917-1986). In the voice-over, Sokurov tells of the boy born to a merchant family, his early interest in literature, his career in the army as a kamikaze officer in the Pacific War, his infatuation with Miho, a schoolteacher. He was to be sent on a mission that would end his life; a distressed Miho was about to commit suicide. Then, "as in a novel," word arrives that the war is over. The couple marry, and he begins his writing career. Then, one day. Miho reads his diary and discovers that her husband has a mistress. She goes mad and is institutionalized; Toshio tends her and almost goes insane himself. The couple's eleven year old daughter, Maya, is traumatized, becomes mute and her body stops growing. When Miho is released from hospital, Toshio resettles his family in Amani Oshima, a remote southern island near where Miho was born, where he resumes his writing career. His wife copies and edits his manuscripts. Happiness returns, and then the novelist dies of a stroke in 1986.

Twenty years later, Sokurov went to the island and asked Miho to act "in such a way that spectators may understand your life." He made this additional request: "Do whatever you want and remain sincere." In the time present of the film, accompanied to music by Bach, Miho reenacts three great emotional calamaties she has experienced—the death of her mother, the death of her father and her profound guilt that she has somehow caused the disabilities inflicted on her daughter. She does not refer to her husband in any of the three monologues, although she does pray briefly before a shrine to his memory. Her mother died before her marriage to Toshio: "Mother, why did you go away?" she laments. She visited her mother's grave every evening for years. Her father's physical appearance was majestic. When his wife died, he confessed to his daughter: "My life, too, has ended."

In the third sequence, Miho, dressed in a kimono, descends the stairs in her home and then Maya—dressed like an adolescent—walks down and embraces her mother, who tells her: "You are the center of my life. I am happy with you every day. Let's be together." She then tells Maya that she must work and goes into the room where her husband's shrine is located.

Only at this point does the camera show Maya's withered, somewhat demented-looking countenance. In the room to which she has retired, Miho asks herself: "Where did I go wrong? Was my sin in word and deed? Why are you [Maya] going through such ordeals? Do I understand her enough?" She then recalls a note her daughter once wrote her: "I'm as strong as my mother. Even stronger." Only at this point does it become obvious that Maya has entered the room and is listening. The two smile at each other; Maya closes the door; Miho smiles but asks herself: "How shall I go on living?" She professes her belief—thus the *dolce* (a musical term referring to softness or delicacy) of the title—that here will be t in her life, but these words are voiced against a visual of pine trees in the midst of a tremendous rain storm.

The film concludes with a title stating "Pages from the Life of Toshio Shimao," but that has not really been the subject matter of the film, which might best be described as "The After Effects of the Life of Toshio Shimao." Guilt is not necessarily being assigned to the novelist, however. Rather, the suggestion seems to be that Miho was always a particularly vulnerable person. That point is reinforced several times to cuts to a sequence where a woman clings to some rocks that are being battered by waves. Miho is someone who has managed to survive despite major hurdles. The novelist is written out of the film in an intriguing way that implies that his wife has been able to overcome more obstacles than her husband's unfaithfulness and her incarceration in an asylum.

In all three documentaries, the heroic role of Japanese women as survivors is foregrounded: the old woman who is the principal ghost in *Elegy*, the old woman of the mountain in *A Humble Life*, Miho in *Dolce*. Taken together, these three documentaries are celebratory: life offers unprecedented opportunities for discouragement, but the three women do their best to surmount the tragic. They are deeply stoic. Japanese documentary filmmakers have not been as lenient in looking at their native land.

THROUGH JAPANESE EYES

No Japanese documentary has proved as controversial as Ichikawa's *Olympiad*, upon which extraordinary resources were bestowed: 164 cameramen with over one hundred cameras, including five Italian Techniscopes; fifty-seven sound recordists; 165,000 feet of tape. The resulting film offended both sides of the political spectrum, was disliked by the Emperor and initially rejected by the Olympic organizers, who had commissioned it. However, *The Olympiad* was acclaimed at the 1965 Cannes film festival and became at the time the highest grossing film ever released in Japan.

Disdain for the film evidently originated in the claim that the film was not sufficiently uplifting in tone; also, the absence of depictions of some of the Olympic facilities meant that a viewer of the film could forget or not know where the competitions had been held. Moreover, there were not enough shots of Japanese athletes or of the children who performed in the opening ceremonies. The film was seen to be too artistic and not to have followed the lead of Leni Riefenstahl's *Olympia* (1938), which, of course, highlighted the accomplishments of the German athletes. (The irony is that Ichikawa was a great admirer of Riefenstahl and attempted to incorporate some of her techniques into his film.)

Eric Cazdyn has isolated a conflict incorporated into the film's basic structure, a conflict between Japan's remarkable recovery from the war signaled in its role as host of the 1964 Olympics and a corresponding "end of a certain utopianism in Japan: not only was there a deMarxification in the universities and public discourse...but there was also a redoubled acquiescence to the rhetoric of the Japanese 'economic miracle.'"[9] Ichikawa may show the Olympic events, but there is

the constant spotlighting of the banal within the spectacle of the Olympics....All of this seems to indicate that there's something else to see when watching the Olympics, there's something else without which the spectacle of the Olympics...would not exist. Without the sacrifice of the postwar Japanese (sacrificing not only their bodies and labour but their immediate postwar ideals of democracy, freedom, and individualism) the Olympics would not have reached Tokyo.[10]

Ichikawa's acknowledgement of the "something else" and his willingness to display it is probably what made the film initially unacceptable. In choosing to incorporate a "hidden" Japan in a film meant to celebrate new political realities, he made one vastly different from his German predecessor. He had subtly undermined the power base that had financed his film by producing one that displays some of the conflicts inherent at the time in Japanese society. He had refused to make a simple-minded propaganda piece.

[Some footage from the 1964 Olympics is used in Charles Walters' fiction film *Walk, Don't Run* (1966), Cary Grant's last movie role, where he plays Sir William Rutland, who unexpectedly must find accommodation in Tokyo when he arrives two days early. This crisis leads him to share space with Christine Easton (Samantha Eggar). Rutland then acts as a matchmaker to ensure that Christine finds happiness with Steve Davis (Jim Hutton), an architect who is also an Olympic athlete. This film is a romantic comedy that uses Tokyo and the Olympics as a backdrop. There is one jarring note, however when reference is made to the fact that Rutland provided the technology for the Americans to manufacture the bombs used at Hiroshima and Nagasaki.][11]

Nagisa Ôshima's *Kyoto: My Mother's Place* (1991) is a documentary shot through with wistful ironies. The director, who was born in Kyoto in 1932 but left there soon after his birth, returned to that city with his mother and sister after his father's death in 1937. Rather than telling the story of his mother's life in a straightforward way, he links her existence to that of Kyoto, the former imperial capital. For Ôshima, Kyoto is a highly codified, ornate and, ultimately, claustrophobic place.

Much time is devoted to the type of house in which his mother and her friends lived: a *machiya*. The word is best translated as "capital town house." Specifically, these were homes where merchants and artisans lived and worked; their owners used the front portions of these incredibly thin-looking places as shops. The houses are extremely narrow because property taxes were determined by the width of the front, and these structures were often referred to as "beds of eels," meaning that a great number of skinny houses side-by-side proliferated on various streets. The first floor of *machiya*—although they often have small gardens in the middle—are cramped and dark. The second floors are usually brighter and, ordinarily, they are reserved for the man of the house as a place where he can pursue his hobbies. Ôshima remembers the first-floor kitchen of his mother's house as freezing cold in winter; the entire first floor was hot and humid in summer, but breezes often relieved the heat on the second floor.

The only surviving friends of Ôshima's mother are two elderly women, born and bred in Kyoto. Only towards the end of the film does the filmmaker's uncle tell him that he and his sister were not born in Kyoto but arrived there as young children. What is the significance of my mother not being born in this city?, Ôshima wonders. She probably tried even harder to fit in, he concludes. Then he ponders the full significance of what that means. The two women he interviews have never been outside Kyoto; they are attentive to their neighbors if one of them needs assistance; they do not meddle or gossip about others; they respect authority; they are especially careful about fire because the *machiya* are highly flammable; above all, they practice patience. Reluctantly, Ôshima concludes that his mother never lived for herself because she felt compelled to be the perfect Kyoto woman. She became, as her brother recalled, a "hard" person because society did not value women. She obviously had to find a way to survive.

As a teenager, Ôshima hated Kyoto. In fact, he wanted to burn the entire place to the ground. For him, it was the symbol of a Japan that was uncompromisingly caught in the past. Yet, as an older person, he recognized that he was formed by Kyoto and, at the very same, he arrived at a sort of understanding of his mother's struggles, about which he did not wish to know anything as a young man.

Ôshima's film is about accepting one's own reality and, in the process, that of one's parents. Kyoto is seen as a beautiful but, as far as he is concerned, a dreary place in which to exist. This famous city in Japan may be physically beautiful, but that beauty can be stultifying. By the process of indirection, Ôshima draws a bittersweet sketch of Kyoto, paints a sober but touching portrait of his mother, and portrays himself as a somewhat callous young man who now recognizes that he was irrevocably formed by Kyoto. At the end, he forgives his younger, awkward self.

Ôshima had been scheduled to direct the extraordinary *The Emperor's Naked Army Marches On* [*Yuki Yukite Shingun*; 1987) but handed the project on to Kazyo Hara, who had already done two strong-minded documentaries, one on cerebral palsy, the other on his ex-wife's sex life. The subject of this film is Kenzo Okuzaki, a tall, gaunt man who served in the Japanese army in New Guinea during the Pacific War. He subsequently spent ten years in prison for murdering a real estate broker in 1956. Thirteen years later, he shot pachinko pellets with a sling at the Emperor in his palace (he was incarcerated for eighteen months); in 1976, he scattered pornographic handbills depicting the Emperor (14 months in jail) and in 1981 he was accused of plotting to murder former prime minister Tanaka (he was not indicted). In the film's opening sequence, he attends a wedding for which he acted as matchmaker. At that ceremony, he denounces both the Emperor and marriage as redundant institutions.

The documentary focuses on Okuzaki's pursuit of vigilante justice against two men in the Japanese army who committed murder (he claims) after the war had ended. Okuzaki does not seem to consider his inner motives in pursuing vengeance except to claim—frequently—that he wishes to console the dead. This seems an unreasonable proposition when contrasted to the bantering and hectoring he unleashes at those whom he is stalking; he sometimes becomes violent and injures those who will not co-operate with him or confess in a manner he deems appropriate. He does not mind lying when it suits his purposes. When he no longer has relatives of supposedly murdered soldiers willing to accompany him in pursuit of the truth, he makes up a false name for his wife so that she can masquerade as a victim's sister and has a well-known anarchist pose as a brother. Throughout the film, he suddenly appears at peoples' doorsteps to hector them; those paid the surprise visits are unfailingly courteous to this rude person.

The director and his crew never interfere with Okuzaki, even when he becomes violent, and it soon becomes obvious that the vigilante is an exhibitionist who enjoys having himself filmed. After all, any confession garnered will then be on the public record. What becomes clear quite soon is that, towards the end of the war, starving Japanese soldiers in New Guinea practiced cannibalism. There seems to be some doubt as to whether Japanese soldiers consumed the flesh of other Japanese, but cannibalism is described as a gruesome fact.[12]

The film begins with Okuzaki visiting an extremely sick man recuperating in hospital from a major operation. Okuzaki is polite, but he insists the former soldier tell him the full story of how he murdered someone in New Guinea. The interrogator reminds the ill man self-righteously that he may have a criminal past (he seems quite proud of it) but that he never murdered anyone while in the army. The story of Okuzaki and the sick man is resumed only at the end of the film. Having returned home, the patient is desperately unwell, but Okuzaki assaults him when he refuses to admit to what his questioner claims is the verifiable truth. Later, the sick man admits that he followed orders to kill because the victim was cannibalizing his fellow Japanese. If he did not follow this (unofficial) order from other units, he would have been murdered. For him, it was a plain case of kill or be killed.

The middle of the film consists of Okuzaki—accompanied by real or false relatives—trying to find out how and why Colonel Koshimizu had two men (named Yoshizawa and Nomura) executed. According to Okuzaki, the men were in fact murdered because they died after Japan surrendered and thus not subject to execution; according to others, the two were deserters who were executed because a formal order to do so was given. Of course, those who carried out the edict claim that soldiers always obey an order from a superior officer.

Gradually, it becomes (somewhat) clear that Yoshizawa and Nomura may have become runaways because they were known to have become cannibals. They became "deserters" to escape that charge. The families of the two men feel that this is not the case: the two men were executed because they were opposed to cannibalism and would have levied that charge against Koshimizu.

After confronting several subordinates, Okuzaki uncovers the fact that the two men were executed as deserters under orders from Koshimizu. However, when the Colonel is interviewed, he admits to giving the order but denies he was present at the double execution. That evidence goes against what several subordinates claim.

At one point, Okuzaki informs Koshimizu that, like other soldiers under his command, he hated the way he conducted himself as an officer: for example, he made his subordinates sing before they were allowed to eat. The former officer claims he was simply following orders from on high. At the very end of the film, an important event is recorded but not seen: well after the interactions of Okuzaki and Koshimizu seen in the film, the vigilante attempted to murder Koshimizu. However, he seriously wounded the Colonel's son and, as the film closes, is spending another ten years in prison.

At one point, Okuzaki informs someone he is haranguing: "Your story can change the world." He never explains how this might happen except that one result might be the repudiation of the Emperor by the Japanese: if Hirohito could be shown to be a genuine war criminal, he would be eternally disgraced. However, Okuzaki never seems to make any link between the Colonel's supposed villainy and the Emperor's.

Okuzaki is very much a performance artist; his behavior is really rooted in his exhibitionistic streak. His demented conduct seems fuelled by the possibility of becoming a movie star. At one point, he complains to one of the men he is questioning: "Your wife seems to dislike making a film like this." The victim tartly responds, as if his honor has been called into question, "I'll punish her." Okuzaki also proudly announces: "Violence is my forte." He also claims that his violence is justified because he possesses the capacity to make good decisions. Of course, Okuzaki is prosecutor, judge and jury in the scenario that he constructs.

This documentary takes the viewer into the chilling world of a man who has ventured into madness. He may be raising some valid issues, but his conduct vitiates the cause he supports. Truth should be revealed but should it be annunciated in such a perverse way? Like Ôshima, Kazyo Hara's Japan is one where disturbing realities lay behind apparent tranquilities. Unlike Sokurov, Okuzaki remained convinced that Hirohito was a war criminal.

The three Japanese documentaries discussed here deal realistically and sometimes caustically with the facts of life in modern Japan. They refuse to entertain any kind of idealizing perspective; instead, they confront some very real limitations and deprivations in Japanese existence. Even Ichikawa's *Olympiad* can be read as an attack upon authority. Kim Longinotto, Jano

Williams and Jean-Jacques Beineix have been similarly uncompromising.

DISSENTING VIEWS

Kim Longinotto and Jano Williams eschew the idea of perfection in their documentaries about Japan. These five films certainly avoid any kind of valorization of Japan as the exotic Other. *Eat the Kimono* (1989), done by Longinotto alone, is a biography of the performance artist Hanayagi Geshu. In the opening sequence, Geshu is in conversation with a man seated next to her in a train. She advises him, contrary to most Japanese recipes for success, to lose control and in that way discover his real self.

Geshu, appearing in an elaborate kimono at a performance, sings and refers to herself as someone the press calls, unflatteringly, "a big-mouthed woman." Dressed conservatively and elegantly, she is interviewed on another train journey, where she speaks against the injustices visited upon the burakumin. The adage, "Let sleeping dogs lie," is a common one in Japan, a nation that wants to overlook injustices. Geshu has many friends in Hiroshima, and they have told her that people treated for the effects of the bomb were placed in preferential categories: Japanese, Koreans and, finally, the burakumin. She has witnessed such prejudices still very much in operation. She refers several times to Japan as a "pyramid system" with an elite at the top and the poor at the bottom.

As part of her performances, Geshu tells the story of her early life. Born in a tent to parents who were travelling players, she lived in extreme poverty and was the victim of bullying. In fact, she went to prison when she beat up one of her tormentors. When she was released, her father admiringly remarked: "I didn't know you had it in you!" Subsequently, in her life as a performer, she has been vilified and threatened by the right wing. She has concluded that the Japanese system cannot be reformed—it must be destroyed. She is virulent in her dislike of

Hirohito, "a murderer," whose birthday is still celebrated in Japan.

The kimono comes from Japan's "feudal past" and, as such, represents the confinement of women. "It eats up women. You mustn't be eaten by the kimono; you mustn't be consumed by it." Rather, in her performances in that costume, she does not accept that garment's restrictions to her movements: "You must eat up the kimono, gobble it up." Geshu's job, as she sees it, is to apply "culture shocks." She would certainly agree wholeheartedly with Mizoguchi's indictment against the institution of geisha.

The Good Wife of Tokyo (1992) centers on Kauko Hohki's return to Tokyo after living in England for fifteen years. She is back in Japan to perform with her punk band, Frank Chickens, and, at her mother's behest, to get married to her boyfriend, who has the unlikely name of Grant Showbiz. Although she is attempting to be a dutiful daughter by agreeing to marry (a ceremony performed by Mother), her return home prompts Hohki to reflect on why she left Japan. Her first effort to examine the past is a "post-wedding hen party" at which she asks her women friends about their relationships with men. In almost every instance, women are seen in Japan as the second sex: their roles in life are to follow male inclinations, although, they admit, arranged marriages, once a common barometer of male subjugation of women, are no longer common. However, Japanese men deliberately "trim themselves small" in order to fit into society and be successful in business. In the opening sequences, "good wife" is a term used ironically: it signifies how women become virtuous by fitting into male-dominated conventions; Hohki also turns the term against herself since she has agreed to become a wife.

Longinotto and Williams, who allow Hokhi to tell her own story in voice-over, then turn the camera's attention to the marriage of Hohki's parents, which is far from perfect. Father has his hobbies that are carefully segregated from his wife's devotion to her career as a minister in a religious group, The House of

Development, which combines Buddhism with Christian Science.

As a minister, Mother is flamboyant, emotional, determined, devoted and courageous. She counsels other women as to what constitutes a good marriage, and she is reduced to tears when a woman relates the events leading up to her husband's suicide. Meanwhile, father's tea is not being made; he removes himself to a separate part of the house when his wife is conducting her meetings. However, he is not critical of his wife's behavior: he is both tolerant and affectionate, although he does not mind poking fun at his partner.

"Why did Mother become a minister?" Hohki asks herself. When she confronts her directly, Mother tells her that this happened when her father had become increasingly cold to her. At that point, Mother informs Hohki, she became physically and emotionally ill. She turned to religion and discovered that it is better to give love than receive it. She joined The House of Development and offered her insights to other women who had endured some of the same agonies she had experienced.

Some of Mother's advice may seem trite: for instance, you cannot control your feelings of unhappiness, but you can modulate your feelings by forcing your mouth to make a smile. She also leads her followers in chanting sentiments such as "Our family is happy" in the hopes that such assertions will become realities. "Are you happy you married? Do you talk to father?," the daughter wonders. Yes, Mother assures her: she is happy that she is married, and she has always had friends with whom she could converse freely. She does not need father for that. At this point, Mother becomes The Good Wife of Tokyo, but the irony first vested in the title has begun to vanish: this woman and her spouse have been good companions and, with sometimes considerable difficulty, managed to make their relationship function. It is possible to be a good wife and a successful woman. However, mother's request that her daughter marry seems a trifle eccentric.

Why must the daughter conform to conventions when it is obvious that mother has in practice very little regard for many of society's constrictive regulations?

In the last major sequence in the film, Hohki invites her sister-in-law, Yukiko, to visit her. Hohki loves her brother, she tells us, but she is sad about the plight of Yukiko, who has failed to be the "perfect housewife" her husband desires. Yukiko sees businessmen like her husband as "company soldiers," and she wishes no part of that world. "Please don't inconvenience me," her husband requests. Are you going to comply?, Hohki asks. No, she is not going to do any such thing, Yukiko claims. Her demeanor demonstrates that she is unable to conform because it is not in her to do so, but her body language also makes it clear that she does not believe in such conventionality. Yokiko does not intend to be a good wife of Tokyo, although she acknowledges that her in-laws have had a successful marriage.

At the end of the film, the Frank Chickens proclaim: "We are ninja, not geisha." In this documentary, marriage for most Japanese women becomes a form of geisha-hood, but the clear implications is that Mother is a form of ninja, a genuine role model for her daughter in her search for individuation.

Dream Girls from 1994 is about the The Takarazuka Revue, the troupe upon which Hana Ogi's Matsubashi Theatre in *Sayonara* is based (Michener refers to the group by its real name in the novel.) Ichizo Kobayashi, an industrialist-turned-politician and president of Hankyu Railways in Takarazuka, founded the Takarazuka in 1913. That city was the terminus of a Hankyu line from Osaka and already a popular tourist destination because of its hot springs. Kobayashi believed that it was the ideal spot to open an attraction of some kind that would boost train ticket sales, draw more business to Takarazuka, and thus increase use of his railway. Since Western song and dance shows were becoming more popular and Kobayashi considered Kabuki old-fashioned and elitist, he decided that an all-female theater group might be well received by the public.

The Revue had its first performance in 1914. Ten years later, the company had become popular enough to obtain its own theater in Takarazuka, called the *Dai Gekijō* (Grand Theatre). Today, the company owns and operates another theater, the Takarazuka, in Tokyo. Currently Takarazuka performs for 2.5 million people each year, the majority of its fans being women. Part of the novelty of Takarazuka is that women play all parts. The women who play male parts are referred to as *otokoyaku* (literally "male role") and those who play female parts are called *musumeyaku* (literally "daughter's role"). The costumes, set designs and lighting are lavish, the performances extravagantly melodramatic.

In this documentary Longinotto and Williams, like Michener, examine the gender reversal at the heart of the Takarazuka, where the biggest stars are the women most proficient in male roles. The women whose specialty is playing female characters seek to be even more feminine than "real women" so that they can thereby give full support to the "maleness" of the lead stars. Those playing female roles "have to stay in the background...and end up boosting the men." In Japan, one of the lead "males" explains, "Women respect and serve men. Here [in the theatre], the same situation must prevail." In other words, the privileging of male over female remains intact—even in this theatrical construction. The "males" customarily receive hundreds of love letters daily from women all over Japan; many lovelorn girls wait for these "men" at the stage door. Housewives secretly visit the theatre and then return to their everyday existences as wives and mothers. "They give you a dream so that you forget reality," one woman asserts. "Real life often isn't fun. In difficult times you go to the Takarazuka and escape into a different world. The men on stage are endlessly kind to their women. They show real sensitivity."

Of central importance is that a strong sexual chemistry be

established between the "males" and "females." In contrast, the young apprentices are dressed in severely cut uniforms that resemble garments worn by nuns. From the moment they are chosen (there are forty successful candidates per year) they must specialize in male or female roles and have little contact in their real lives with men. In fact, they spend most of their time in first year learning how to clean the school properly; those moving on to second year teach newcomers this particular art.

A top star can be so for only two years; she must then retire. All the women in the troupe, aware that they should wed before the age of twenty-five, are especially anxious to learn the proper Takarazuka etiquette of smiling gracefully and acquiescing gently. Such skills help them in their stage work, but such talents ultimately make them marriageable. They learn to become disciplined to play their roles as good wives. The early training at the school also teaches women to endure bad treatment: "However cruelly they treat you, you get tougher mentally. You're persecuted, but it won't kill you. You lean to endure."

One teen-age fan acutely observes that if "real" men were acting in the Takarazuka plays, the results would be "coarse"; here, women "can create ideal men that women really want." Her friend agrees: men only value work; they do not care about their wives; work is so vital that men sacrifice their families to it. In the instance of the title, the word "dream" is used with shades of irony: only women can become dream men.

Similar gender issues are explored by Longinotto and Williams in *Shinjuku Boys* (1995) and *Gaea Girls* (2000). In the former, the lives of three hosts at the New Marilyn Club in the Shinjuku district in Tokyo are explored. The clientele at the New Marilyn are almost exclusively heterosexual women who have become dissatisfied with born men. They find the transgendered women or *onnabe* who interact with them at the Club "ideal" or "dream" men. Usually, *onabe* identify as non-female, sexually desire women and cross-dress female to male; however, being an *onnabe* neither presupposes identification as a man nor implies exclusive sexual relations with female-born women.

FIGURE 25 The three subjects of *Shinjuku Boys* (Kazuki, Tatsu and Gaishi, left to right).

The film centers on three *onnabe*. Tatsu lives with a girl friend; Kazuki has a relationship with Kumi, a man who lives as a woman and works as a cabaret dancer. Gaishi is a "playboy" type: he has many short-lived relationships with bar customers. Neither Kazuki nor Gaishi have fully enacted sexual relationships. Gaishi is quite open on this topic: "I don't want to be touched and I don't want [my unclothed body] to be seen." Tatsu's girlfriend is unequivocal about their relationship: "With or without a penis, Tatsu is Tatsu." She loves Tatsu and so any construction or definition imposed by others is irrelevant to her.

Kumi is a "manufactured virgin," who has had her penis removed and does not have sexual dealings with her partner. Gaishi, as a high school student, had a three-year relationship with a woman teacher, who then left him to get married. "You can't trust women because they want to get married," he observes. He, of course, operates in the opposite direction. Why does he have casual "affairs" with women?: "They need me, that's why I do this work."

Kazuki, long on the outs with his mother who pleaded with him not to work at the New Marilyn, has a conversation with her towards the end of the film in which he is informed that he will be warmly welcome at home. Having thought things over, mother reveals that she was a victim of sexual oppression as a youngster and can, as a result, be empathic towards her child; the implication is that any kind of sexual transgression can be understood and forgiven. The film also follows the story of Sampei, who is first glimpsed applying for a job at the club; he is seen gradually acclimatizing himself to his new profession.

Gender is not a simple biological issue of male and female the film demonstrates. Rather, gender is performative, and labels such as "lesbian" are not necessarily either useful or truthful. Both Simone de Beauvoir and Judith Butler have argued that a woman is not born but, rather, becomes a woman. More particularly, gender is stylized through the body. The three subjects of *Shinjuku Boys* are doing exactly this and, at the same time, rejecting societal pressures to appear heterosexual, especially during *tekireiki* (the time when a woman is of marriageable age).

The destruction of accepted gender molds can be found in *Gaea Girls* in which the president, the glamorously-attired Yuka Sugiyama, and, the chief trainer, the deliberately-male looking Chigusa Nagayo, of the Gaea club are attempting to train new recruits to become Japanese professional female wrestlers (*joshi puro*), a sport established in the 1940s.

Nagayo debuted in 1960 and went on to considerable success as half of a tag team known as The Crush Girls; after she and her partner—Lioness Asuka—split up, Nagayo won the World Heavyweight title but lost it the following year to Lioness Asuka. The film shows a subsequent match between the two in which a very bloodied Nagayo sprays fire in Lioness Asuka's face and then pins her to win the confrontation.

In the training of would-be Gaea girls, it is necessary to be cruel in order to be kind: if a woman is not professionally disciplined, she can be hurt in the ring, disappoint her audience and, of course, lose her match. "Are you being soft on yourself?," the teacher asks. The disciple admits: "I didn't change inside."

Being "soft" on a trainee is the worst possible approach. In this job, you can only become successful if an inner transformation facilitates the acquisition of physical skills. Of course, those skills are what are often deemed masculine. Anger is an essential ingredient: if you cannot access a huge helping of it, you will not do well. Traditional Japanese notions of politeness have to be cast aside.

A trainee also has to be desperate. One of the trainees wears a t-shirt with *RESERVOIR DOGS* inscribed on it. The cruel, sadistic male behavior seen in Tarantino's film is the paradigm imposed on the Gaea trainees. However, in a deft piece of intimidation, Nagayo tells a student: "I should have had children by now, but I did not because you are my child." She can play the role of the disappointed mother when it might possibly motivate someone. This film may be showing a microcosm within Japanese society, but one clear implication is that ruthlessness is the only way to get ahead professionally.

The Longinotto-Williams' films resist notions of the Exotic or the Other. For them, new ideas about gender and sexuality are challenging normative ideas that have long been scripted in traditional Japanese society.

Jean-Jacques Beineix's *Otaku* (1994) is about a different kind of obsession than those found in Longinotto's films. In modern Japanese slang, *otaku* refers to someone's hobby, such as the collecting of manga, comic books, video games, and, especially, "idols" (representations of young women, particularly film stars). This documentary focuses on what it means to have "virtual relationships" in the privacy of one's own home with

229

objects rather than having dealings with other people. What does this growing national pastime say about contemporary Japan? The term can be extended to mean that you express commitment only to what interests you and disregard everything else. Put another way, *otaku* becomes an expression of personal desire, inclinations often suppressed in Japanese culture. You can, if you so desire, become lost in the world of objects.

The idols who populate Beineix's films are teenage girls, whose physical presences are not hyper-sexualized; in fact, they are incarnations or goddesses who are not perceived as real girls, just like the women in the Takarazuka imitate "real" men and women. As such, the idols provide a kind of safety valve or protection against relationships. However, there is a more "advanced" kind of *otaku* that manifests itself in pornographic videos and movies.

In addition, there are plastic model *otaku*—based on photographs of real schoolgirls—that are for home use. One model for such a device claims that she is not embarrassed posing almost nude. "Does she worry about what men might do with the representation of her in the privacy of their own homes?" Nonchalantly, she replies: the people who buy the dolls have "problems." If the dolls make them less afraid of real women, she implies, that is a good result.

One hobbyist talks to his favorite doll. She cannot reply but, in his heart, he can make her say what he wants. He has a sense of protecting his dolls. In contrast, real dealings with women always end in pain.[13]

Another form of *otaku* are military camps, where participants engage in battles. They dress as soldiers, carry real weapons, join various armies (of Japan, The United States, even Hitler's Germany) and then fight. One woman, her glance decidedly shy, confides that she has just had the thrill of killing someone. "You were happy to kill?" the female voice-over inquires. "Yes. It was a good feeling." For some, such exercises reinforce the idea of national identity and a shared (frequently, diminishing) communal sense of being Japanese.

One man gave up medical school in order to stay at home to make model airplanes. He is happy to be cut off from society. The models are fragile, he realizes, but this is beside the point: his pleasure resides in constructing the planes. His wife was upset at first, but then she beheld the pleasure the models gave him. She would like to have children, but she now realizes that is an unlikely prospect.

Bondage comics are another much sought-after collectible. It also becomes an activity. For one aficionado, participation establishes full trust in a relationship. She allows herself to be bundled up in order to experience the exhilarating freedom of escaping. She is awestruck by a friend who allowed herself to be couriered across Japan by her husband. "Such trust is admirable." Some women sell their underpants to *otaku*, who approach them on the street.

Beineix is interested in perversion, and he finds many examples of it in contemporary Japan. Longinotto and Williams venture away from any pre-conceived ideas about Japan. They make no statements validating or invalidating the Japanese experience. Their Japan is a nation embroiled in gender identity/performance issues that are universal. The films in the next chapter are set in contemporary Japan, a place of many contradictory impulses.

CHAPTER EIGHT

CONTEMPORARY VACILLATIONS

Western films about contemporary Japan show it in transit. Japan has become an unstable entity, a distinction it shares with every other nation. Truth disappears just as one thinks one is about to pin it down, to impose a rationale upon it. As in the nursery rhyme about Humpty Dumpty, everything is in the process of falling apart, and no one quite knows how to put everything back together—or if it is even worth the effort.

Some of these film narratives examined in this chapter insist that present-day Japan is like every other nation on the planet. Others persist in envisioning Japan as a sacred entity, in the process bestowing upon it spiritual or quasi-spiritual values. Some films seriously question Japanese values: is it not, when all is said and done, a place where patriarchal authority remains strong?

There are more narrowly focused narratives. Japan is also a nation that has consistently produced unsettling horror films. In one instance, Japanese source material is employed to show how Westerners in Tokyo deal with a particular kind of haunting. There is an ingenious re-invention of a classical Japanese literary text. The films studied in this chapter display a wide range of differences in how they "engage" with Japan: some use Japan as a backdrop, some valorize Japan exceedingly, some emphasize the exotic, some propose that Japan is now fully globalized.

The fifth James Bond film, *You Only Live Twice* (1967), provides some valuable clues as to how Japan has been read in the Cold War era and up to the present. All of the Bond films exploit exotic locales as settings for the espionage and sexual adventures of 007. *You Only Live Twice*, set entirely in Japan, tells the story of how

Ernst Stavro Blofeld (Donald Pleasence), the sinister German-born head of SPECTRE, attempts to use Japanese minions to engineer World War III between the United States and the Soviet Union. Blofeld's "front man", Mr Omato (Teru Shimado), the head of a huge industrial firm, uses all the resources at his command to bring this sinister design to fruition. Of course, he is foiled by Bond (Sean Connery making his fifth appearance in the role).

In keeping with the Bond tradition of taking full advantage of "local color," the Japanese settings include Tokyo, the docks at Kobe, Himeji castle, a fishing village, and an extinct volcano. In order to gain ease of access to the villain's headquarters, Bond must fit in: he becomes Japanese. His eyes are altered, he takes classes in ninja fighting, and, in an elaborate sequence in his new identity, he marries a Japanese woman in a Shinto ceremony.

Although Bond has never been to Japan before, he speaks perfect Japanese (he took a First in Oriental Languages at Cambridge). He visits a sumo match, is followed by kimono-clad women operatives, and knows the right temperature at which sake should be served. The film's travelogue sequences establish the physical facts of Japan. More importantly, however, Japan's place as a subordinate power is emphasized. The big players are the United States, USSR, Britain and SPECTRE.

The ruthless Omato's corporate headquarters is vast and imposing. He seems in perfect control until the wily Bond evades him. For his lack of success, he is shot dead by Blofeld, someone even more cunning than he is. Omato may be well organized but he lacks the killer instinct of the German. His place is to follow the machinations of someone more sinister than he. Japan's place as a second-rate power is incorporated into the rendering of this alliance, which, of course, replicates Japan's involvement with Nazi Germany.

In addition, two Japans are highlighted. Omato's Japan is technically advanced: he has a huge array of henchmen at his disposal. In fact, Blofeld is completely dependent on Japanese computers and expertise. "Techno-Orientalism" in this film is juxtaposed to the old Japan in the form of ninja. As opposed to samurai, ninja used covert ways of fighting; they were specialists in espionage, sabotage, infiltration and assassination. In *You Only Live Twice*, the ninja who assist Bond are trained in centuries-old traditions, but they are also adept in the use of twentieth-century weaponry. When the dastardly plans of Blofeld are foiled by the ninja, the "old" Japan prevails.

Japan is a place steeped in the past; Japan is in the forefront of technological advancement—it exemplifies efficiency; Japan is the land where women wear kimono, men have hairless bodies, women dive for pearls, and so on. One of Bond's Japanese colleagues proudly claims without a hint of irony, "Men come first in Japan; women second." All of the above stereotypes, fully exploited in the film, demonstrate the wide variety of views that exist in the West's conception of post-Occupation Japan. In this chapter, the various directors whose work is explored tend to concentrate on one of these constructions rather than taking them all on board.

POST-MODERN BOREDOM AND DISENCHANTMENT

One approach to using contemporary Japan as a setting is to display it as a place that engenders the same feelings of ennui and depression found everywhere on the globe. In Sofia Coppola's *Lost in Translation* (2003) Bob, a fifty-five-year-old actor from California, looking bored and oblivious to his new surroundings, is still famous enough to be invited to Tokyo to shoot a Suntory whiskey commercial for two million dollars.[1] As soon as he arrives and is greeted by a smiling, friendly Japanese crew, he gets a fax from his wife Lynda, forty-five-years-old, reminding him that he forgot his son's birthday. The next morning, he spots Charlotte, a twenty-five-year-old recent graduate of Yale, in an elevator full of expressionless Japanese people.

Bob, without putting much effort into it, shoots the whiskey commercial. Charlotte is accompanying her husband John, who is thirty-years-old and a constantly busy photographer, who does not pay much attention to her. She feels sad, lost and alone in her luxurious hotel room. A few days later, Bob and Charlotte have a pleasant short conversation in the hotel bar. For the next few days, they briefly meet, whether accidentally or on purpose. Their sympathy for one another grows.

FIGURE 26 Charlotte (Scarlett Johansson) and Bob (Bill Murray) in a rare moment of exuberance in *Lost in Translation*.

Charlotte invites Bob to join her and friends at a party. Their understanding of each other's feelings deepens. Charlotte reveals to him her fear of not knowing what to do with her life; he tells her about the scary and troubling parts of his marriage. After going back to his room, Bob tries to share his emotions about the party with his wife on the phone, but she remains cold and talks about her chaotic daily routine.

The next day, Charlotte travels to Kyoto and Bob appears as a guest in a popular, prank-filled Japanese TV show. Upset about his appearance in that show, he finds himself again in the hotel bar. Charlotte is not there. The singer from the bar approaches him and the two sleep together. When Charlotte discovers this, she is disappointed.

On his last evening in Tokyo, Bob admits to Charlotte that he wishes he could stay in Tokyo with her. They both know such a wish is a romantic fantasy. They say goodbye without words, hold each other by the hand, and kiss gently. Before he leaves the next morning, he calls to see her again. They part without a kiss, both embarrassed, not knowing exactly how to react. She walks away. On the way to the airport, he spots her from his car. He has his driver stop and rushes toward her. They embrace warmly. He whispers to her. They kiss gently but passionately. They say goodbye again.

In Coppola's telling of the fleeting relationship, she makes the point that the script of Bob's life has been written but Charlotte's has not. In fact, Bob is attracted to the young woman because she has not made irrevocable decisions. In that way, she becomes a possible escape from his present life.

The film abounds with paradoxes: Bob is an actor who has lost the ability to act meaningfully. Charlotte is a would-be intellectual, but she does not know how to focus her intelligence. Bob and Charlotte are in a strange country, but, for the most part, they show little interest in Japan. Coppola goes out of her way to establish that Tokyo has become so much a part of the international global village that it is possible for tourists/strangers to spend time there without ever worrying to ponder what is uniquely Japanese about Japan.

The Park Hyatt Hotel where Bob and Charlotte are staying acts as a cocoon, keeping them away from any real contact with the city. Charlotte asks Bob: "You're probably having a mid-life crisis. Have you bought a Porsche yet?" Yet, she is obviously in the middle of an early life crisis. When she invites Bob to go out on the town, her metaphor is that of the prison break, implying that they are unwilling inmates who need to escape. However, what are they escaping from?

Charlotte attempts to understand her new environment: she decorates her room with cherry blossoms in order to create an "authentic" local environment. However, she seems unmoved by her visit to a temple. When she is steered into an ikebana flower-arranging class at the hotel, she is unaffected by the gentle and peaceful atmosphere. She travels from Tokyo to Kyoto for a day to see a "different" and perhaps "more authentic" Japan but does not seem moved by the temples and a Shinto wedding ceremony. In the Kyoto sequence, her stare and facial movements hint that she is trying to form some sort of attachment to the foreignness of Japanese culture but cannot do so.

FIGURE 27 Charlotte (Scarlett Johansson) at the ikebana exhibition in *Lost in Translation.*

One evening Bob and Charlotte watch Fellini's *La Dolce Vita* on television. The scene highlighted is the celebrated sequence where the glamorous Anita Ekberg, as the unattainable Swedish-American actress Sylvia, cavorts in the Trevi Fountain. A visitor to Rome, Sylvia takes pleasure in seeing that spot and some other famous landmarks. In comparison, Bob and Charlotte take little pleasure in the differences in their new environment. They both suffer from anhedonia, the inability to take enjoyment in anything.

Coppola has been accused of racism (some verbal jokes center on the Japanese tendency to render "r" sounds as "l"; there are references to the diminutive stature of some Japanese), but it could be argued that the director is more intent on showing the "ugly American" sides of both Bob and Charlotte than she is on presenting stereotypical or offensive images of the Japanese.

In fact, the portrait of Charlotte may be in large part autobiographical: Coppola was a photographer before she became a filmmaker, and her marriage to Spike Jonze was unraveling at the time she was making *Lost in Translation*. The screenplay was written by Coppola with Bill Murray in mind. In fact, the film would never have made without his participation, and Coppola had some difficulty in pinning him down. Murray is an actor who has always had the propensity to play befuddled, overly narcissistic personality types.

The title of the film comes from the sequence in which the Japanese director of the whiskey commercial communicates his directions about Bob's performance vehemently and passionately; the woman translator gives what Bob feels is an inadequate translation. Something is obviously lost in translation, but Bob is not concerned. In fact, he is indifferent to the director's pleas. He responds flatly when asked to show feeling. This scene is illustrative of the entire film: the American visitors refuse (in Bob's case) or are unable (in Charlotte's) to be penetrated by the Other and, in large part, remain indifferent to it. Of course, Coppola is making the point that contemporary Japan has become so globalized as to have lost its exoticness. In many ways, the Tokyo that Charlotte and Bob visit looks like many American metropolises, and evidence of significant differences have to be searched for carefully. Neither protagonist is interested in such an undertaking. They are, in every sense of the adjective, lost souls.

A similar use of Tokyo as a place of disenchantment inhabits Joseph Losey's earlier *La Truite* (*The Trout*, 1982). As a young girl growing up on her father's trout farm, Frédérique (Isabelle Huppert) learns that men treat women as animals. From that sordid background, she incorporates a kind of kill-or-be-killed attitude towards the opposite sex. At the beginning of the film, she is squeezing sperm out of a dead fish.

Although married, she runs off to Tokyo with a rich man, Saint-Genis (Daniel Olbrychski), who fancies her. There, she has her hair cut in an attempt to alter her identity. When her lover is too busy to spend time with her, she invites a cook at a sushi restaurant to accompany her. In a strange sequence, she is introduced to his mother, who is standing beside a washing machine on the street. When they arrive at *The Golden Bee*, a nightclub where her lover has arranged to meet her, he is already there with a woman who is apparently his Japanese girl friend. Things become a bit more complicated when the cook meets a man on the dance floor and asks him to join their group. The Japanese woman laughs hysterically when a waiter spills a drink on Frédérique. The banker proclaims, "You're a flower that's fallen in our midst!" She asks: "Are you a gardener?"

In the next sequence, Frédérique receives advice from an older woman, Gloria (Alexis Smith), who has made love by her own count 33,000 times in 13 capitals and only in cities with a population of one hundred thousand or more. With her deceased Japanese husband, she reached *satori*, a word she defines as ecstasy of a sexual kind (and not the same as the Buddha's use of the word to mean enlightenment). Gloria advises her new friend to make love that night with her new lover and to forget the Western sense of sin. Instead, Frédérique falls asleep.

The following day, she and Saint-Genis visit the latter's mentor, the elderly Daigo Hamada (Isao Yamagato) at his country home. Hamada, who is suffering from an undiagnosed ailment, tells Saint-Genis: "The closer to death I come, the more I love life." That night, back in Tokyo, Frédérique refuses to sleep with Saint-Genis and then learns that her husband has attempted suicide. On her flight back to Paris to attend to her spouse, Hamada is a fellow passenger, whom she wishes she could have had as her father. He takes delight in flirting with her.

There is much discussion in the Tokyo sequence as to whether Frédérique and Saint-Genis are capable of loving other persons. The film's answer is that they are too damaged to do anything of the sort. The use of Japan (mainly as seen in a luxurious suite in a Tokyo hotel and at Hamada's extravagant retreat) at first glance might seem to be aimed at showing how the Japanese spirit in matters of love is vastly different from that of the West. However, Losey uses ironic inversion to demonstrate that the Japanese in the film are just as capable of rudeness, chicanery and self-deceit as their counterparts elsewhere. Many of the characters in the film have bizarre imaginations; all of them lack generosity. In this context, Hamada's observation—"I thought it was only in Japan that people could die of love"—must be taken with a grain of salt.

The Tokyo in Alejandro Gonzàlez Iñàrritu's *Babel* (2006) may be dauntingly and anonymously cosmopolitan, but redemption there is possible. The film is set in four places: Morocco, The United States, Mexico and Japan. The three narratives are linked by one major plot element: a rifle. In Morocco, a herder purchases the gun from a hunting guide so that his sons can use it to protect their herd from jackals. One of the brothers attempts to discover if the range of the rifle will allow him to shoot a bus some distance away. He seriously wounds an American tourist (Cate Blanchett); her husband Richard (Brad Pitt) attempts to save her. Meanwhile, back in San Diego in the United States, the couple's two children are being looked after by their nanny, Amelia (Adriana Barraza), who wishes to attend her son's wedding in nearby Mexico. When she cannot find anyone to look after the children, she takes them with her in a car driven by her feckless nephew Santiago (Gael Garcìa Bernal); she and the children eventually get stranded in the desert. The .270 caliber rifle had been bestowed upon the hunting guide by Yasujiro Wataya (Kôji Yakusho), whose daughter Chieko (Rinko Kikuchi) is a deaf mute.

The circularity of the plot is meant to insinuate that in the global village many seemingly interconnected things are now easily connected, but the title in referencing the Hebrew verb *balal* (to confuse or confound) enforces the notion that contemporary life is full of disconnects. In each of the three plot elements, children suffer: the brother of the boy who shoots the rifle is himself shot to death by the police investigating the crime; the two American children almost perish in the desert; in Tokyo, Chieko is enduring a psychological death.

Chieko is an alienated young woman. She is a prisoner of her deafness, but she is also grieving the death of her mother. She tells her father that he pays no attention to her, but she is really telling him that she cannot complete the rite of mourning.

In the first sequence in which she appears, this young woman is ejected from a volleyball game when she is rude to the umpire. At a restaurant soon afterwards, she is humiliated by a boy who feigns interest in her. She attempts to get back at him by removing her underwear and allowing him and his friends to see her vagina. She then goes to a dentist whom she kisses with her tongue and then forces his hand on to her vagina. Affronted, he asks her to leave his office.

Two police officers investigating how the rifle traveled from Japan to Morocco arrive at her flat. Later, she and some friends hang out with some boys who give them whiskey and pills. At a disco they visit, her friend passionately embraces a young man who had previously shown an interest in Chieko; she obviously feels betrayed. Arriving back at her flat, Chieko contacts the young, attractive police officer, Detective Mamiya (Satoshi

Nikaido). Since he is investigating the mystery of the rifle, he is puzzled by her request. "What did you want to tell me?" he asks. She writes a series of notes stating that her father was asleep when his wife committed suicide by jumping to her death. "You saw her jump?" Yes. She assures him. "Does your father still hunt?" he asks. No. She tells him.

Chieko then leaves the room and returns naked, walking towards the police officer. He is obviously attracted to her, but he insists she stop: "This is wrong. You're a girl." Then, in an extremely graceful sequence, he accepts her embrace but responds to it with compassion, not eroticism. In the next shot, Mamiya and Chieko (covered by his trench coat) converse; she writes him a note but does not allow him to read it in front of her. He leaves the apartment but encounters Wataya in the foyer. Mamiya explains why he has been searching for him, and Wataya confirms that he gave the gun to the Moroccan guide. As they part, the detective says that Chieko has told him about his wife's death by throwing herself from the balcony. "What balcony?," Wataya asks. "She shot herself in the head." When Wataya enters his flat, he finds a nude Chieko on the balcony. He goes over to her, stands next to her and extends a hand, which she gratefully accepts.

Mamiya goes to a bar, has a drink and then takes out the note from Chieko, which is lengthy and not translated for the viewer. The note does not have to be rendered into any language because the detective has previously demonstrated remarkable compassion. The viewer realizes that Chieko has informed him of the truth surrounding her mother's death, probably apologized for her behavior and may have indicated that her inter-action with him was a genuine communication—clarity rather than confusion—that has led to some sort of breakthrough that has allowed her to replace melancholia with mourning. She no longer has to indulge the fantasy of killing herself by leaping from the balcony.

In these three films, Japan retains a neutral subject position. Tokyo is large, chaotic, overpopulated. There is nothing special in this distinction and nothing remarkably negative. Contemporary metropolises as a genre are everywhere places of profound alienation and loneliness.

ENLIGHTENMENT ON OFFER

Dorris Dörrie envisions Japan as a repository of spiritual values essentially different from the West's, but she is quite willing to excoriate that country when necessary. Her *Enlightenment Guaranteed* (*Erleuchtung garantiert*; 1999) and *Cherry Blossoms* (*Kirschblüten—Hanami*; 2008) are both centered on the spiritual enlightenment Japan provides some visitors. The earlier film — on digital video — concerns two brothers from Munich: Uwe (Uwe Ochsenknecht) and Gustav (Gustav-Peter Wöhler). Although Uwe is a prosperous seller of kitchens, he is a malcontent at home: he screams at his children and berates his long-suffering wife. In contrast, Gustav *seems* happily married and works as a *sheng fui* consultant. When Uwe's wife and children leave him, he is distraught and, in a drunken frenzy, decides to accompany his brother on a spiritual pilgrimage to Japan. Uwe is so out of touch with his brother that he mistakes his tabletop Zen garden for an ashtray.

In Tokyo, the brothers see a city very much like many others in Europe: everyone is using cell phones, the streets are crowded, and the impersonality of urban existence is stressed. Quite soon, the two are reduced to near destitution: they get lost, and their ATM cards do not function. They live as street people until Gustav meets a fellow German, a woman, who takes them in and finds work for them in a Japanese version of a German beer garden. She also assists them in finding their way to Gustav's real destination: the Sojiji Soin Father Temple, a Zen monastery in Monzen outside of Tokyo.

At the monastery, the two men are subject to the monastic

rules: cold showers, meditation early in the morning, rigorous cleaning of the wooden floors. The abbot instructs Uwe: if you hate your wife so much, give yourself over to that emotion to the exclusion of all others. He is telling the disciple that for him this will be the only way of ultimately killing that feeling. To the other brother, the monk offers an insight. Gustav has always been a person who blames himself for being prone to making mistakes. Making mistakes is a condition of humanity, he tells him, and he assures him that he is an acceptable person no matter what errors he has made.

When they return to the hubbub that is Tokyo, the brothers have changed. Gustav tells his brother he is gay. "How long have you been gay?," Uwe asks. "Always," is the response. His sexual identity has obviously caused Gustav to make mistakes in his previous life. He and Uwe place the tent they acquired earlier in Tokyo on a vacant lot and, in the film's final sequence, begin to recite one of the sutras they learned at the monastery. The process of internalization is becoming complete.

Dörrie dramatizes the changes in Uwe by his use of his video camera. When his wife first abandons him, he records himself proclaiming self-pitying accusations against her. In Tokyo, he starts to record his brother; then Gustav records him and also himself. The two start to talk about their dead mother, and, they become friends. When the overweight Gustav has trouble cleaning the floors, Uwe gives him tips on how to do it. Both brothers begin to realize that the physical act of cleaning is meant to assist spiritual cleansing. At the beginning of the film, when Gustav recites some of the teachings of Buddha, Uwe smirks. Later, he realizes that enlightenment resides in letting go of interior selfishness, something he has never been able to do before.

The use of DV gives *Enlightenment* an extremely intimate look, almost as if the director was shooting a documentary. When Dörrie arrived with her actors at the monastery, the abbot informed her: "You can shoot your film here, but you have to undergo the entire procedure: get up at 3, meditate until 4, then sing sutras and clean the monastery from 6:30 a.m. to 7 at night." She did not think he was serious, but she soon discovered, "I was the only one in our little group who could not take the rules at all. I felt fenced in. Whenever I would stand around and talk to my actors, one of the monks would come and give me a broom. So I had something to do."

This film does not idealize Japan: Tokyo is shown to a high-tech neon jungle; the discipline at the monastery is arduous. What the film dramatizes is a change in attitude undergone by the siblings wherein each becomes more tolerant and forgiving of himself. Japan is an important part of the process, but the brothers' renewed closeness allows spiritual refurbishment to take place. *Guaranteed* in the title is meant to be read ironically: the only way to reach a state of self-accord is through abandoning over-concern with one's ego.

In its opening forty-five minutes, *Cherry Blossoms* is set in Germany: in a small town in Bavaria, Berlin and, finally, Ostsee, a seaside resort. When Trudi (Hannalore Elsner) learns that her husband Rudi (Elmar Wepper) is fatally ill, she puts off her plans to visit Tokyo, where one of her sons, Karl (Maximilian Brückner) lives.

Instead, husband and wife go to Berlin, where their two other adult children are not much interested in seeing them. In a manner similar to Noriko in *Tokyo Story*, Franzi (Nadia Uhl), their daughter's lesbian partner (an outsider) is the person who takes an interest in the couple. In Berlin, Trudi attends a butoh performance with her daughter and her daughter's partner; Rudi, who has no interest in things Japanese, simply wanders off. Disappointed with their children who do not have time for them, the couple goes to Ostsee, where Trudi dies in her sleep.

The German sequences are deliberate reenactments of plot elements from Ozu's *Tokyo Story*. When his wife dies, Rudi

245

reflects: "If I had known what was going to happen, I would have been kinder to her." Franzi attends the funeral with her father-in-law, who tells her that he has never met a nicer girl than her. In a manner reminiscent of Noriko, she replies: "I'm not so nice. That's embarrassing." At this point it as if the viewer is being taken back to the end of *Tokyo Story* so that a new narrative can emerge. And that is exactly what happens.

In the early part of the film, Rudi has expressed no interest in visiting Japan: for him, for example, Mt. Fuji is simply a large mountain. The children feel that dealing with their widower father is going to be an arduous task. "Mama could have gotten along. But him? What do we do with him?"

Franzi tells Rudi about Trudi's ambition to become a butoh dancer (a reproduction of Hokusai's *Red Fuji* is in back of her in this sequence). "Maybe," she wonders, "there was another woman inside her who nobody saw?" Rudi did not like his wife's attraction to butoh in which her face was covered with heavy white makeup, her body clothed in black tights. Unknown to everyone but the viewer, in the night before she dies, Trudi feels sexually energized and dreams of herself performing butoh.

Butoh, as created by Hijikata Tatsumi in 1959, is a dance form that eschews rigid lines, structure and formality. It often has grotesque and sexually charged movements. One practitioner explained to Dörrie that butoh is really the dance of the dead, where the dead are dreaming of the living. In the instance of *Cherry Blossoms*, the director was directly inspired by a performance she witnessed of Kazuo Ono performing the character of La Argentina, a flamenco dancer:

The spotlight settles on a flamboyant figure perched on the edge of an orchestra seat. A 79-year-old man, face and hands painted white, lips bright red, wears an old-fashioned black velvet dress, a crumpled pink hat, and high-heeled shoes. He adjusts his hat, dabs his face, lowers his eyes and flutters his eyelids. With mincing arms, he becomes the grotesque shadow of a young coquette. He drapes himself across the edge of the stage in the serpentine curves of traditional femininity, then kicks his foot high like a carefree young lover. To the slow koto music, he skips, flutters, and poses. Finally, he smiles, drops one shoulder and tilts his chin like a scared and puzzled child, curtseys, and tiptoes away.[2]

In the wake of his wife's death, Rudi admits that his dead wife's interest in butoh embarrassed him. "I didn't want her to keep it up. We kept her locked up." Not only had he repressed his wife, he is very much a repressed person. On the evening before Trudi died, she attempted to perform butoh with Rudi, but he claimed that it was foolish to dance in the middle of the night. "What's with you?," he asked angrily. Of course, she was trying to connect with her husband, whom she felt was about to die.

Rudi, accompanied by his wife's clothing, visits Japan in an attempt to make some sort of spiritual contact with Trudi. The Tokyo to which he arrives is similar to that in *Enlightenment*; Karl has a small flat in a huge apartment complex. He attempts to be courteous to his father but cannot quite manage to do this. His behavior is often perfunctory. Like the brothers in *Enlightenment*, Rudi finds it difficult to find his way in Tokyo; he goes to a strip show; he gets a massage at a sex parlor but breaks down in tears. One day he gets lost—his son remonstrates with him about the resulting inconvenience.

Father and son continue to have bitter arguments. In a drunken outburst, Karl complains: You "hid himself in your office...You never knew mama! You old fool!" During his walks around Tokyo, Rudi comes upon Yu (Aya Irizuki), who, in some ways, becomes his alter ego. She is performing butoh in a park during cherry blossoming in order to get in touch with her dead mother. Back at the apartment, Rudi overhears his son complaining to one of his siblings about him on the phone: "He can't cope. He has mama's clothes with him. You'll have to take him!" Rudi has taken his wife's clothing to Japan (and wears them under his own clothes) because he wants to show Japan to Trudi. For him, the clothes are transitional objects that allow him to stay in touch with his wife.

Yu informs Rudi that anybody—alive or dead—can become a butoh dancer. This is the way that the daughter ensures that her mother remains alive within her. Rudi prepares some of Trudi's recipes for Karl, who breaks down: "I was so dependent on her that I ran as far as I could away from her. I came to the place she most wanted to visit, and she never saw it." In the park, Rudi is taught to dance by Yu, whom he follows to her tent in a place reserved for homeless people (there are similar sequences in *Enlightenment*). Karl is furious when Rudi brings Yu back to the flat to take a shower.

FIGURE 28 Under the tutelage of Yu (Aya Irizuki), Rudi (Elmar Wepper) learns to dance butoh in *Cherry Blossoms*.

Yu accompanies Rudi to a pilgrimage to a "shy" Mt. Fuji: for two days, the mountain remains covered in mist. On the third night, Rudi sweats profusely, rises early in the morning and finally beholds a resplendent Fuji in the darkness. Dressed in his wife's clothing, he rushes to a nearby beach, where he performs butoh. In this sequence, his deceased wife joins him. At the end, he collapses. Like Kazuo Ono, he embodies male and female attributes. Arguably, he dies fused physically and spiritually with his dead wife.

Many of the Tokyo sequences take place at the time of cherry blossoming. For the Japanese, this annual event symbolizes the permanence and impermanence of human existence: the cherry trees blossom every year but they do so for only a tantalizingly brief period. Rudi finally discovers in his imagination the fulfillment that had previously eluded him. Having come into bloom, he dies.

Rudi's three children have no understanding of their father's actions in the last two weeks of his life and possess no sense of the enlightenment he has undergone. They remain disappointed in him. What they do not realize is that their father had undergone a complicated process wherein the melancholia he had experienced was dissipated by the mourning process that butoh provided.

Disappointment is also a major theme in Aaron Woolfolk's *The Hariyama Bridge* (2009). Daniel Holder (Bennet Guillory), a retired, long-widowed Afro-American photographer from San Francisco, was alienated from his artist son (Victor Grant) long before Mickey's death in a road accident. Daniel's father had died in the Pacific War, and he retains strong anti-Japanese feelings as a result. He was furious when Mickey seized upon a "great chance" to live and work in Japan. For him, this was a terrible betrayal.

In the time present of the film, Daniel travels to Koichi to reclaim his son's paintings. This is an act of retribution, not reclamation. He is rude to Yuiko Hara (Misa Shimizu) and Mickey's other former colleagues. In fact, Daniel is insistent that he is the real owner of the paintings that Mickey gave to colleagues and friends, especially Mickey's wife, Noriko Kubo (Saki Takaoka). Daniel's sentiments begin to change when he learns that Noriko was pregnant with a daughter, Mariya, at the time her husband died. Furthermore, Daniel learns that Noriko's decision to wed Mickey was disapproved of by her parents, especially her father.

Daniel is aware that some Japanese have racist sentiments towards him, but he is shaken when he learns that Noriko has experienced similar experiences of estrangement, particularly from her parents. At first, Daniel wants to take Mariya back to the States with him; he is startled to discover that she speaks only Japanese. His daughter-in-law reminds him that his grand-daughter is Japanese and speaks that language.

In the course of his interactions with Yuiko and Noriko, Daniel's resistance wanes. He recalls that his father once smuggled him into the Palace of Fine Arts in San Francisco in the dead of night because blacks were discriminated against there. Then his father disappeared from his life. Much later, when an exhibition of his own photographs was on display in New York City, Daniel took Mickey with him to see that show. Instead of visiting the Statue of Liberty and the Empire State Building, father and son spent their time looking at art in various museums and galleries.

Then father and son grew apart. The son immigrated to Japan. As he experiences Japan, Daniel buys a camera and starts to photograph the lush, meticulous landscapes he sees. Furthermore, he decides that he does not wish to return to San Francisco with his son's art. Nor does he wish to remove Mariya from her mother, who is having a severe identity crisis in being a mother, particularly as she has no emotional support from her parents. Daniel decides to move to Japan so that he can be a part of his granddaughter's life.

The title of the film refers to the bridge that stands in the middle of urban Kôchi. According to legend, a young Buddhist priest met a young woman there and fell instantly in love with her, gave her a hairpin and was delighted when she informed him she reciprocated his love. However, a city official overheard their plans and the two were forbidden to meet again (in those days, Buddhist priests were not allowed to marry). That narrative obviously casts its shadow on the "forbidden" love between Afro-American male and Japanese female, but in the film's resolution the wounds of the past are in the process of being healed. Daniel's wife and his colleagues provide a safe space in which Daniel can undergo transformation.

ALIENATED YOUTH

The two films by Western directors considered here are so attuned to the subjectivities of their young Japanese protagonists that, in each instance, they do not seem to be films made by *gaijin*.

John Williams's *Firefly Dreams* (*Ichiban utsukushi natsu*; 2000) concerns a young woman from Nagoya, who, unconsciously, is reacting to the impending breakup of her parents' marriage. Naomi (Maho) is sent away by her father to his sister, who, with her husband, runs a hotel in a rural setting. Naomi finds her cousin, Yumi, irritating, and, in general, remains bored and dissatisfied.

Naomi's aunt has taken a special interest in the old and fragile Mrs. Koide (Yoshie Minami), who lives a few miles away. Naomi is assigned the task of looking after this woman, who has a mysterious past. Shortly after they married many years before, her husband died in the army while fighting in China. She never remarried, although she was exceptionally beautiful. There was some sort of rumors about her and another man, but this gossip is never fleshed out.

One of the claims made about Mrs. Koide, who used to live in Tokyo, is that she acted in films. When Naomi asks her about this, the elderly woman remarks that such information is nonsense. However, it gradually transpires that she did act in one film and had felt betrayed by a man who was involved in some aspect of the making of the film. (Earlier, Yoshie Minami acted in a number of films, mainly small parts; the directors included Ozu, Kurosawa and Kobayashi.)

Naomi teases her cousin and develops a passing romantic relationship with a delivery boy. Her affection for Mrs. Koide becomes stronger, but her rural life is interrupted by the death of her father. He had been a distant but kind parent, unlike Naomi's mother, who at the outset of the film had been on the verge of leaving her family (because of a boyfriend). The film does not state it, but the implication is that Naomi's father committed suicide.

At this point, the young woman dreams about her father. In one sequence, he walks away from her; in another, he is showing her a cage that contains a firefly. These encounters with the past are intertwined with Naomi's increasing fascination with the old woman, who lives more and more in the past. She is astounded when Mrs. Koide reprimands her for wearing a particular kimono (Naomi is not wearing a kimono) and then, in a non sequitur, asks that they practice their lines. Mrs. Koide disintegrates further and has to be hospitalized. When Naomi visits her, she thinks that she is someone called Mariko. "I don't know any Naomis," Mrs. Koide insists.

The next time Naomi visits, she asks: "Is that you, Naomi? Come here so that I can see you better." She then wishes they could have been friends together as girls. Naomi tells her: "We are friends now, aren't we?" When she is queried about the film in which she appeared, the old woman is vague: "What was its name? Sometimes I don't think it happened. It seems like someone else's life."

Back in Nagoya, Naomi searches for a video of Mrs. Koide's film. She is unsuccessful until she comes across a VHS copy in a flea market. The film, called *Among the Fireflies*, shows a young

Mrs. Koide with a man wandering in a field, and then cuts to a view of her looking directly at the viewer. She then turns and walks away, very much like the father does in Naomi's dream.

Both her father and Mrs. Koide walk away from Naomi, but the film ends on a positive note. In the course of the summer, Naomi loses her father, but she forms an attachment to the old woman who tells her that she is an exceptionally attractive young woman; she is "cute." Naomi responds: "Cute and beautiful are different." Naomi has been show as "cute" during most of the film, but she develops an interior beauty when she internalizes the affection bestowed upon her by Mrs. Koide.

Tokyo Eyes (2001) is a French-Japanese coproduction and, like *Firefly Dreams,* the cast is entirely Japanese. The eyes in the title refer to those K or Four Eyes (Shinji Takeda), the young, alienated protagonist. The style of the film is distinctly Gallic, very much in Nouvelle Vague fashion. Four Eyes, as he is called by the police, puts on thick glasses that blur his vision and then fires an automatic pistol at strangers in the streets of Tokyo (using his methodology, he feels he can never harm anyone). When panic ensues, the police desperately try to find this would-be killer before anyone actually gets hurt. The investigation is headed by Roy (Tetta Sugimoto) who shares a flat with his younger sister, Hinano (Hinano Yoshikawa). When she sees a sketch of the culprit, Hinano realizes that it resembles a young man she saw on a subway train. She searches for him, finds him and falls in love with him. There is a great deal of symbolism: a bird in a cage in K's flat and a t-shirt emblazoned with the kanji for "foreign" on it.

There are many French and Japanese films that show disenfranchised youth, use cramped interiors, emphasize back alleys, buses and subway trains, and underscore the absence of parents, impersonal metropolises, and the resultant ennui. This film follows that formula.

Four Eyes achieves a sense of excitement and meaning by

becoming a false terrorist, and Hinano eventually succumbs to his charms. In order to resolve the tricky situation she and K are in, Hinano decides to tell her brother that she has become romantically entangled with Four Eyes. Roy determines not to tell his colleagues, whom he labels a "bunch of bureaucrats." He also assures his sister: "morality changes with the times." Meanwhile, K, having decided to abandon his activities as Four Eyes, sells his no-longer needed weapon to a bumbling, middle-aged yakuza, who has never risen high enough in his gang to be entrusted with a gun of his own. The actor-director Takeshi Kitano (often known as Beat Takeshi; he plays Hara in *Merry Christmas, Mr Lawrence*), some of whose films are in the yakuza genre, plays this role. There is only one bullet left in the gun, but, in hapless fashion, the yakuza manages to shoot K with it, thus allowing the film to end with one real and ultimately fatal killing.

In *Firefly Dreams*, a supposedly-lost or perhaps non-existent film, turns up, assisting the plot's trajectory to imply that fantasy can become reality, that the dead father and the deceased Mrs. Koide can somehow be internalized by Naomi. In *Tokyo Eyes*, the over-activated imagination of K leads to his death. Both *Firefly Dreams* and *Tokyo Eyes* demonstrate the abilities of their *gaijin* directors to work convincingly with Japanese casts to treat the themes of isolation, loneliness, and identity. Neither director imposes an enforced paradigm of Orientalness on his chosen material.

EXPLOITATION JAPANESE-STYLE

In an attempt at ingratiation, a Japanese salary man tells the Belgian-born Angela (Chloé Winkel) that a "woman who looks like her cannot be from this planet—she is from the stratosphere." This remark explains the title given to Matthias X. Oberg's *The Stratosphere Girl* (2004). Unsure of what do with her life, Angela, at her high school graduation, becomes infatuated with a disk jockey, Yamamoto (Jon Yang) and decides, based on his recommendation, to fly to Japan to work at a hostess bar. She has only met Yamamoto once but determines that her meeting with him is the turning point in her life.

Before leaving for Japan, Angela draws avidly in a *manga*-like manner: these sketches are extremely autobiographical. She continually recounts incidents in her life by fashioning them into images. At the very same time, she sees herself as a modern day heroine, very much in the mode of some *manga* comics. "A hero never gives up," she reminds herself. Such a person must also be alert.

The hostess bar where Angela finds employment is a seedy place where European-born women (mainly blondes) entertain salary men, who crave stimulation. These women make conversation with the clientele and, to a certain extent, the work of these women—which is illegal since they do not have work visas—is meant to remind the viewer of geisha. Of course, in this narrative about how the West sees Japan, this is racism in reverse wherein blond women become fetishized objects.

Oberg seems, at first, to be providing an almost documentary-style account of the ways in which these women allow themselves to be exploited. Angela is in Japan, her voice-over assures the viewer, because she wishes to reconnect with Yamamoto. Gradually, she becomes aware that Larissa, a Russian-born hostess, disappeared suddenly after she performed at a party (held outside her club) hosted by the ingratiating but sinister Kruilman (Filip Peeters), also a Belgian. (Presumably, his name can be read symbolically as Cruel Man.) Gradually, Angela uncovers several possible scenarios, in one Larissa was murdered by some men dressed as women and in the other, she was killed by some jealous colleagues because of her outrageous sexual behavior.

Angela illustrates both versions of the "truth" and when she finally meets up with Yamamoto, she tells him her speculations as to the awful fate that overtook Larissa. She informs him that she can offer him "proof" by fetching her drawings for him to study. When she returns to her abode, Kruilman is there inspecting her work. He threatens her, but she flees with her work into the arms of Yamamoto, with whom she spends the night in a love hotel. When she awakens, her drawings have vanished, and she is summoned to Kruilman's. She wonders if she is about to be murdered, but she soon discovers that Larissa is living there and is alive, well and angry with her. In order to silence Angela, she is offered a contract as a *manga* artist by Yamamoto, who has obviously been in cahoots from the outset with Kruilman. She now becomes a "visitor in [her] own world" because the story of a hero "has to come to a good end."

Oberg's film becomes confused about what it is trying to accomplish. As an expose of a very sordid world where foreign women are exploited in Tokyo, it works well. The heroine's determination to uncover what happened to Larissa, however, disintegrates when, upon learning what really did happen, she decides, presumably because she is infatuated with Yamamoto, to accept a contract so that she can pursue a career as an artist. In the process, she becomes another kept woman.

Exploitation of a European woman—but of a very different kind—is explored in Alain Corneau's *Fear and Trembling* (*Stupeur et tremblements*; 2003) in which Amélie (Sylvie Testud), a Belgian, decides to return to Japan, the land of her birth. In order to do this, she takes a job as a translator in a large Japanese corporation.

Amélie's first task is to write a letter accepting an invitation extended to Saito (Tarô Suwa), her department head, to play golf. He finds her first and subsequent versions unacceptable and rips them up (without really inspecting them). He then peremptorily tells her to report to Miss Mori (Kaori Tsuji), her immediate supervisor, who in Amélie's opinion is a living work of art. Soon, Amélie is asked to serve coffee for thirteen at a meeting. She disgraces herself by speaking Japanese: a foreigner should not be speaking perfect Japanese. Further efforts by her lead to futility: she is a failure at making photocopies of the rules of Saito's golf club. They are, in her boss's opinion, not perfectly centered.

Looking for an opportunity to display her skills, she assists a department head in writing a report on low-fat butter. The report is a great success, but the department head is labeled a traitor for using her. In fact, Miss Mori has reported her disgraceful behavior. When Amélie confronts her, Miss Mori tells her that she will forgive her if she apologizes. Further, she tells Amélie that she does not understand that the rules of corporate life take precedence over friendship.

Amélie then begins "living without pride and intelligence," but she is a signal failure at the tasks assigned by Miss Mori, who comes to consider her underling mentally challenged. As a child, Amélie wanted to be God, then Christ and finally a martyr. Now, she settles for the last role. Her downward spiral continues, and she becomes a washroom attendant.

The European woman then makes her most significant faux pas when she attempts to comfort Mori after the Japanese woman has been publicly humiliated. This, another employee informs her, is the worst thing she could have done. Amélie subsequently asks Mori if she has seen *Merry Christmas, Mr Lawrence*? Mori replies that she thought the plot ridiculous but liked the music. In Amélie's imagination, she has become David Bowie's Celliers to Miss Mori as Ryuichi Sakamoto's Yonoi. She imagines the scene where Yonoi removed a lock of Celliers' hair and then saluted him; according to her, this was a "beautiful way to die." Amélie offers this interpretation to Mori, who counters, "You aren't like David Bowie." For Amélie, the Japanese film is about the desperate desire of people from other cultures to understand each other.

Determined to be Japanese in spirit by sticking out the last seven month of her contract, Amélie does exactly that and then approaches Mori: "I regret I cannot renew my contract. I am externally grateful for the opportunity, but I am not competent enough." A gleeful Mori wants even more self-flagellation and receives it. Amélie admits that the Western brain is inferior to the Asian and that she is stupid (as opposed to pretending to be stupid). The European goes on to observe that the perfect job for her would be as a garbage collector. These admissions are so strong that they seem to give Mori an orgasm. In this instance, Amélie has played her role perfectly—she has acted with the necessary "fear and trembling before the Emperor."

The satire in *Fear and Trembling* cuts in two directions. Japanese xenophobia is looked at scathingly. The Japanese business world wants to participate in the global economy but is rigidly resistant to the outside world. The actions of many of the Japanese salary men are robot-like. On the one hand, a foreigner with perfect skills in Japanese is offered a contract; on the other, that person cannot be trusted to perform any real task because they are not Japanese. The Japanese codes of honor, obligation, and loyalty are so stretched (in a manner reminiscent of Itami) as to become empty parodies of themselves. The mindlessness of corporate bureaucracies is excoriated; the meaninglessness of much of the concern for "saving face" and avoiding public humiliation is ruthlessly examined.

Many of the standard prejudices (and stereotypes) against the Japanese are aired and validated very much in the manner of the French Prime Minister, Edith Cresson, in 1991. However, Amélie does not escape heavy ironic censure. She is shown to be single-mindedly and somewhat insensitively trying to be Japanese. From the moment she arrives at the corporation, she looks out a window and imagines herself flying over the city of Tokyo: this is obviously a part of her childhood fantasy of being God. Amélie is a rigid thinker who ultimately cannot perform the most basic accounting skills by using her hand-held calculator. She is aware and yet not aware of her erotic feelings for Mori (as reinforced by the references to Ôshima's film). The film's sound track continually plays excerpts from Bach's *Goldberg Variations* to remind the viewer that Amélie's conception of the world remains Eurocentric.

The film's source is Amélie Nothomb's *Stupeur et tremblements* (1999), an autobiographical novel in which the author, who was born in Kobe to Belgian diplomats, returned to Japan for a year. In the book and film, Amélie realizes at the end of her stay in Japan that she wants to become a writer. In fact, her sojourn in Japan solidifies that ambition and allows her to find her voice as a writer. As both the book and the film narrative conclude, the heroine comes to terms with her previous inflexibility and loosens herself a bit from her narcissistic preoccupations.

Amélie is a modern-day Sisyphus in Corneau's film: she is assigned repetitive, meaningless tasks that must be re-done. In order to rekindle her preoccupation with being Japanese, she submits to the ordeal but finally comes to her senses. The Japanese corporate world is shown to be one where kindness sometimes intrudes, but it is one dominated by a rigidly constructed world-view stuck in the past.

The theme of xenophobia is reversed in Fred Schepisi's *Mr Baseball* (1992). Jack Elliot (Tom Selleck) is an aging slugger for the New York Yankees who, against his will, is sent to Japan to play in Nagoya for the Chunichi Dragons. This assignment is a major demotion that Jack does not handle well. He sees the Japanese as a bunch of small people rushing around madly; to him, Nagoya looks like Cleveland, Ohio except for the fact that he cannot understand the road signs. He adopts a wise-guy attitude that quickly places him at odds with his manager, Uchiyama (Ken Takakura), who believes in harmony as the essential ingredient in his team's chemistry. All Jack does is mock what he considers irrelevant idealism. For him, being a star is what being a major league baseball player is all about. He refuses to take the good advice about curbing himself offered by Max Dubois, the "Hammer" (Dennis Haysbert), an American who has played much of his career in Japan. Max has come to understand and respect how the Japanese mindset differs from the American one.

Jack is dumfounded when a newspaper report claims that he has determined to shed his laziness under the guidance of his new manager. Angry at Yoji (Toji Shioya), his interpreter, for putting these words of "harmony" in his mouth, Jack confronts him and is told that the sentiment was attributed to him in order to save his face. Otherwise, he would have been seen as a disrespectful person.

Disrespectful is certainly how Jack acts towards his manager, who tells him in no uncertain terms that he has a hole in his swing. When his manager asks him to bunt (something many major-league hitters do not know how to do or wish to do), Jack strikes out. Meanwhile, Jack begins an affair with Hiroko, the woman who handles commercials for the team. She counsels him: you must accept before you learn; acceptance of yourself and your situation are the first real steps in making progress. He confesses to her that the worst possible thing that ever happened to him was that he once tried "not to miss the ball" rather than simply hitting it.

After he causes a near-riot by arguing with an umpire's call, Jack's manager is on the verge of being fired because his handling of Jack has become a "disgrace to the team." Shortly afterwards, Hiroko and Jack make a call at her ancestral home, on which occasion a very surprised Jack learns that his manager is Hiroko's father. At lunch, Jack learns that slurping one's soup can be seen as polite in Japan, but, when he attempts to imitate that sound, he makes too loud a sound. When a heated confrontation later takes place between Jack and Uchiyama, the manger informs him that his rebellious daughter has obviously planned this difficult situation. At this point, Jack decides to put himself in his manager's hands.

Before he allows him to hit, Uchiyama demands that Jack get

FIGURE 29 Unlike the serenity displayed in this still, Jack (Tom Selleck) and Uchiyama (Ken Takakura) are frequently at odds in *Mr Baseball*.

himself into the best possible condition. Jack, who begins to realize the errors of his previous ways, apologizes to the team for his past bad behavior. "Now you are ready to hit," Uchiyama informs him. In turn, Jack offers advice to his manager: he treats baseball as a profession rather than seeing that it as a game in which grown men are paid handsomely to have fun. Meanwhile, Jack's agent telephones to tell him that he is coming to Japan with a representative of the Los Angeles Dodgers: they are ready to sign him. When she learns that Jack might accept this offer, Hiroko is furious.

At the big game against the Tokyo Yomiuri Giants, there is the possibility that Jack might break Uchiyama's record for most consecutive home runs. When he comes to bat in a situation that would usually call for bunting, Uchiyama tells Jack to swing away. However, when he gets a pitch that seems appropriate, Jack successfully bunts. During the game, the manager says: "We're losing." Jack counters: "We're behind." At the end of the game, the Dodges decide upon "Hammer" Dubois over Jack, who is not a bit upset.

In one of the film's final sequences, Uchiyama goes to his daughter's apartment on Jack's behalf. From now on, he tells Hiroko, he intends to speak to his daughter only from his heart, something he has never done before. The final sequences take place at the Detroit Tigers' spring camp, where Jack has become a coach. Sitting in the stands is his wife, Hiroko.

People have to accept themselves, the film argues, and, when they do, they tend to perform their best. Jack may have dedicated his life to baseball but, as an older man, he has become afraid of missing the ball. This preoccupation has made him arrogant rather than humble, so afraid is he of failure. In a similar way, Uchiyama's fear of failure has led him to be afraid of demonstrating his strong feelings of affection to his players and his daughter. Jack helps him to rid himself of those inhibitions. In this film narrative, each culture learns from the other.

Unlike *Mr Baseball*'s search for authenticity, the Japanese setting in Pramrod Chakravorty's *Love in Tokyo* (1966) is really a pretext for the combination of melodrama, song and dance melodies, comic turns, and ingenious plot twists characteristic of Bollywood. The film, shot shortly after the 1964 Olympics, contains two of the most beloved songs from Indian cinema: "Love in Tokyo" by Rafi Mohamed and "Sayonara" by Lata Mangeshkar.

Ashok (Joy Mukherji) is being pressured to marry a woman he does not love. He is relieved when his elderly mother provides an excuse to leave India: she asks him to travel to Tokyo to pick up his eight year old nephew, a recently orphaned boy named Chikoo whom no one in India has met because his family disowned his older brother after he married a Japanese woman.

Ashok arrives in Tokyo only to discover that Chikoo has no intention of going to live in India, a country he has never seen. Ashok hopes to win his nephew over by taking him on an expensive shopping trip, but the boy escapes when his uncle's attention is diverted by a beautiful woman named Asha (Asha Parekh), whom he sees performing a traditional Indian dance on television. Asha was also orphaned as a child and raised by her uncle in the Indian community of Tokyo. Asha's uncle wants her to marry a man she despises: the boorish, chain-smoking airline pilot, Pran. Asha absconds when she discovers that the two men have cooked up a fiendish plot to get their hands on her sizable inheritance.

Chikoo and Asha both end up in the same hiding place and form an alliance against their uncles. Asha protects the boy by posing as a Sikh until she realizes that she has fallen in love with Ashok. She later pretends to be Chikoo's Japanese aunt in order to win Ashok's heart without her identity being revealed. Ashok falls in love with the aunt but asks the Sikh for wooing advice.

The movie has a subplot involving a friend of Ashok's named Mahesh (Mehmood) who comes to Tokyo to marry a woman from a higher class. In one scene, Mehmood fools his potential father-in-law by posing as an "international geisha" who just happens to speak Hindi fluently.

HAUNTED TOKYO

In the West, the horror film is a well-established genre with many sub-divisions. Recently, however, there have been some American films that are adaptations of Japanese films in this genre (*The Ring I* and *The Ring 2* —set in the Pacific Northwest—are based on the two Japanese *Ringu* films.). The only American film of this kind set in Japan is *The Grudge* (2004) based on *Ju-On* (2002).

The plot unfolds as a series of bizarre encounters with a spectral-looking boy in a house where a father killed his wife and his son; the murderer then committed suicide. Lodged in the attic of the house are the ghosts of the dead women and her son. Once another person moves into that house (or even has contact with someone from that place), he or she can be invaded or killed by the sense of fury and quest for revenge of the murdered woman and her child. This curse extends to the police who investigated the original misdeeds and those officers who seek to uncover what is happening in the film's present. The power of the angry ghosts has the strength of a virus. In the film's reality, it is easy to become infected, almost as if the victims' (inner) immune systems are being ravaged.

Takashi Shimuzu made his first film in 2001, but he achieved acclaim in Japan a year earlier with a two-part straight-to-video version of *Ju-On*. The movie, based on the second video, is divided into chapters, each of which plays out in identical fashion: an intensifying mood of trepidation, an intimation of a ghostly presence, a sudden appearance by this ghost, and a climactic scene where the victim succumbs to a black vapor or some other grisly but unspecified fate. There are overlapping time frames: in the world of these films, time collapses at the same time identities dissolve and are destroyed.

FIGURE 30 Takashi Shimuzu directing Sarah Michelle Gellar in *The Grudge*.

Most of the grisly happenings take place in the murder house, which looks like an unremarkable, ordinary place. The film also features isolated corridors and nocturnal street scenes. The cumulative effect implies that almost anyone could be the victim of these ghosts. Very ordinary people are at risk.

Sam Raimi, who directed *Spider Man* and *Spider Man 2* plus a number of horror films including *The Evil Dead*, claimed *Ju-On* was "the most frightening film I've ever seen, leaving you no time to catch your breath." He made this statement after he became executive producer of the remake. He hired Shimuzu to direct the English-language version and shoot the film in Tokyo using the same house as in the earlier film. The second film is glossier in appearance than its predecessor; there is no division into chapters; and there is a decided attempt to get a more coherent flow as opposed to the deliberately choppy pace of the Japanese version.

Of course, the addition of American actors to the second version makes a decided difference. Karen (Sarah Michelle Gellar), a social work student, has come to Japan to be with her boyfriend; Peter (Bill Pullman), a professor, takes a job in Tokyo and is accompanied by his wife. Matthew (William Mapother) and his wife live in Tokyo and purchase the house to accommodate his mother (Grace Zabriskie). No attempt is made to discuss any of the Americans' response to Japan as a new environment, although it is stated that the United States is different from Japan. Another layer is introduced into the film by the use of Gellar, who achieved celebrity status as Buffy the Vampire Slayer; in this film, however, she is the hapless victim of sinister forces.

The American film ties up the loose ends left by its Japanese counterpart. Before the original murders and suicide took place in the house, the Japanese woman was a student of Peter's and infatuated with him. Her deeply jealous husband murdered her and their son. Both before and after her death, the woman wrote love letters to Peter, who has only a passing recall of who she is. When he finally shows up at that place, the grudge infects him. He then commits suicide by jumping from the balcony of his apartment.

Matthew, his wife and mother take up residence in the house and are, of course, destroyed by it. Karen visits the house in order to look in on the mother and becomes involved with its goings-on. In a scene that brings together the present and the past, Karen encounters (the now dead) Peter in the house and begins to understand what has been happening. Unfortunately, her boyfriend is infected and killed.

The Japanese version of *The Grudge* treats horror as an unknowable entity whereas the American version introduces closure: the horror has to be contained. The differences in endings demonstrate that Raimi did not feel an American audience would respond favorably if answers were not provided. The success of the earlier Japanese version may indicate that a Japanese audience can more easily tolerate uncertainty as a necessary part of the human condition.

THE FRANCHISE FILM EXPLOITS TOKYO

Wasabi (2002), *Into the Sun* (2005) and *The Fast and The Furious: Tokyo Drift* (2006) employ Japan as a decorative accessory, very much in the manner of *You Only Live Twice*. In a sequence near the end of the first film, Hubert Fiorentini (Jean Reno) eats several mothfuls of wasabi and remarks to his colleague Momo (Michel Muller) how delicious it is. When Momo follows suit, he burns the inside of his mouth. This scene is symptomatic of the entire film. The writer Luc Besson admires—and delights in— contemporary Tokyo, but he is not completely certain what he is doing with it. In turn, the film is comical and sentimental.

In France, Hubert, a Dirty Harry type of police officer, arrests a transvestite bank robber on suspicion of planning a bank robbery, but, in the course of doing so, he manages to punch the son of the chief of police. Although asked to go on leave by his superior, he is reluctant to do so until he receives a phone call from Tokyo from a lawyer acting for a recently deceased Japanese woman. She has appointed Hubert the executor of her estate. He immediately accepts the summons.

Nineteen years before, when living in Tokyo, he was married to this woman. For unknown reasons, she disappeared from his life. He has been mourning her loss to the extent that his boss tells him to "drop the cop and become a man." On arrival in Tokyo, Hubert learns that he and his wife had a daughter, and he and Yumi (Ryoko Hirosue) soon develop a love-hate relationship, although she does not know that he is her father.

Hubert and his former colleague Momo eventually piece together the secrets of the dead woman. She abandoned her husband when she became an undercover operative who infiltrated the yakuza. She was murdered when her identity was uncovered, but she did manage to obtain 200 million Euro of mob money. The gang boss wants his money back and so goes after Yumi. Eventually, in another bank robbery sequence, the yakuza and his henchmen are killed by Leon.

Symptomatic of the uncertainties of what director Gerard Krawczyk and writer Luc Besson sought to accomplish is their treatment of the yakuza. In a sequence in a department store, Hubert bests his opponents in a series of comic turns; the same observation can be extended to the opening bank heist. However, the other attempted bank robbery at the end of the film is pure action violence.

The headline introducing Kaori Shoki's review in the *Tokyo Times* reads: "Think Léon in Tokyo, then ask why." This observation is apt. Besson and Reno enjoyed great success with *The Professional* (1994) in which Léon, a professional assassin, befriends Mathilda (Natalie Portman), a young girl whose family has been killed by drug dealers. At her request, he teaches her to be a professional killer, but he later has to rescue her when she is captured. In that film, violence and sentimentality are also conjoined.

Wasabi was obviously devised as a vehicle for Reno, although the relationship between father and daughter is more broadly comic and less complicated than that between "father figure" and "apprentice" in the earlier film. More central to this film's existence is Reno's turn as comedian-gunman. Although, for example, a contrast is drawn between the aptitude young people might demonstrate in video games full of guns and their inability, unlike Reno, to perform the same in real life, the point being made could be extended to any culture. Places such as the Shinjuku area of Tokyo are exploited as backdrops, but the film never attempts to harness and thus focus its use of Japan in any serious way.

In a similar fashion, *Into the Sun* was conceived as a showcase for Steven Seagal and his brand of phlegmatic, stoic action hero performances in which he is costumed in a long, black leather coat. When Takayama, the Governor of Tokyo is assassinated, former CIA agent Travis Hunter (Seagal) is summoned to investigate with the assistance of Sean Mack (Matthew Davis), a rookie

FBI agent. Hunter's fiancée Nayako (Kanako Yamaguchi) is also working with him. Hunter and Mack discover that Kuroda (Takao Ôsawa), the leader of a new style yukaza gang, is in league with Chen, a Chinese Tong gang leader, to build a giant drug-dealing network. Hunter seeks the assistance of Kojima, the second-in-command of an old-school yakuza gang.

Hunter, born, raised and resident of Tokyo, is sympathetic to the older generation of gangsters as opposed to the brash upstart types. For much of the film, Hunter takes a wait-and-see approach, but he cannot do this once Mack, Nayako, and the head of the old school yakuza are murdered.

The film may be formulaic, but it comments on two aspects of gang warfare in Japan. At one point, a member of an older yakuza family observes, as in *Black Rain*, that his new-style counterparts lack *jingi*, a term that can be loosely translated as "honor and humanity." There was once a proper way to be a criminal, but that tradition is waning. Linked to that observation is the fact that Chinese gangs have taken over the massage parlors, strip shows, gambling dens in the Kabukicho district of Tokyo: "Our biggest problem," one Japanese gangster has observed, "is the rise of the Chinese mafia. The difference between us is that Japanese yakuza think of long-term business relationships, but the Chinese mafia thinks just of the short-term. Their only goal is money, money, money."[3] *Into the Sun* reflects and comments upon a genuine socio-economic phenomenon and, in the process, sides with the older generation.

The Fast and The Furious: Tokyo Drift (2006) is another franchise film, the third of four in the series.[4] At the outset, Sean (Lucas Black) is an American teenager fascinated with illegal street racing. In order to straighten him out, his mother sends him to Japan to live with his father, a career Navy man stationed in Tokyo. Someone who always sees himself as an outsider, Sean is made to feel more so by his *gaijin* status. His father demands he attend school, which he means he must wear a uniform. He is one of the few non-Asians there, finds it strange to wear slippers to class, and quickly becomes entranced with Neela (Nathalie Kelley), whose dead mother was Australian. Another "military brat" named Twinkie befriends him and soon Sean is immersed in the world of drift racing, where the driver executes turns by briefly taking his foot off the throttle and then using it and the steering wheel to guide the car's resulting "drift" motion.

Neela is romantically involved with a yakuza called D.K. (Brian Tee), who challenges Sean to a race. Of course, Sean wrecks that expensive car, which is owned by Han (Sung Kang), a rich outsider who is not interested in the monetary value of cars. Rather, he wants to find someone he can trust and apparently Sean fits that bill.

Sunny Chiba (as he did in *Kill Bill Volume I*) makes a cameo appearance as Kamata, D.K.'s powerful uncle and yakuza boss, who discovers that Han, D.K.'s business partner in crime, has been stealing money: the books do not balance. After an enraged D.K. confronts Han, a car chase ensues leading to Han's death. D.K. attempts to kill Sean, who is saved by his father's intervention.

Sean, who refuses to leave Japan despite his father's pleading, decides to confront Kamata. He returns the missing money, apologizes and offers a solution—a race between himself and D.K. with the "loser leaving town for good." Sean's father even assists him in refurbishing a wrecked car. Not surprisingly, the race (and the preparation for it) occupies the last part of the film. D.K. dies when he crashes his car. Of course, Sean gets the girl.

The Japanese settings in these three films are merely backdrops against which a series of predictable exploits can be displayed.

POST-MODERN INGENUITY

Sei Shônagon's *Pillow Book*—to which Marker refers in *Sans soleil*—was written during the time she served the Empress

Consort Teishi during the 990s and early 1000s. This narrative incorporates various kinds of lists, including personal reflections, court gossip, and poetry. During the Heian period, this kind of writing—collections of notes and notebooks known as *zuihitsu*—became extremely popular. Peter Greenaway, who revels in dividing his films into sections and subsections, was obviously drawn to this propensity in Shônagon. The resulting film allowed the director to comment on the significance of texts in peoples' lives by showing calligraphic texts being inscribed on the human body. What does it mean to write a text on a body?

FIGURE 31 In an early sequence, Nagiko (Vivian Wu) is being written on in *Pillow Book.*

Does the significance of the text change as a result?

When Nagiko (Vivian Wu) was a child, beautiful calligraphy was inscribed on her by her father. As an adult, she seeks to be written upon by men and then, at the instigation of a lover, Jerome (Ewan McGregor), she begins writing on male bodies. At one level, Greenaway's narrative is decidedly Oedipal: Nagiko wishes to be penetrated by men in the same manner her father previously wrote on her; later, she rejects that stance and becomes a creator in her own right. In the course of the film she discovers her own considerable sense of agency. As such, the film takes a decidedly feminist stand.

Being Japanese in subject matter, this *Pillow Book* (1996) is also about revenge. Every year at the same time, Nagiko's father (Ken Ogata) visited his publisher (Yoshi Oida). Only later does Nagiko discover that the publisher forced her father to have sex with him. In this context, this is homosexuality as a hostile act, an intrusive inscription.

Later, as an adult, Nagiko submits a book to the publisher, who rejects it; at the very same time, she learns about his dealings with her dead father. In the course of the film, she sends the publisher thirteen anonymous books inscribed on the bodies of men. Only on the last one—on the body of a sumo wrestler hired by her to kill the publisher—does she reveal her identity and confront the culprit with his misdeeds. The wrestler slits the publisher's throat.

The notion of inscribing male bodies with texts and sending these men to the publisher is Jerome's. He delivers *Book One: The Book of Agenda* to the publisher, who immediately has scriveners copy down the text.

THE FIRST BOOK
THE AGENDA
I want to describe the Body as a Book
And this Body and this Book
Will be the first Volume
Of Thirteen Volumes.[5]

However, to Nagiko's consternation, Jerome dallies with the publisher. After Nagiko and Jerome meet at the significantly named Café Typo, crestfallen and depressed Jerome agrees to fake his own death. However, he takes too many pills and dies, whereupon Nagiko writes *Book Six: The Book of the Lovers* on his corpse.

This is a book and a body
That is so warm to the touch
My touch.....
May I keep this book forever.
May this book and this body outlast my love.
May this body and this book love me as I love its
Length, its breadth, its thickness, its text,
Its skin, its letters, its punctuations, its quiet
And its noisy pages.[6]

When the publisher is slain by the wrestler, she writes: "*This is the writing of Nagiko Kiyohara no Motosuke Sei Shônagon, and I know you to have blackmailed, violated and humiliated my father.... You have now committed the greatest crime—you have desecrated the body of my lover. You and I now know that you have lived long enough.*"[7] Upon recovering the book written on Jerome's corpse after the publisher's death, Nagiko buries it under a bonsai tree and subsequently gives birth to a baby girl fathered by Jerome. In the film's Epilogue, she writes on the child's face.

An extremely intellectual filmmaker, Greenaway observes "there's evidence in all my films of a sneaking admiration for the encyclopedic point of view. All the great artifacts, certainly of western art, have somehow been encyclopedic in their concept."[8] In turning to a Japanese source but placing Nariko's affair with a Westerner at the center of his film, Greenaway is signaling that he wanted to examine the inter-actions between East and West in a cinematic form of encyclopedia.

Japanese painting and prints explore two-dimensional space in a manner that fascinated Western artists at the end of the nineteenth century. Greenaway has claimed: "My films could be better appreciated, better understood, if people applied the aesthetic of painting to them. A great delight is a concern for surface, in using two-dimensional organizations of objects across the screen as though they were two-dimensional....This concern for surface...is not a concern for any other filmmaker. Their prime concern is getting performances from actors and to hell with the picture-making. This is greatly under-selling the cinema."[9] Exploiting the surface is of primary importance in understanding *The Pillow Book* and points to its use of aesthetic ideas Japanese in origin. In this context, Greenaway is inscribing a film text on to the consciousness of his viewers.

There is another curious strand woven through the film by its oscillations between Kyoto and Hong Kong as mise en scènes. In comparison to unrelentingly cosmopolitan Hong Kong, Kyoto could be deemed provincial. Nagiko is inscribed by her father in Kyoto; she becomes the inscriber in Hong Kong. The former imperial capital can be associated with xylography (or woodblock presses) whereas the publisher's Hong Kong press is obviously of more recent technology. The name "Swindon's," associated with his firm, affirms the presence of his publications in the English-speaking world and perhaps beyond. As signifiers, the use of the two cities insinuates that Japan remains a nation entrenched in the past whereas the new China lives in the frenetic present of globalization. Greenaway may be implying that Japan, in comparison to China, has become an economic backwater, but, if that is so, he may be slyly hinting that this may be a cause for rejoicing.

Nagiko's concern throughout the film is with her appearance. Gradually, she redefines what she means by appearance. Rather than being decorated, she will do the decorating. It is a crucial turning point when she paints the male body. When she embroiders surfaces, she forever changes her life and the existences of those around her. For her, surface remains every-thing. In effect, Nagiko refuses to be subordinate, to be a member of a secondary sex.

Put another way, Nagiko at the film's outset can be perceived as Japan, a country that can be rendered female and therefore subjugated. At the film's conclusion, in a bold twist, the post-colonial subject vanquishes the male master.

EPILOGUE

"REAL" JAPAN

This book concludes by examining two recent films. In one Japan and the Japanese are portrayed in an extremely negative way. The other, by a Taiwanese director, imagines contemporary Japan in the guise of an update of Ozu. Japan is now a member of the global village, where traditions are being relentlessly erased and, of course, eradicated.

Idealism is cast aside in *The Cove* where Japan is perceived to be acting in an exploitative manner, conducting itself in a way usually associated with Western corporate greed. *The Cove* is a no-nonsense indictment of the Japanese attitude towards dolphins and of Japan's refusal to come to grips with the issue of mercury poisoning. Its disturbing evidence goes a long way to remove any tendency on anyone's part to see Japan in idealized terms.

In *Café Lumière*, a theme introduced by Ozu—the gradual destruction of the family as the basic social unit holding the fabric of Japan together—is reformatted. Yes, the social fabric of Japan has been thrown asunder, but there remains the hope that some remnants of what it is to be Japanese will survive intact. Specifically, *Café Lumière* may be a homage to Ozu in its use of trains and its concentration on the family, but the film is resolute in showing that the disintegration of the family has deepened considerably. Traditional values are disappearing, perhaps never to return. The film, however, offers a glimmer of hope in its final moments.

EATING FLIPPER

Guilt and the attempt to avoid guilt are the subjects of *The Cove*

(2009). Although, as has been well publicized, Japan has attempted for years to modify or lift the ban on hunting whales, Louie Psihoyos's documentary concerns the capture and slaughter of dolphins in Taiji in Wakayama Prefecture. In the process, the director shows how some Japanese have evaded the spirit—if not the letter—of the law.

Picturesque Taiji has been a whaling town since the seventeenth century but suspended the hunt in 1988 as a result of the International Whaling Commission (IWC) ban. Instead, the fishing industry there now concentrates on capturing dolphins, a species not regulated by the IWC.

Ric O'Barry, who became famous as the trainer of Flipper in the legendary television series from 1964-7, has come to believe that the capturing and incarceration of dolphins for amusements parks is inherently against nature, especially because these cetaceans are extremely intelligent and have emotional lives that are destroyed by such environments. He is obviously even more outraged by the killing of these mammals so that their flesh can be sold (usually labeled as whale meat).

The fishermen in Taiji have found a way of forcing the dolphins into a cove by disrupting their sonar navigation. Once, the animals have been snared, they are made available to buyers from aquariums and other such institutions for about $150,000 each. The animals that are not selected in the cull are slaughtered and their meat sold. That meat has a concentration of mercury that is extremely toxic.

Taiji has resisted any kind of documentation of the slaughter, and this is what Psihoyos and his crew decided had to be established. Much footage in the early part of the film is expended showing and describing the high-tech equipment that was sent to Japan in 47 suitcases. Other passages show how the cameras were hidden in rocks in the cove so that the killing of the dolphins could be recorded. The townspeople of Taiji, very much on the defensive, are hostile to anyone seeking to document what is transpiring. Eventually, the director and his crew do manage to place their cameras in position, and the slaughter is recorded towards the end of the film.

The premise of the film is established on two levels. First, dolphins should not be captured, sold or slaughtered. Second, dolphin meat infused with mercury is extremely toxic and could lead to further instances of Minamata disease, a neurological syndrome that was first discovered in Minamata in Kumamoto prefecture in 1956.

Twenty-three thousand dolphins are slaughtered in Taiji every year, and the resulting meat for sale is perhaps slight when considered against the size of Japan's population. However, O'Barry points out that stomping out this particular atrocity will pave the way for other wrongdoers to be halted. Taiji's way of handling this matter is simply to maintain silence.

The Japanese attitude seems to be that outsiders are once again telling them how to live their lives. In "A Message from the People of Taiji, Japan" dated May 23, 1994 [before the IWC ban and the filming of *The Cove*], this point is made tellingly:

No matter how viciously the environmentalists and animal rights activists condemn us, we will not give up whaling. We simply cannot do that, because it would mean to us not only a significant economic loss but also a loss of our pride and the unique culture of our own. A small village like Taiji would be wiped out completely by the massive forces of industrialization and commercialization without a pride for its own heritage and a strong sense of community identity.

If "dolphin hunting" were substituted for "whaling" in the above paragraph, the attitude of Taji township towards the documentarians is encapsulated: Japan has its traditions and intends to stick to them.

The documentary's argument can be summarized another

**FIGURE 32 This poster for *The Cove* emphasizes the revelations
it makes public.**

way: any cruelty towards animals is illegitimate and should be
made illegal; in the case of dolphins, who seem to be a highly

evolved species with the ability to experience feelings of sorrow and depression, it is a particularly heinous act to enslave or kill them. The countervailing claim of the Taiji fishermen is that they have made their living from the sea for generations and should be allowed to continue. Either of these positions can be debated. What upsets the Japanese position is the presence of mercury, with which the meat of the dolphins is filled. As well, dolphin meat is not advertized as such: it is usually labeled whale meat.

Japanese opposition to the ban on whaling is well known. That fact has been publicized in the media for many years. However, the documentary is unusual because it shows Japan, a country often valorized in Western documentaries, in an extremely negative way. Moreover, the film's message has been further legitimized by its winning of the 2010 Oscar for best documentary film. The evidence gathered in *The Cove* is especially poignant when juxtaposed next to Richie's *Inland Sea*, a film that predicted that Japanese oneness with the sea was fast disappearing.

THE PRESENCE OF THE PAST

There is no *Café Lumière* (*Kohi jiko*) in Hou Hsiao-Hsien's film from 2004. There is the Café Erica, which the protagonist Yoko (the pop star Yo Hitoto) sometimes frequents. There is also the no longer-extant Café Dat, whose former existence is something Yoko is researching. The Lumière in the title refers to the celebrated siblings, Auguste Marie Louis Nicolas and Louis Jean, who were among the earliest filmmakers. Their surname means light, which adds another layer of meaning to the title of a film, which is about the nature of filmmaking as an art and about films as a place of inner light.

At the outset, Hou's film was conceived as a three-part portmanteau picture to mark the one-hundredth anniversary of Ozu's birth in 1903. When the other two directors opted out, Hou decided to make the entire film. Although he has often been compared to Ozu, their work is actually very different. Ozu allows his plot lines to emerge slowly but very precisely. Hou favors more rambling exposition. Moreover, Hou does not establish scenes in the manner of Ozu's signature location shots, and he likes to work in a much more minimalist way: he allows his camera to rest on a person long after a dramatic point seems to have been reached and passed. He seems to do this so that the viewer is forced to inhabit even the boredom and dailyness of his fictional subjects. This indwelling is a marked aspect of his style, an entry point offered to the audience to share intimate moments with the filmed subjects.

Both directors, however, share an interest in family structures and how this unit of society survives at the same time it is becoming looser and less intact. There is the same fascination with trains. In Ozu, the trains connect cities or at least places far apart. In *Café Lumière*, the trains are for the most part subway cars and trams part of the transportation system of contemporary Tokyo.

In a deliberate tribute to *Tokyo Story*, Yoko's parents travel from their home in the country to visit her in Tokyo; there is also a sequence in which Yoko gives a pocket watch to her close friend, Hajime (Tadano Asonu). Hajime is completely fixated by the Tokyo transit system and frequently makes recordings of its sounds. In one scene he is in a car that passes one in which Yoko is a passenger: they do not see each other.

The story in Hou's film is both simpler and more diagrammatic than any film by Ozu. Yoko, who is researching the life of Jiang Wen-Ye (1910-84), the Taiwanese-born composer who immigrated with his family to Japan in 1923, arrives back in Tokyo from Taiwan. She visits her friend Hajime, returns home to visit her parents (father and step-mother) during the O-bon festival and assists them in grave cleaning, tells them she is pregnant by her Taiwanese boyfriend, returns to Tokyo where she tells Hajime she is pregnant, interviews Jiang's first wife (whom he abandoned), receives a visit from her mother and father in which she reiterates her decision not to marry but keep the baby, takes a subway train where she falls asleep but is awaken by Hajime, who has been standing over her with his recording machine. *Café Lumière* is a film in which not much apparently happens but that is partially because Hou is much more interested than Ozu in investigating the interiority of his subjects.

Although pleasant acting, Yoko is disconnected from others and their wishes. She is mindless of the need for even basic courtesies in exchanges between her father and her mother (years before, her biological mother became a religious fanatic who abandoned husband and child). Yoko experiences morning sickness but other than that does not really wish to discuss her pregnancy. She does not observe basic social etiquette with her neighbor in Tokyo and does not bother to shop for food when she is expecting the visit from her parents. However, she does bestow a pocket watch on Hajime early in the film: this item, which commemorates the 116th anniversary of the Taiwan Railway, is something she knows he will appreciate.

The biggest clue to understanding Yoko is when she tells Hajime (before he knows she is pregnant) that she has had "another" disturbing dream: this one is about an unhappy mother whose baby becomes old and wrinkled; the infant, who is made of ice, then melts. Hajime informs her that this is a European myth of some sort and offers to find a book that retells the story. He subsequently comes up with a copy of Maurice Sendak's illustrated children's book *Outside Over There* (1981), which Yoko recalls having read one day years before in a large hall while she was waiting for her now long absent, biological mother.

Ozu does not use elaborate intertexts in his films such as Hou's exploitation of *Outside*, in which a young girl, Ida, takes care of her baby sister while her father is away from home and her mother is in the garden but is, in any case, emotionally absent. Goblins steal the baby and replace it with an ice statue replica, which begins to melt. Guided by her father's voice and a magic horn, Ida climbs out her window, goes "outside over there" and saves her sibling by subduing the goblins into a dream-like state.

In the Sendak, the mother is both depressed and withdrawn.[1] This forces Ida to set out on a quest by herself. She obviously learns to be independent, perhaps hyper-independent. In many ways this has been the story of Yoko's life until she becomes pregnant. Is her baby going to turn to ice because she, as a mother, neglects him or her? The dream is articulating fears she does not wish to confront in her waking life. Does she wish to be a parent? If she does, what kind of parent? Is she going to be an absent one like her own mother? The drawings in *Outside Over There* are employed by Hou to carry further the burden of the film's meaning: there is the outer world, and there is the turbulent inner world, which is full of opportunities to accept or repair disconnects.

In a key sequence that uses a different kind of intertextual evidence, Hajime arrives unexpectedly at Yoko's apartment to show her a self-portrait he has made on his computer. Hajime is removed from the other city dwellers around him. Except for Yoko, he does not inter-act with anyone else in the film, and his energy and time is spent recording train noises. He feels more connected to trains than to human beings.

Hajime's disconnect from others is most apparent in the way he views himself through the computerized self-portrait. In this image, he is represented as a baby with a microphone and a recorder around its neck inside a womb of trains. Emanating from the baby are train tracks and lines with the major Tokyo station names marked. (In fact, the Yamanote Line —the major JR line in downtown Tokyo —is circular in shape and envelops the core of the city). Hajime's drawing is indicative of his and fellow Tokyoites' existence; trains actually do wrap and wind themselves around the city and the lives of its inhabitants. In Hajime's depiction, trains become mother figures supporting and guiding their children's lives. Hajime calls himself a "train baby": he is an offspring of the JR Lines and hence, a contemporary Tokyoite. Yet, at the same time, the "Hajime baby" in the drawing is disconnected from the womb of trains.

Yoko and Hajime describe the infant in the drawing as lonely and close to tears as it floats in a pool of crimson blood. The description of the baby symbolizes the alienated condition in which Hajime and Yoko live. He is surrounded by a deluge of trains and identifies with them, but they also enclose him from the outside world, severing him from human connection. As Hajime is disconnected from the womb that holds him, Yoko has yet to connect with the child she is carrying inside her womb.

Trains, trams and subway cars carry people to and away from each other. In a sense, every passenger is connected with other travelers on vehicles on which they travel simultaneously; in another sense, they do not know or wish to know each other. Ian Johnston has commented on Hou's use of trains as being idiosyncratic: "At times, there's definitely an outsider's perspective operating. A Japanese filmmaker would surely never dwell so long on the streams of passersby at the train station or in the streets, let alone offer repeated shots of fascinated close-ups of a train driver's white-gloved hands" [2] Hou seems to agree with this observation:

Tokyo Metro is a very important means of transportation where no Japanese directors dare to make a film. They usually opt for the private lines, which are easier to borrow from. They simply opt for the alternative. Tokyo JR is virtually impossible. But then I thought, this script tells a story about Tokyo, it doesn't make any sense if I can't shoot about JR, for it's the most important setting. Chuo Line and Yamanote Line are both very important settings. If we can't shoot anything about them it will be ridiculous. Tokyo without the Metro or the train is no Tokyo at all.[3]

If he wanted to talk about the identity of a modern-day Tokyoite, Hou obviously had to use the JR line.

Yoko is investigating a dead Taiwanese composer; Hou the Taiwanese is making a film about Ozu. This self-referencing by Hou is obviously intentional. In contemporary Tokyo, Yoko is attempting to retrace Jiang's steps and reclaim parts of his existence: this is exactly what Hou is setting out to do regarding Ozu.

This is an especially significant topic for this Taiwanese film director making his first film in Japan since Japan's colonization of Taiwan is the subject of many of his previous films, including *A City of Sadness* (1989). In his Japanese film, he wishes to allude to this fact of history without overly emphasizing the disparities between the two nations.

However, there was much discord in Jiang's life. After great success in Japan, he abandoned his Japanese wife (interviewed briefly by Yoko) and immigrated to mainland China in 1938 in the middle of the second Sino-Japanese war. After Japan's surrender in 1945, he was deprived of his Japanese nationality and became a composer for the People's Republic, where he was regarded as a corrupt modernist. In order to survive, he had to recast his form of composition to meet the needs of the Communist party.

Jiang and Ozu are from the recent modernist past. However, the film is centered on contemporary life. At the end of the film, after Hajime has awoken his "sleeping beauty," they emerge from the subway together. This is the closest approximation to an imposed meaning or sense of closure that the film allows. The couple are together—they are no longer crisscrossing Tokyo in parallel trains without seeing each other. Are they babes in the wood who will find the path home together "outside over there"? Or will they remain apart? A film by Ozu would have bestowed a sense of closure. Hou cannot do so because he does not feel that such an ending would be in keeping with contemporary life. After all, there is no Café Lumière. There is, however, cinema that can bestow light on the shadowy parts of contemporary existence.

ADAPTATION VERSUS ADOPTION

Ours is an age in which the idea of national cinema is constantly debated. Does the concept of nationalism have much relevance in the twenty-first century? This book obviously does not enter into this kind of argument. Rather, its focus has been on how the West cinematically constructs Japan. What is seen by outsiders to be— correctly or incorrectly—intrinsically Japanese? What does Japan mean to outsiders?

The study of how a foreign land is adopted, adapted and appropriated in film may be a novel approach to studying films, but it can reveal a great deal about the artistic and socio-economic circumstances influencing film production. Film, when all is said and done, is an art form completely different from *written* fiction, and film creates, as I have argued, its own distinct form of truth.

Moreover, Japan as a setting allows non-Japanese filmmakers to discuss issues in a way that their national cinemas cannot—or it permits a forum in which key issues can be examined in new lights and thus creates an alternative history.

On the surface, these films may be explorations of a foreign land, but they tend to become, as I have suggested, self-reflexive meditations. As such, they reveal a great deal about how foreigners perceive Japan, about how the concept of Japan can be made to have various meanings, and thus about how the Other is dealt with cinematically.

Some of the Western films examined in this book have felt free to inscribe on to Japan whatever issues and sentiments they desire. This is a quasi-libidinal activity in which Japan is perceived as a female upon whose body the Westerner can gaze, write and perhaps transform. However, this is wishful thinking because Japan resists any attempt to reduce it to a simple binary in handy opposition to the whims of the Occidental.

For the most part, in this book Japan has been seen as a place that can be witnessed in multiple new ways: as a palimpsest on which various kinds of auteurs can inscribe themselves; as an idealized, utopian place that is distinct from the West and its (corrupt) values; as a dangerous location with suspicious values; as a locale in which Western-inspired values become highlighted in ways that could not be attained in traditional Western settings—that is, the difference in place helps to produce meaning; and as a nation that has become part of the world-wide phenomenon of globalization. For some filmmakers, Japan's resistance to symbolic structures of meaning is central. For them, the Japanese integration of surface and symbol resists Western heteronormative scripts that prescribe the alignment of sexuality, gender identity, and gender roles.

In any event, Japan remains a conundrum to the West. This is how is should be. Many of the directors whose work is studied in this book realize that Japan may invite their creative attention but that it must always remain a separate entity. Only when differences are respected can the West learn and appreciate the East. In the end, the West can adapt Japan, but Japan can never be adopted.

NOTES

CHAPTER ONE

[1] I am referring specifically to my discussions of Kurosawa, Ozu, Mizoguchi, Resnais, Schrader, Sokurov, Greenaway, Fuller, Logan, Wenders and Marker. In his ground-breaking study of Kurosawa, Mitsuhiro Yoshimoto attempts to redefine the ways in which the Japanese film is discussed and evaluated in the West. For example, Yoshimoto argues against the dangers inherent in auteur theory. He states his arguments well, but there are nevertheless some directors who do indeed engrave their personalities into their film products, and this fact of life should be recognized when it occurs.

[2] Edward Zwick's *The Last Samurai* (2003) is set during the Satsuma Rebellion (1877), but is heavily-fictionalized. Nathan Algren (Tom Cruise), a disgruntled Army captain, travels to Japan to train the Emperor's Army in the latest technologies of war. However, after being captured by Katsumoto (Ken Watanabe), the samurai who is the head of the rebellion, Algren develops an affection for the way of bushido. At the film's conclusion, the samurai rebellion to which Algren has committed himself is crushed but Algren convinces the Emperor not to sign a commercial treaty with the United States.

The United States had no involvement in the Rebellion; Algren is a composite figure; the Satsuma Rebellion was led by Saigō Takamori. What the film does show is how Western-style technology in war did lead to the Rebellion being crushed; however, the "old" Samurai values are enshrined. The Meiji Revolution may have modernized Japan, but it did so at a considerable price to Japanese traditional values. *The Last Samurai* displays Western achievement at the very same time it suggests that foreign values helped to destroy traditional Japanese values.

[3] The word "alterity" is often used in recent critical discourse to describe the Other, but this term carries a considerable baggage (especially in regard to notions of primitivism) that I have avoided it here.

[4] See Shahat (1997).

[5] Schrader (2004, p. 175).

[6] Nygren (2007) makes the crucial point that the sense of "otherness" between the West and Japan has been reduced in the past twenty to thirty years, but he argues, 'this is not the same as saying that all constructions of self are identical. Again, this is not an issue that can be simply clarified, but invites complex models of incommensurable cultural contexts, as the limits of narrative identity and identification.' (xi). I agree. The construction of "otherness" in Western films made from the Occupation to about 1985 is often extremely different from that in more recent films. In any event, specific cultural contexts always have to be investigated.

Nygren's *Time Frames* concentrates on how Japanese films since 1951 have been interpreted in the West. My study goes in the other direction to see how the Japanese are constructed in a number of films.

[7] This point of view is expressed a bit differently by Nygren (2007, p. 7): "Japan's postwar American Occupation, although profound in its rupture with the past, was brief and came late in its modernizing development. If we are to begin to imagine what sometimes seems impossible, an intercultural set of relationships not governed entirely by the principles of domination and hegemony, there is no better place than Japan."

[8] I do not discuss some key issues in the study of Japanese films because they are not relevant to this book's purview. For example, I do not examine the "Pure Film" issue and the idea of a Japanese nationalist cinema. Also, I do not comment on the censorship of Japanese films undertaken during the Occupation, and I do not examine Hollywood's attempts to manipulate the

Japanese market to make its products more popular. See the Select Bibliography for the relevant scholarship on these three issues by Gerow (2010), Hirano(1992) and Kitamura (2010).

[9] Rosenstone (2006, p. 37).

[10] Ibid, pp. 160, 163.

[11] Metz (1974, p. 44).

[12] Woolf (1926, pp. 308-10).

[13] Benedict. (2005, p. 43).

[14] *Independent on Sunday*, 21 January 1991.

[15] Wilde (1986, p. 82).

[16] Barthes (1982, p. 108).

[17] Cited by Huang (2008, pp. 25-6).

[18] Huang (2010, p. 194).

[19] Miyao (2007, p. 1).

[20] Koppes and Black (1987, p. 60).

[21] Clayton R. Koppes and Gregory D. Black in *Hollywood Goes to War: How Politics, Profits and Propaganda Shaped World War II Movies* (New York: The Free Press, 1987) and Robert L. McLaughlin and Sally E. Parry in *We'll Always Have the Movies: American Cinema During World War II* (Lexington: The University Press of Kentucky, 2006) provide excellent accounts of how American films showed the Japanese during World War II.

[22] High, (2003, p. 161).

[23] Ibid, 163.

[24] Ibid, 284.

[25] von Sternberg, (1965, p. 289).

[26] Ibid, 165, 167.

[27] Ibid, 285.

[28] Ibid, 290.

[29] Ibid, 291.

[30] Interview with Philip French in *The Observer*, 25 February 2007.

[31] Turim (1998, pp. 169-84) provides a deft, close reading of this film. I agree with most of her arguments, although I have emphasized other aspects of the film in my reading.

[32] This incident does not occur in *The Sower and the Seed* and is one of the most significant changes introduced by Ôshima. There is the distinct possibility that Hara realizes from the outset that Yonoi is homosexual and that is the reason he keeps knowledge of the Korean soldier's infraction from him. Such a reading heightens the contrast being drawn between the aristocratic patrician and his working-class subordinate.

[33] "Propos de Nagisa Ôshima," *Revue de Cinéma: Image et Son 385* (July/August 1983), 21.

[34] Yoshimoto (2000, p. 176).

[35] Ibid, p. 178.

[36] "*Tokyo Story* has invited a range of moral and spiritual interpretation that we might usefully remember in closing that it is typical of Ozu's works in arising from immediate concerns of his historical moments. The shots of Tokyo construction were topical during the postwar building boom. Contemporary observers remarked that postwar economic organization was eroding the traditional *ie* system, and care of the elderly became a more pressing problem. A popular book of the early 1950s was called *Children Who Do Not Look After Their Parents*. Even at their most evocative, Ozu's films are always referential": Bordwell (1994, pp. 332-3).

[37] Terasaki (1985, p. 7).

[38] Ibid, p. 139.

[39] Marchetti. (1993, p. 170) Marchetti's narrative shows how racism pervades films such as *A Bridge to the Sun* and *Sayonara*. Her arguments are well argued and sustained, but I remain unsure that these two films are as race-conscious (in a negative way) as she argues.

[40] I disagree with Gina Marchetti's reading of the film, although she states her point-of-view brilliantly. "....even though Gwen does receive her domestic education through motherhood and Terry becomes the emblem of Japanese capitulation to the moral and cultural superiority of America, *Bridge to the Sun* allows no

concrete representation of a new domestic order that could accommodate its interracial couple.... *Bridge to the Sun* calls for racial tolerance but insists on it only within the boundaries of traditional patriarchal relations and remains vague about the viability of any multiracial domestic relationship.": Marchetti (1993, p. 175). First. The film is based on a factual account (an autobiography). Second. Terry was an opponent of the Japanese war movement, and it is not fair to say that he capitulated to a notion of American superiority. Third. The film and its source accept the fact that there may be some differences between East and West that cannot be understood completely.
[41] Benjamin (1992, p. 90).

CHAPTER TWO

[1] Terasaki (1985, pp. 210-11).
[2] Monaco (1979, p. 18).
[3] Kreidl (1979, pp. 38-9).
[4] Monaco, op. cit., p. 27.
[5] Monaco, op. cit., p. 28.
[6] Kreidl, op. cit., p. 54.
[7] Duras (1961, p. 112).
[8] Ibid., p. 109.
[9] Some *hibakusha* (Hiroshima survivors) felt that the film's sensuality was an insult to those killed by the bomb. Robert Jay Lifton, *Death in Life: The Survivors of Hiroshima* (London: Weidenfeld and Nicolson, 1967) 468.
[10] Duras, op.cit., p. 19.
[11] Ibid,, p. 25.
[12] On this point, Wilson (2006) observes: "one of the risks of the film is the way it appears to allow the trauma of Nevers to take precedence over the mass horror of Hiroshima. This appears confirmed specifically in the way in which the film pays little or no attention to the Japanese man's recollection, to his perspective." (p. 53) However, Wilson also cites Resnais'

affirmation: "We are *opposing* the immensity, vastness and unreality of Hiroshima and the trivial little story of Nevers." (pp. 53-4). In my discussion of the film, I am attempting to demonstrate the truthfulness of the director's assertion and to show how the film positions the two place names in relation to each other.

[13] Duras, op. cit., p. 63.

[14] Ibid., p. 68.

[15] Ibid., p. 73.

[16] Ibid., p. 54.

[17] Ibid., p. 9.

[18] When Donald Richie saw the film he especially "like[d] the feeling of intimacy achieved by two actors and a camera; and the hallucinatory final scenes of an apparently completely empty, moon lit Hiroshima." He immediately perceived Okada as a Western-type Japanese male. However, he was bothered by the implausibility of such a couple getting together. In addition, "I cannot imagine a Japanese man allowing intimacies in public like that, and the face-slapping scene is nonsense: what Japanese would do that? Would do it to a Japanese woman all right, but not a foreign one." Overall, "why Hiroshima? The use of that particular city seems to equate the atrocity with the simple shearing of the heroine, it makes a false connection—unless Resnais wanted two symbols of war: the dead city, the near-dead girl in the basement. All other slips are because Resnais knew nothing of the Japanese and made people do unlikely things." Richie (2005, p. 126) Entry for 25 January 1960.

[19] Roth (1995, p. 99).

[20] Van der Kolk and van der Hart (1991, p. 448).

CHAPTER THREE

[1] Although the biopic has a dubious reputation in the West, its potential is ably discussed by Bingham (2010, p. 10) in *Whose Lives Are They Anyway?*: "The appeal of the biopic lies in seeing

an actual person who did something interesting in life, known mostly in public, transformed into a character. Private behaviors and actions and public events as they might have been in the person's time are formed together and interpreted dramatically. At the heart of the biopic is the urge to dramatize actuality and find in it the filmmaker's own version of truth. The function of the biopic subject is to give the spectator a story. The genre's charge, which dates back to its salad days in the Hollywood studio era, is to enter the biographical subject into the pantheon of cultural mythology, one way or another, and to show why he or she belongs there."

2 Donald Richie, who had been a good friend of Mishima's, told Schrader in the pre-production phase of the film's making: "I say that Mishima himself would have probably have sided with Paul; that he would not, I think, have approved of the amount of censorship that Yôko is exercising. He was enough of an exhibitionist to want to project a little of the truth—to tantalize his audience if nothing else.' Richie did not express his feelings about the film's proposed structure: "Talks of how he is going to structure his film: Mishima in real life, then Mishima as a boy, then Mishima as one of the characters in his various novels. These three will have a kind of conversation, and somehow in the exchange he hopes that something like the real author will appear—and that Yoko will not notice." (Richie 2004, p. 196). Entry for 17 June 1983.

3 This portion of the film was deliberately filmed to resemble sequences from Z (1969) and State of Siege (1972) by Costa-Garvas.

4 Specifically, Ichikawa places great emphasis on the architectural elements of the Golden Temple (as is evident, for example, in the opening credits, where various architectural drawings are displayed); the music of Toshiro Mayuzumi combines chanting with a discordant modernist score. Schrader's set emphasizes the space occupied by the Temple as separate from ordinary existence, and his choice of Glass to compose his score may have

been influenced by how Ichikawa handled this issue.

"..*Enjô* goes beyond the cinematic convention of the time by its experimental play with widescreen format and with elements of *taiozoku* film—in particular the recurring story of cruel youth that indicated underlying dislocation in Japan in the late 1950s.": Washburn (2001, p. 172).

[5] Schrader (2004, pp. 28-9).

[6] Ibid., p. 29.

[7] In "Ways of Seeing Japanese Prints and Films: Mizoguchi's *Utamaro*," in *Cinematic Landscapes: Observations on the Visual Arts of China and Japan*, ed. Linda C. Erlich and David Desser (Austin: University of Texas Press, 1994), 217-240, Dudley Andrew examines the background of the film, its relationship to John Berger's *Ways of Seeing*, and the ties between the flat surface of ukiyo-e woodcuts and cinema.

[8] Ibid 97.

[9] On viewing *Utamaro*, George Gercke of CIE (Civil Information and Education Section) expressed the opinion that "showing a character killing to avenge her failure in love was not desirable because it could influence young people harmfully, even though this particular story was not a contemporary one." Hirano (1992, pp. 75-6),

[10] For example, Sokurov ignores the convincing, abundant evidence of Hirohito's close involvement in the running of the war found in Bix (2001).

[11] Brands (2006) makes it quite clear that MacArthur was not an architect of American foreign policy towards Hirohito.

[12] Custen (1992, p. 7).

[13] Heilbrun, (1993, pp. 295-304).

CHAPTER FOUR

[1] "A silence of nearly sixteen years was broken when I received a cable from Humphrey Bogart, who wanted me for a picture. About to make *Tokyo Joe* for Columbia Pictures," Hayakawa

recalled, "he made a specific request of the studio that I be signed to appear in it with him. 'From what I remember of him, he's perfect for the part,' he told Robert Lord, the producer. 'I want him to do it with me, so get him!' Robert Lord took a dubious view of my qualifications, for he cabled the Paris offices of Columbia. 'Is Hayakawa too old and feeble to stage a good fight with Bogart?' ": Hayakawa (1960), p. 211.

[2] Fuller (2002, p. 316).

[3] *Slant Magazine*, 6, June 2005.

[4] Fuller (op.cit., p. 323).

[5] 15 December 1945.

[6] Dower (1999, p. 216). This book contains the best and most detailed account of the social history of the Occupation.

[7] Quoted by Dower (op. cit., p. 216).

[8] The depiction of GIs is comparatively rare in Japanese cinema, but there is an important exchange between a soldier and a woman in Ichikawa's *Enjô*. A woman and a GI are arguing in the garden at Shukaku. She slaps the man and runs away heading in the direction of the pavilion. The soldier yells at her that she must have an abortion. Mizoguchi, the protagonist, informs the woman she must not harm the temple, struggles with her, and she falls off some steps. The accident causes a miscarriage, whereupon the GI thanks Mizoguchi by presenting him with two cartons of cigarettes. "You saved us a lot of trouble by getting rid of the baby," the GI tells him. In the novel, Mizoguchi deliberately steps on the woman's stomach. Other Japanese films that actually show American servicemen during the Occupation include Kenoshita Keisuke's *Nihon no higeki* (1953), Taniguchi Senkichi's *Akasen ichi* (1953), and Jun'ya Satô's *Ningen no shômei* (1977).

[9] Okinawa had been a separate nation before the Meiji Restoration. Four years after the Restoration, the Japanese government, through military incursions, officially annexed the kingdom and renamed it Ryukyu. At the same time, the Qing

Dynasty asserted sovereignty over the islands of the Ryukyu Kingdom, since it was also a tributary nation of China. Ryukyu became Okinawa Prefecture of Japan in 1879. Following the Battle of Okinawa and the end of the Pacific War in 1945, Okinawa was under United States administration for twenty-seven years. During the trusteeship rule the United States Air Force established numerous military bases on the Ryukyu Islands. The language of Okinawans varies significantly from modern Japanese.

[10] Manso (1994, p. 409).

[11] Littlewood (1996, p. 74).

[12] Fuller (op.cit., p. 323).

[13] The correct name is given in Michener's *Sayonara*. For a discussion of this group, see the discussion of Kim Longinotto and Jano Williams's *Dream Girls* in Chapter Seven.

[14] Butler (1997) contains a great deal of useful information about the relationship between gender confusion and depression.

[15] Manso (op.cit., p. 421).

[16] Ibid., p. 422.

[17] The relationship of Kelly and Katsumi is more a Madame Butterfly story, although an inverted one. The navy man marries his Japanese sweetheart, and then cannot bear to be parted from her. He and she then take their lives.

[18] My reading of *Sayonara* varies considerably from Marchetti (1993, p. 143), although I agree with her on this point: "Although ostensibly a critique of racism sugarcoated by a Romeo and Juliet love story, *Sayonara*, more profoundly perhaps, exists as a historical document that illustrates how the dominant ideology deals with social and cultural change by both acknowledging and squelching it. Although the film implies that Gruver and Hana Ogi ultimately live happily ever after as husband and wife, the rumblings of class and gender inequalities heard within the film's subplots do not seem to be wrapped up neatly."

Marchetti is correct to point out that the suicide of Kelly and

Katsumi is deeply problematic. Why, after all, can't Kelly go home to the States and then return to Japan to be with his wife? This common-sensical solution is never considered. Also, Katsumi seems to revere her American husband as some sort of god. This raises all kinds of questions about equality.

However, the film's handling of Eileen—she is presumably going to have some sort of relationship with Nakamura—suggests that women can find in the East a way out of the constrictions visited upon them in the West. My reading of the film emphasizes the transforming power that Hana Ogi has over Gruver's previously diminished view of his own masculinity.

CHAPTER FIVE

1 Interview with Tamara Wieder, *Boston Phoenix* October 10-17, 2002.

2 Littlewood (1996, p. 109).

3 Golden (1997, p. 433).

4 Wieder, op. cit.

5 The casting of three Chinese actresses in major roles caused a stir. Zhang Ziyi (Sayuri) and Gong Li (Hatsumomo) are Chinese, whereas Michelle Yeoh (Mameha) is ethic Chinese from Malaysia. Zhang Ziyi was outspoken on this issue: "A director is only interested in casting someone he believes is appropriate for a role. For instance, my character had to go from age 15 to 35; she had to be able to dance, and she had to be able to act, so he needed someone who could do all that. I also think that regardless of whether someone is Japanese or Chinese or Korean we all would have had to learn what it is to be a geisha, because almost nobody today knows what that means—not even the Japanese actors on the film. *Geisha* was not meant to be a documentary. I remember seeing in the Chinese newspapers a piece that said we had only spent six weeks to learn everything and that that was not respectful toward the culture. It's like saying that if you're playing a mugger, you have to rob a certain number of people. To

my mind, what this issue is all about, though, is the intense historical problems between China and Japan. The whole subject is a land mine. Maybe one of the reasons people made such a fuss about *Geisha* was that they were looking for a way to vent their anger": Interview with Ingrid Sischy, *Interview* July 2006. Roger Ebert film pointed out that a Japanese-owned company financed the film, and that Gong Li and Zhang Ziyi outgross any Japanese actress even in the Japanese box office.

As far as another issue regarding authenticity is concerned, it was decided by the producers that contemporary Japan looked much too modern to film a story which took place in the 1920s and 1930s and it would therefore be more cost-effective to create sets for the film on soundstages and locations in the United States, primarily in California.

[6] Le Fanu (2005, pp. 69-95) provides an excellent guide to the intricacies of Mizoguchi's treatment of geisha.

[7] In this role, the most celebrated in his entire career, Hayakawa regained his earlier fame, but the characterization is of a deeply introverted, twisted person. He is neither a matinee ideal nor the incarnation of a form of Oriental Evil. "Saito brutally tortures Major Nicholson (Alec Guinness), locking him up in a small cell under the sun: 'an oven,' when Nicholson refuses his order to do manual labor, insisting that the code of the Geneva Convention prohibits officers from being forced to do it. Saito's barbarous act is specifically connected to Japanese militarism. He says to Nicholson: 'what do you know of the soldiers' code, *Bushido*? Nothing! You are unworthy of command!' Saito does have his own principles in the form of *bushido*, but they are not understandable to British and American soldiers...Thus despite his apparent gentleness, refinement, and Westernization, Saito is characterized as despotic, uncivilized, and inassimilable.... When Nicholson wins the silent battle against Saito and obtains permission to work not as a manual laborer but as a commander to build a bridge over the River Quai, a high angle log shot

shows the back of Saito, who is crying severely alone in his room. This is the last emotional outburst of Saito that the viewers witness in the film. After this shot, Saito turns into a completely receptive, meek, and defeated character." Miyao (2007, pp. 276-7).

CHAPTER SIX
[1] Kaplan and Dubro (2003, p. 141).
[2] Schilling (2003, p. 13) provides a masterful history of the yakuza genre. He gives a particularly apt summary of it before and after the Pacific War. "In the silent era, these films remained a subset of the samurai period drama, which was then the most popular domestic genre. Their heroes were usually Robin Hood types from the feudal past who may have made their living from their winnings, these men often wandered the countryside, poor and lonely, but faithful to the gangsters' code. In the upheavals that followed Japan's defeat in World War Two, the gang films changed. With old values discredited and new Western influences flooding in, audiences demanded fresh cultural affirmations of Japanese identity.... The zeitgeist had shifted. Gangsters no longer were romantic figures from a distant past but a present-day reality in every black market or entertainment district. Ruthless and dangerous, they swaggered where others cowered, flourished where others starved. These men attracted a new kind of admiration, not for their virtue, like the old-time gamblers of story and song, but rather their power and élan. Films thus began to appear about these postwar gangsters in the hard-boiled style of Hollywood noir." (13)
[3] Scott (2005, p. 66).
[4] Ibid., p. 65.
[5] Ibid.
[6] Ibid., p. 66.
[7] Ibid., p. 133.

CHAPTER SEVEN

[1] King, Homay (2010), 126.

[2] Wilson (2006, p. 195) provides an excellent description of Marker's post-Resnais films: "....the directors whose work and whose cinematic trajectory since the 1950s bear closest comparison to Resnais are his early collaborators Chris Marker and Agnès Varda, whose relation to the Nouvelle Vague was, like Resnais's, tangential, and whose very different works over subsequent decades are yet equally marked by attention to memory, virtuality and mourning on the one hand, and to the textures, shapes and surfaces of the material world on the other."

[3] Lupton (2005, p. 101). Lupton also argues that *The Koumiko Mystery* "gleefully sends up the contemporary vogue for statistical surveys, and market research."

[4] Marker's extraordinary ambition in *Sans soleil* is evident in this reference. Tarkovsky's film was seen from the time of its release as a major statement about the human condition, although exactly what is being related is difficult to comprehend. It depicts an expedition led by a Stalker, who bring his two clients to a site known as "the Zone", which has the supposed potential to fulfill a person's innermost desires.

[5] Lupton (op. cit., p. 153) defines the Zone in this way: "Yamaneko believes that the graphic mutations of the Zone are in many senses more truthful than the illusory presence conjured by conventional film footage and photographs, since they can depict quite literally the shifting and transforming action of time and recollection upon the images of the past." She also points out that the form of Marker's film resembles a musical composition with recurrent themes and the like.

[6] Marker's camera pays close attention to posters advertising Kurosawa films in *The Koumiko Mystery*.

[7] Richie (2004, pp. 293-4) found Wenders' behavior objectionable. On 10 December 1992, Richie went to Atsuta Yoshun's wake. "He survived by over thirty years the director who made him famous.

Moreover, when people talked with him, they only wanted to talk about Ozu. I remember Wim Wenders going after him, pushing, probing, demanding, until the poor man burst into tears on camera, with Wim gloating through the view-finder."

[8] Richie (2002, p. 15).

[9] Quandt (2001, p. 330).

[10] Ibid.

[11] Miiko Taka (Hana Ogi from *Sayonara*) plays Aiko Kurawa, a colleague and friend of Christine Easton.

[12] Cannibalism among Japanese soldiers is treated in Kon Ichikawa's *Fires on the Plain* (*Nobi*, 1959).

[13] Hirokazu Koreeda's *Air Doll* (*Kûki ningyô*; 2009) is about an inflatable sex doll that comes to life and acquires a heart.

CHAPTER EIGHT

[1] Sammy Davis Jr. appeared in a series of Suntory commercials in the early 1970s. In the late 1970s Kurosawa directed a celebrated series of commercials featuring American celebrities on the set of *Kagemusha*. One of those featured was Francis Ford Coppola (an executive producer of the film). This incident obviously inspired Sofia in the making of *Lost in Translation*. Suntory is also seen on-screen in *Babel*.

[2] Stein (1986), 107.

[3] Kristof and WuDunn (2001, p. 320).

[4] In *Lost in Translation*, the crass American actress Kelly (Anna Faris) is in Tokyo to promote her latest film, "Midnight Velocity," a martial-arts action movie which supposedly stars Keanu Reeves.

[5] Greenaway (1966, p. 102).

[6] Ibid., p 107.

[7] Ibid., p. 112.

[8] As cited by Bridget Elliott and Anthony Purdy in "Skin Deep: Fins-de-Siècle and New Beginnings in Peter Greenaway's *The Pillow Book*" (p. 271) in Willoquet-Maricondi and Alemany-

Falway (2008).

[9] Ibid., p. 275.

EPILOGUE

[1] André Green (2001) discusses the phenomenon of the "dead mother" complex (whereupon a severely depressed or withdrawn mother can offer no psychic sustenance to her child) in *Life Narcissism/Death Narcissism* (Andrew Weller, trans.). London, New York: Free Associations Books.

[2] "Train to Somewhere," *Myspacetv* Issue 48 (May 2005).

[3] *Metro Lumière*: an interview with Hou on the DVD of *Café Lumière*.

FILMS ABOUT POSTWAR JAPAN MADE BY FOREIGN DIRECTORS, 1949-2009

1949: *TOKYO JOE*
Director: Stuart Heisler
Story: Steve Fisher
Adaptation: Walter Doniger
Screenplay: Cyril Hume, Bertram Millhauser
Producers: Henry S. Kesler, Robert Lord
Cast: Humphrey Bogart (Joe Barrett), Alexander Knox (Mark Landis), Florence Marly (Trina Pechinkov Landis), Sessue Hayakawa (Baron Kimura), Teru Shimada (Ito), Hideo Mori (Kanda), Rhys Williams (Colonel Dahlgren)

1950: *ORIENTAL EVIL*
Directors: George P. Breakston, C. Ray Stahl
Screenplay: C. Ray Stahl
Cinematography: Ichirô Hoshijima
Editing: Martin G. Cohn
Music: Albert Glasser
Producers: George P. Breakston, Irene Breakston, C. Ray Stahl
Cast: Byron Michie (Thomas Putnam, alias Roger Mansfield), Martha Hyer (Cheryl Banning), Tetsu Nakamura (Noritomu Moriaji)

1951: *TOKYO FILE 212*
Directors and Writers: Dorrell McGowan, Stuart McGowan
Story: George P. Breakston
Cinematography: Ichirô Hoshijima, Herman Schopp
Editing: Martin G. Cohn
Music: Albert Glasser
Producers: Dorrell McGowan, Stuart McGowan, C. Ray Stahl
Cast: Florence Marly (Steffi Novak), Lee Frederick (Jim Carter as

Robert Peyton), Katsuhiko Haida (Taro Matsudo), Reiko
Otani (Namiko), Tatsuo Saito (Mr Matsudo), Byron Michie
(Mr Jeffrey)

1952: *BACK AT THE FRONT*
Director: George Sherman
Book: Bill Maudlin
Writer: Oscar Brodney
Screenplay: Lou Breslow, Don McGuire
Cinematography: Clifford Stine
Editing: Paul Weatherway
Music: Henry Mancini, Herman Stein
Producer: Leonard Goldstein
Cast: Tom Ewell (Willie), Harvey Lembeck (Joe), Mari Blanchard
(Nina), Russell Johnson (Johnny Redondo), Richard Long
(Sergeant Rose), Gregg Palmer (Captain White), Barry Kelley
(Brigadier General Dixon), Vaughan Taylor (Major Lester
Ormsby), Benson Fong (Rickshaw driver)

1952: *GEISHA GIRL*
Directors: George P. Breakston, C. Ray Stahl
Screenplay: C. Ray Stahl
Music: Albert Glasser
Producer: George P. Breakston
Cast: Archer MacDonald (Archie McGregor), Steve Forrest
(Rocky Wilson), Martha Hyer (Peggy Barnes), Tetsu
Nakamura (Tetsu Nakano), Dekao Yoko (Zoro), Heihachirô
Ôkawa (Police inspector), Tatsuo Saito (Professor)

1953: *ANATAHAN*
Director, cinematography and screenplay: Josef von Sternberg
Novel: Michiro Maruyama
Editing: Mitsuzô Miyata
Art direction: Takashi Kono

Music: Akira Ifukube
Producer: Kazuo Takimura
Cast: Akemi Negishi (Keiko Kusakabe), Tadashi Suganuma (Kusakabe), Kisaburo Sawamura (Kuroda), Shôji Nakayama (Nishio), Josef von Sternberg (voice-over)

1955: *HOUSE OF BAMBOO*
Director: Samuel Fuller
Cinematography: Joseph MacDonald
Editing: James B. Clark
Art Direction: Addison Hehr, Lyle R. Wheeler
Music: Leigh Harline
Producer: Buddy Adler
Cast: Robert Ryan (Sandy), Robert Stack (Eddie Kenner aka Spanier), Shirley Yamaguchi (Mariko), Cameron Mitchell (Griff), Brad Dexter (Captain Hanson), Sessue Hayakawa (Inspector Kito), Biff Elliot (Webber)

1956: *SACRIFICE (GISEI)*
DIRECTOR: Donald Richie
Sacrifice is one of a number of coterie films made by Richie: others include *Wargames* (1962), *Atami Blues* (1962), *Dead Youth* (1967), *Five Philosophical Tales* (1967) and *Cybele* (1968)

1956: *THE TEAHOUSE OF THE AUGUST MOON*
Director: Daniel Mann
Book: Vern J. Sneider
Screenplay: John Patrick
Cinematography: John Alton
Editing: Harold F. Kress
Art direction: William A. Horning, Eddie Imazu
Music: Saul Chaplin
Producer: Jack Cummings
Cast: Marlon Brando (Sakini), Glenn Ford (Fisby), Machiko Kyô

(Lotus Blossom), Eddie Albert (Captain McLean), Paul Ford (Colonel Wainwright Purdy III), Jun Negami (Mr Seiko), Harry Morgan (Sergeant Gregovich)

1957: *SAYONARA*
Director: Joshua Logan
Novel: James Michener
Screenplay: Paul Osborn
Cinematographer: Ellsworth Fredericks
Editing: Philip W. Anderson, Arthur P. Schmidt
Art direction: Ted Haworth
Music: Franz Waxman
Producer: William Goetz
Cast: Marlon Brando (Lloyd Gruver), Red Button (Joe Kelly), Miiko Taka (Hana Ogi), Miyoshi Umeki (Katsumi), Patricia Owens (Eileen Webster), Ricardo Montalban (Nakamura), Martha Scott (Mrs. Webster), Kent Smith (General Webster), James Garner (Mike Bailey)

1958: *THE GEISHA BOY*
Director and screenplay: Frank Tashlin
Story: Rudy Makoul
Cinematography: Haskell B. Boggs
Editing: Alma Macrorie
Art direction: Tambi Larsen, Hal Pereia
Music: Walter Scharf
Producer: Jerry Lewis
Cast: Jerry Lewis (Gilbert Wooley), Marie McDonald (Lola Livingston), Sessue Hayakawa (Mr Sikita), Suzanne Pleshette (Sergeant Pearson), Nobu McCarthy (Kimi Sikita)

1959: *HIROSHIMA MON AMOUR*
Director: Alain Resnais
Screenplay: Marguerite Duras

Cinematography: Michio Takahashi, Sacha Vierny
Editing: Jasmine Chasnev, Henri Colpi, Anne Sarraute
Production design: Minoru Esaka, Mayo, Peri, Lucilla Mussini
Music: Georges Delerue, Giovanni Fusco
Producers: Anatole Dauman, Samy Halfon
Cast: Emmanuelle Riva (Elle), Eiji Okada (Lui), Stella Dassas (Mother), Pierre Barbaud (Father), Bernard Fresson (German lover)

1961: *BRIDGE TO THE SUN*
Director: Etienne Périer
Book: Gwen Terasaki
Screenplay: Charles Kaufman
Cinematography: William J. Kelly, Seichi Kizuka, Marcel Weiss
Editing: Monique Isnardon, Robert Isnardon
Art Direction: Hiroshi Mizutani
Music: Georges Auric
Producer: Jacques Bar
Cast: Carroll Baker (Gwen), James Shigeta (Hidenari), James Yagi (Hara), Tetsurô Tanba (Jiro), Yôko Takahashi (Kyoko Takahashi),Hiroshi Tomono (Ishi),Ruth Masters (Aunt Peggy)

1961: *CRY FOR HAPPY*
Director: George Marshall
Novel: George Campbell
Screenplay: Irving Brecher
Cinematography: Charles Lawton Jr.
Editing: Viola Lawrence
Art direction: Robert Peterson
Music: George Anthell
Producers: Robert Lord
Cast: Glenn Ford (Andy Cyphers), Donald O'Connor (Murray Prince), Miiko Taka (Chiyoko), James Shigeta (Suzuki), Miyoshi Umeki (Harue), Howard St. John (Vice Admiral

Junius B. Bennett), Joe Flynn (John McIntosh), Harriet E. MacGibbon (Mrs. Bennett)

1962: *MY GEISHA*
Director: Jack Cardiff
Screenplay: Norman Krasna
Cinematography: Shunichiro Nakao
Editing: Archie Marshek
Art direction: Makoto Kikuchi, Arthur Lonegran, Hal Pereira
Music: Franz Waxman
Producer: Steve Parker
Cast: Shirley MacLaine (Lucy Dell), Yves Montand (Paul Robaix), Edward G. Robinson (Sam Lewis), Robert Cummings (Bob Moore), Yoko Tani (Kazumi Ito)

1965: *THE KOUMIKO MYSTERY (LE MYSTÈRE KOUMIKO)*
Director, cinematography, screenplay, narration, editing: Chris Marker
Sound: SIMO
Music: Toru Takemitsu
Production: Apec Joudioux, Sofracima, service de la Recherché de l'ORTF
Cast: Koumiko Muraoka

1966: *LOVE IN TOKYO*
Director: Pramrod Chakravorty
Screenplay: Sachin Bhowmick
Cinematography: V.K. Murthy
editing: Dharamvir
Art direction: Shanti Dass
Music: Jakishan Dayabhai Pankai, Shankarsinh Raghuwanshi
Producer: Lakshmi Chakravorty
Joy Mukheriee (Ashok), Asha Parekh (Asha), Pran (Pran), Shubha Khote (Sheela)

1966: *WALK, DON'T RUN*
Director: Charles Walters
Story: Robert Russell, Frank Ross
Screenplay: Sol Saks, Garson Kanin
Cinematography: Harry Stradling Jr.
Editing: Walter Thompson, James D. Wells
Production design: Joseph C. Wright
Music: Quincy Jones
Producer: Sol C. Siegel
Cast: Cary Grant (Sir William Rutland), Samantha Eggar (Christine Easton), Jim Hutton (Steve Davis), John Standing (Julius D. Haversack), Miiko Taka (Aiko Kurawa), George Takei (police captain)

1967: **YOU ONLY LIVE TWICE**
Director: Lewis Gilbert
Story: Ian Fleming
Screenplay: Roald Dahl
Cinematography: Freddie Young
Editing: Peter Hunt
Production Design: Ken Adam
Music: John Barry
Producers: Albert R. Broccoli, Harry Salzman
Cast: Sean Connery (James Bond), Akiko Wakabayashi (Aki), Tetsurô Tanba (Tiger Tanaka), Teru Shimada (Mr Osato), Donald Pleasence (Ernst Stavro Blofeld), Bernard Lee (M)

1974: *THE YAKUZA*
Director: Sydney Pollack
Story: Leonard Schrader
Screenplay: Paul Schrader, Robert Towne
Cinematography: Kôzô Okazaki
Editing: Don Guidice, Thomas Stanford
Art direction: Yoshiyuki Ishida, Stephen Grimes

Music: Dave Grusin
Producer: Koji Shundo
Cast: Robert Mitchum (Harry Kilmer), Ken Takakura (Tanaka Ken), Brian Keith (George Tanner), Eiko Kishi (Eiko)

1982: *THE CHALLENGE*
Director: John Frankenheimer
Screenplay: Richard Maxwell, John Sayles, Ivan Moffat
Cinematography: Kôzô Okazaki
Editing: John W. Wheeler
Art design: Yoshiyuki Ishida
Music: Jerry Goldsmith
Producer: Lyle Poncher
Cast: Scott Glenn (Rick), Toshirô Mifune (Toru Yoshida), Donna Kei Benz (Aiko Yoshida), Calvin Jung (Ando)

1982: *THE TROUT (LA TRUITE)*
Director: Joseph Losey
Novel: Roger Vailland
Screenplay: Monique Lange, Joseph Losey
Cinematography: Henri Alekan
Editing: Marie Castro-Vasquez
Design: Alexandre Trauner
Music: Richard Hartley
Producer: Christian Ferry
Cast: Isabelle Huppert (Frédérique), Jean-Pierre Cassel (Rambert), Jeanne Moreau (Lou), Daniel Olbrychski (Saint-Genis), Isao Yamagata (Daigo Hamada), Alexis Smith (Gloria)

1982: *SUNLESS (SANS SOLEIL)*
Director: Chris Marker
Cinematography: Sandor Krasna
Special effects: Hayao Yamaneko
Production: Argos Films

1983: *MERRY CHRISTMAS, MR LAWRENCE*

Director: Nagisa Ôshima
Novel: Laurens van der Post
Screenplay: Nagisa Ôshima, Paul Mayersberg
Cinematography: Toichiro Narushima
Editing: Tomoyo Ôshima
Art direction: Andrew Sanders
Music: Ryuichi Sakamoto
Producers: Geoffrey Nethercott, Eiko Ôshima
Cast: David Bowie (Jack Celliers), Tom Conti (John Lawrence), Ryuichi Sakamoto (Captain Yonoi), Takeshi Kitano (Sergeant Gengo Hara), Jack Thompson (Group Captain Hicksley)

1985: *A.K. (PORTRAIT OF AKIRA KUROSAWA)*

Director and editing: Chris Marker
Cinematography: Frans-Yves Marescot
Music: Toru Takemitsu
Production: Serge Silberman/ Greenwich Film Productions, Herald Ace, Herald Nippon

1985: *MISHIMA: A LIFE IN FOUR CHAPTERS*

Director: Paul Schrader
Japanese script: Chieko Schrader
Writers: Paul Schrader, Leonard Schrader
Cinematography: John Bailey
Editing: Michael Chandler, Tomoyo Oshima
Art Direction: Eiko Ishioka, Kazuo Takenaka
Music: Philip Glass
Producers: Francis Ford Coppola, George Lucas
Cast: Ken Ogata (Yukio Mishima), Junkichi Orimoto (General Mashita), Naoko Ôtani (Mother), Haruko Kato (Grandmother), Yasokuke Bando (Mizoguchi), Kenji Sawada (Osamu), Setsuko Karasuma (Mitsuko), Toshiyuki Nagashima (Isao)

1985: *TOKYO GA*
Director: Wim Wenders
Cinematography: Edward Lachman
Editing: Solveig Dommartin, Jon Neuberger, Wim Wenders
Music: Laurent Pettigand
Producers: Chris Sievernich, Wim Wenders
Cast: Chishû Ryû (himself), Yuharu Atsuta (himself), Werner Herzog (himself), Chris Marker (himself)

1989: *NOTEBOOK ON CITIES AND CLOTHES (AUF ZEICH-NUNGEN ZU KLEIDERN UND STÄDTEN)*
Director: Wim Wenders
Writers: Wim Wenders and François Burkhardt
Cast: Yohji Yamamoto and Wim Wenders

1989: *BLACK RAIN*
Director: Ridley Scott
Screenplay: Craig Bolotin, Warren Lewis
Cinematography: Jan de Bont
Editing: Tom Rolf
Art Direction: John J. Moore, Herman F. Zimmerman
Music: Hans Zimmer
Producer: Craig Bolotin
Cast: Michael Douglas (Nick Conklin), Andy Garcia (Charlie Vincent), Ken Takakura (Masahiro), Kate Capshaw (Kate), Yûsaku Matsuda (Sato)

1989: *EAT THE KIMONO*
Directors: Kim Longinotto, Jano Williams
Cinematography: Kim Longinotto
Editing: John Mister
Cast: Genshu Hanayagi (herself)

1991: *THE INLAND SEA*
Director and screenplay: Lucille Carra
Book: Donald Richie

1991: *INTIMATE STRANGER*
Director, Producer, Cinematographer, Editor: Alan Berliner
Cast: Joseph Cassuto (himself)

1992: *THE GOOD WIFE OF TOKYO*
Director: Kim Longinotto
Cast: Kazuko Hohki, Yukiko Hohki, Chika Nakagawa, Grant
Showbiz (themselves)

1992: *MR BASEBALL*
Director: Fred Schepisi
Story: Theo Pelletier, John Junkerman
Screenplay: Gary Ross, Kevin Wade, Monte Merrick
Cinematography: Ian Baker
Editing: Peter Honess
Production design: Ted Haworth
Music: Jerry Goldman
Producer: John Kao, Susumu Kondo, Jeffrey Silver
Cast: Tom Selleck (Jack Elliott), Ken Takakura (Uchiyama), Aya
Takanashi (Hiroko), Dennis Haysbert (Max Dubois)

1994: *DREAM GIRLS*
Directors: Kim Longinotto, Jano Williams
Cast: Miki Maya (herself), Anju Mira (herself)

1994: *OTAKU*
Director and Producer: Jean-Jacques Beineix
Cinematography: Rémy Boudet
Editing: Jackie Bastide

1995: *SHINJUKU BOYS*
Directors: Kim Longinotto, Jano Williams
Cinematography: Kim Longinotto
Editing: John Mister
Music: Nigel Hawks
Producer: Alan Bookbinder
Cast: Gaishi, Tatsu, Kazuki, Abe, Kumi (themselves)

1996: *ORIENTAL ELEGY (VOSTOCHNAYA ELEGIYA)*
Director, screenplay and narrator: Aleksandr Sokurov

1996: *THE PILLOW BOOK*
Director and screenplay: Peter Greenaway
Story: Sei Shônagon
Cinematography: Sacha Vierny
Editing: Peter Greenaway, Chris Wyatt
Producers: Terry Glinwood, Jean-Louis Piel, Tom Reeve, Dennis
    Wigman
Cast: Vivian Wu (Nagiko), Yoshi Oida (The Publisher), Ken
    Ogata (The Father), Hideko Yoshida (Aunt/Maid), Ewan
    McGregor (Jerome)

1997: *A HUMBLE LIFE (SMIRENNAYA ZHIZN)*
Director and screenplay: Aleksandr Sokurov

1998: *TOKYO EYES*
Director: Jean-Pierre Limosin
Writers: Jean-Pierre Limosin, Santiago Amigorena, Philippe
    Madral, Yûji Sakamoto
Cinematography: Jean-Marc Fabre
Editing: Danielle Anezin, Thierry Demay
Art direction: Masami Kobayashi
Music: Xavier Jamaux

1999: *ENLIGHTENMENT GUARANTEED (ERLEUCHNTUNG GARANTIERT)*
Director: Doris Dôrrie
Screenplay: Doris Dôrrie and Ruth Stadler
Cinematography: Hans Karl Hu
Editing: Inez Regnier, Arne Sinnwell
Art direction: Ruth Stadler
Producer: Louis Saul
Cast: Uwe Ochsenknecht (Uwe), Gustav-Peter Wôhler (Gustav), Petra Zieser (Petra), Ulrike Kriener (Ulrike), Anica Dobra (Anica)

2000: *DOLCE*
Director and screenplay: Aleksandr Sokurov
Story: Toshio Shimao
Cast: Miho Shimao, Maya Shimao (themselves)

2000: *GAEA GIRLS*
Directors and screenplay: Kim Longinotto, Jano Williams
Cast: Chigusa Nagayo, Meiko Satomura, Yuka Sugiyama, Saika Takeuchi (themselves)

2001: *FIREFLY DREAMS*
Director, editing and screenplay: John Williams
Cinematography: Yoshinobu Hayano
Set decoration: Tsutomu Nagaoka, Tsutomu Obokori
Music: Paul Rowe
Producers: Kazuaki Kaneda, Martin B. Z. Rycroft, John Williams
Cast: Maho (Naomi), Tsutomu Niwa (Masaru), Etsuko Kimata (Yumi), Kyoko Kanemoto (Naomi's mother), Atsushi Ono (Naomi's father), Yoshie Minami (Mrs. Koide)

2001: *WASABI*
Director: Gérard Krawczyk

Writer: Luc Besson
Cinematography: Gérard Sterin
Editing: Yann Hervé
Music: Julien Schulthei, Eric Serra
Producers: Luc Besson, Shohei Kotaki, Kanjiro Sakura
Cast: Jean Reno (Hubert Fiorentini), Ryoko Hirosue (Yumi Yoshimodo), Michel Muller (Maurice), Carole Bouquet (Sofia), Yoshi Oida (Takanawa)

2003: *CAFÉ LUMIÈRE*
Director: Hsiao-Hsien Hou
Screenplay: Hsiao-Hsien Hou and T'ien-wen Chu
Cinematography: Pin Bing Lee
Editing: Ching-Song Liao
Production design: Toshiharu Aida
Music: Yôsui Inoue
Producers: Ching-Song Liao, Hideji Miyaima, Fumiko Osaka, Ichirô Yamamoto
Cast: Yo Hitoto (Yôko), Tadanobu Asano (Hajime Takeuchi), Masato Hagiwara (Seiji), Kimiko Yo (Yôko's step-mother), Nenji Kobayashi (Yôko's father)

2003: *FEAR AND TREMBLING (STUPEUR ET TREMBLE- MENTS)*
Director and screenplay: Alain Corneau
Novel: Amélie Northomb
Cinematographer: Yves Angelo
Editing: Thierry Derocles
Production design: Valérie Leblanc, Philippe Taillefer
Producers: Christine Gozian, Kenzô Horikoshi
Cast: Sylvie Testud (Amélie), Kaori Tsuji (Fubuki), Tarô Suwa (Monsieur Sato), Bison Katayama (Monsieur Omochi), Yasunari Kondo (Monsieur Tenshi)

2003: *KILL BILL: VOLUME 1*
Director and Screenplay: Quentin Tarantino
Cinematography: Robert Richardson
Editing: Sally Menke
Art direction: Daniel Bradford, Hidefumi Hanatani, Minoru Nishida
Music: RZA
Producers: Erica Steinberg, E. Bennett Walsh, Bon Weinstein, Harvey Weinstein
Cast: Uma Thurman (The Bride), Lucy Liu (O-Ren Ishii), Vivica A. Fox (Vernita Green), David Carradine (Bill),Julia Dreyfus (Sofie Fatale), Chiaki Kuriyama (Gogo Yubari), Sonny Chiba (Hattori Hanzo)

2003: *LOST IN TRANSLATION*
Director and Screenplay: Sofia Coppola
Cinematography: Lance Acord
Editing: Sarah Flack
Art direction: Mayumi Tomita, Rika Nakanishi
Music: Kevin Shields
Producers: Francis Ford Coppola, Fred Roos
Cast: Bill Murray (Bob Harris), Scarlett Johansson (Charlotte), Akiko Takeshita (Ms. Kawasaki), Giovanni Ribisi (John), Anna Faris (Kelly), Catherine Lambert (jazz singer)

2004: *THE GRUDGE*
Director: Takashi Shimizu
Screenplay: Takashi Shimizu and Stephen Susco
Cinematography: Hideo Yamamoto
Editing: Jeff Betancourt
Art direction: Kyôko Yauchi
Music: Christopher Young
Producers: Doug Davison, Joseph Drake
Cast: Sarah Michelle Gellar (Karen), Jason Behr (Doug), William

Mapother (Matthew), Clea DuVall (Jennifer), KaDee Strickland (Susan), Grace Zabriskie (Emma), Bull Pullman (Peter)

2004: *THE STRATOSPHERE GIRL*
Director and screenplay: Matthias X. Oberg
Cinematography: Michael Mieke
Editing: Peter Alderliesten
Art Direction: Tim Pannen
Music: Nils Petter Molvaer
Producers: Karl Baumgartner, Christoph Friedel
Cast: Chloé Winkel (Angela), Jon Yang (Yamamoto), Rebecca Palmer (Rachel), Filip Peeters (Kruilman), Togo Igawa (Oshima)

2005: *INTO THE SUN*
Director: Mink
Story: Steven Seagal, Joe Halpin
Screenplay: Steven Seagal, Joe Halpin, Trevor Miller
Cinematography: Don E. FauntLeRoy
Editing: Michael Duthie
Production design: Peter Hampton
Cast: Steven Seagal (Travis Hunter), Matthew Davis (Sean Mack), Takao Ôsawa (Kuroda), Eddie Jones (George), William Atherton (Block)

2005: *MEMOIRS OF A GEISHA*
Director: Rob Marshall
Book: Arthur Golden
Screenplay: Robin Swicord
Cinematography: Dion Beebe
Editing: Pietro Scalia
Production design: John Myhre
Art decoration: Patrick M. Sullivan, Jr.

Producers: Gary Barber, Roger Birnbaum, Bobby Cohen, Patricia
   Whitcher
Cast: Ziyi Zhang (Sayuri), Togo Igawa (Tanaka), Li Gong
   (Hatsumomo), Michelle Yeoh (Mahema), Ken Watanabe (The
   General), Cary-Hiroyuki Tagawa (The Baron), Kôji Yakusho
   (Nobu), Randall Duk Kim (Dr. Crab)

2005: *THE SUN (SOLNTSE)*
Director and cinematography: Aleksandr Sokurov
Writers: Yuri Arabov, Jeremy Noble
Editing: Sergei Ivanov
Music: Andrey Sigle
Producers: Igor Kalyonov, Marco Mueller, Andrey Sigle
Cast: Issei Ogata (Hirohito), Robert Dawson (Douglas
   MacArthur), Kaori Momoi (Empress Kojun), Shirô Sano (the
   chamberlain), Shimei Tsuji (old servant), Taijirô Tamura),
   Georgi Pitskhelauri (MacArthur's warrant officer)

2006: *BABEL*
Director, story idea, producer: Alejandro González Iñárritu
Screenplay: Guillermo Arriaga
Cinematography: Rodrigo Prieto
Editing: Douglas Crise, Stephen Mirrione
Art direction: Rika Nakanishi
Music: Gustavo Santaoialla
Cast: Brad Pitt (Richard Jones), Cate Blanchett (Susan Jones),
   Rinko Kikuchi (Chieko Wataya), Kôji Yakusho (Yasujiro
   Wataya), Yuko Murata (Mitsu), Satoshi Nikaido (Detective Lt.
   Kenji Mamiya), Kazunori Tozawa (Detective Hamano)

2006: *THE FAST AND THE FURIOUS: TOKYO DRIFT*
Director: Justin Lin
Screenplay: Chris Morgan
Cinematographer: Stephen F. Windon

Editing: Kelly Matsumoto, Dallas Puett, Fred Raskin
Art design: Tom Reta
Music: Brian Tyler
Producers: Ryan Kavanaugh, Lynwood Spinks, Clayton Townsend
Cast: Lucas Black (Sean Boswell), Brian Goodman (Major Boswell), Sonny Chiba (Uncle Kamata), Keiko Kitagawa (Reiko), Brian Tee (D.K.)

2006: *LETTERS FROM IWO JIMA*
Director: Clint Eastwood
Book: Tadamichi Kuribayashi
Story: Iris Yamashita, Paul Haggis
Screenplay: Iris Yamashita
Cinematography: Tom Stern
Editing: Joel Cox, Gary Roach
Production design: Henry Bumstead, James J. Murakami
Music: Kyle Eastwood, Michael Stevens
Producer: Paul Haggis
Cast: Ken Watanabe (General Kuribayashi), Kazunari Ninomiya (Saigo), Tsuyoshi Ihara (Baron Nishi), Ryo Kase (Shimizu), Shidô Nakamura), Hiroshi Watanabe (lieutenant Fujita)

2008: *CHERRY BLOSSOMS (KIRSCHBLÛTEN-HANAMI)*
Director and screenplay: Doris Dôrrie
Cinematographer: Hanno Lentz
Editing: Frank C. Müller, Inez Regnier
Producers: David Groenewold, Patrick Zorer
Cast: Elmar Wepper (Rudi Angermeier), Hannelore Elsner (Trudi Angermeier), Aya Irizuki (Yu), Maximilian Brückner (Karl Angermeier), Nadia Uhl (Franzi)

2009: *THE COVE*
Director: Louie Psihoyos

Writer: Mark Monroe
Cinematography: Brook Aitken
Editing: Geoffrey Richman
Music: J. Ralph
Producer: Jim Clark
Cast: Richard O'Barry, Joe Chisholm, Louie Psihoyos, Isabel Lucas and others as themselves

2009: *THE HARIYAMA BRIDGE*
Director and screenplay: Aaron Woolfolk
Cinematography: Masao Nakabori
Editing: John Coniglio
Art direction: Takahisa Taguchi
Music: Kazunori Maruyama
Producers: Danny Glover, Naoshi Yoda
Cast: Bennet Guillory (Daniel Holder), Saki Takaoka (Noriko Kubo), Misa Shimizu (Yuiko Hara), Danny Glover (Joseph Holder)

SELECT BIBLIOGRAPHY

Alter, Nora N. (2006) *Chris Marker*. Urbana: University of Illinois Press.

Barthes, Roland (1982) *Empire of Signs*. Translated by Richard Howard. New York: Hill and Wang.

Benedict, Ruth (2005) *The Chrysanthemum and the Sword: Patterns of Japanese Culture*. Boston: Houghton Miflin.

Benjamin, Walter (1968) *Illuminations*. Translated by Harry Zohn. New York: Harcourt Brace.

Bernstein, Matthew and Gaylyn Studlar, ed. (2007) *Visions of the East: Orientalism in Film*. New Brunswick: Rutgers University Press.

Bingham, Dennis (2010) *Whose Lives Are They Anyway?: The Biopic as Contemporary Film Genre*. New Brunswick: Rutgers University Press.

Bix, Herbert P. (2001) *Hirohito and the Making of Modern Japan*. New York: Perennial.

Bordwell, David. (1988) *Ozu and the Poetics of Cinema*. Princeton: Princeton University Press.

Bordwell, David. (1989) *Making Meaning: Inference and Rhetoric in the Interpretation of Cinema*. Cambridge: Harvard University Press.

Botz-Bornstein, Thorsten (2007) *Films and Dreams: Tarkovsky, Bergman, Sokurov, Kubrick, and Wong Kar-wai*. Latham: Lexington Books.

Brands, Hal (2006) " 'Who Saved the Emperor?': The MacArthur Myth and U.S. Policy toward Hirohito and the Japanese Imperial Institution, 1942-1946." *Pacific Historical Review* No 75, No 2.

Budd, David H. (2002) *Culture Meets Culture in the Movies*. Jefferson: McFarland and Company.

Burch, Nöel. (1979) *To the Distant Observer: Form and Meaning in the Japanese Cinema*. Berkeley: University of California Press.

Buruma, Ian. (2000) *The Missionary and the Libertine*. New York: Vintage.

Buruma, Ian. (2004) *Inventing Japan 1853-1964*. New York: Modern Library.

Butler, Judith (1997). "Melancholy Gender/Refused Identification." *The Psychic Life of Power*. Stanford: Stanford UP. 132-150.

Custen, George (1992) *Bio/Pics: How Hollywood Constructed Public History*. New Brunswick: Rutgers University Press.

Dalby, Liza (2008) *Geisha*. Berkeley: University of California Press.

Davies, Roger J. and Osamu Ikeno. (2002) *The Japanese Mind: Understanding Contemporary Japanese Culture*. Tokyo: Tuttle.

Davis, Darrell William. (1996) *Picturing Japaneseness: Monumental Style, National Identity, Japanese Film*. New York: Columbia University Press.

Davis, Natalie Zemon. (2000) *Slaves on Screen: Film and Historical Vision*. Cambridge: Harvard University Press.

D[esjardins], Chris.(2005) *Outlaw Masters of Japanese Film*. London: Tauris.

Desmond, John E. and Peter Hawkes. (2006) *Adaptation: Studying Film and Literature*. Boston: McGraw Hill.

Dombrowski, Lisa. (2008) *The Films of Samuel Fuller: If You Die, I'll Kill You!* Middletown: Wesleyan University Press.

Dower, John W. (1986) *War Without Mercy: Race and Power in the Pacific War*. New York: Pantheon.

Dower, John W. (1999) *Embracing Defeat: Japan in the Wake of World War II*. New York: Norton and The New Press.

Dower, John W. (2010) *Cultures of War: Pearl Harbor/ Hiroshima/ 9-11/ Iraq*. New York: Norton and the Free Press.

Duras, Marguerite. (1961) Translated by Richard Seaver. *Hiroshima Mon Amour*. New York: Grove.

Ehrlich, Linda C. and David Desser, ed. (1994) *Cinematic*

Landscapes: Observations on the Visual Arts and Cinema of China and Japan. Austin: University of Texas Press.

Fuller, Samuel. (2002) *My Tale of Writing, Fighting and Filmmaking.* New York: Applause.

Gerow, Aaron (2010) *Visions of Japanese Modernity: Articulations of Cinema, Nation, and Spectatorship, 1895-1925.* Berkeley: University of California Press.

Gerow and Abé Mark Nornes (2001) *In Praise of Film Studies: essays in Honor of Makino Mamoru.* Yokohama and Ann Arbor: Kinema Club.

Golden, Arthur (1997) *Memoirs of a Geisha.* New York: Knopf.

Gordon, Andrew, ed. (1993) *Postwar Japan as History.* Berkeley: University of California Press.

Greenaway, Peter (1996) *The Pillow-Book* [sic]. Paris: Dis Voir.

Greene, Naomi. (1999) *Landscapes of Loss: The National Past in Postwar French Cinema.* Princeton: Princeton University Press.

Hayakawa, Sessue (1960) *Zen Showed Me the Way.* ed. Croswell Bowen. Indianapolis: Bobbs-Merrill.

Hayes, John P. (1984) *James A. Michener: A Biography/* Indianapolis: The Bobbs-Merrill Company.

Heilbrun, Carolyn (1993) "Is Biography Fiction?" *Soundings* 76, no. 2-3 (Summer-Fall).

Hersey, John (1989) *Hiroshima.* New York: Vintage, 1989.

High, Peter B. (2003) *The Imperial Screen: Japanese Film Culture in the Fifteen Years' War, 1931-1945.* Madison: University of Wisconsin Press.

Hirano, Kyoko (1992) *Mr Smith Goes to Tokyo: Japanese Cinema under the American Occupation 1945-1952.* Washington: Smithsonian.

Huang, Yunte (2008) *Transpacific Imaginations: History, Literature, Counterpoetics.* Cambridge: Harvard University Press.

Huang, Yunte (2010) *Charlie Chan: The Untold Story of the Honorable Detective and His Rendezvous with American History.* New York: Norton.

Hunt, Leon and Leung Wing-Fai (2008) *East Asian Cinemas: Exploring Transnational Connections on Film*. London: Tauris.

Hunt, Lynn, ed. (1989) *The New Cultural History*. Berkeley: University of California Press.

Hutcheon, Linda (2006) *A Theory of Adaptation*. New York: Routledge.

Ivy, Marilyn (1995) *Discourses on the Vanishing: Modernity, Phantasm, Japan*. Chicago: University of Chicago Press.

Iwasaki, Mineko, with Rande Brown (2003) *Geisha of Gion*. London: Pocket Books.

Kaplan, David E. and Alec Dubro (2003) *Yakuza: Japan's Criminal Underworld*. Berkeley: University of California Press.

Keesey, Douglas *The Films of Petter Greenaway: Sex. Death and Provocation* (2006) Jefferson: McFarland.

King, Geoff (2010) *Lost in Translation*. Edinburgh: Edinburgh University Press.

King, Homay (2010). *Lost in Translation: Orientalism, Cinema, and the Enigmatic Signifier*. Durham: Duke University Press.

Kitamura, Hiroshi (2010) *Screening Enlightenment: Hollywood and the Cultural Reconstruction of Defeated Japan*. Ithaca: Cornell University Press.

Kôjin, Karatani (1998) *Origins of Modern Japanese Literature*. Translated by Brett de Bary. Durham: Duke University Press.

Koppes, Clayton R and Gregory D. Black (1987) *Hollywood Goes to War: How Politics, Profits, and Propaganda Shaped World War II Movies*. New York: The Free Press.

Kouvaros, George (2008) *Paul Schrader*. Urbana: University of Illinois Press.

Kreidl, John Francis (1979) *Alain Resnais*. New York: Twayne.

Kristeva, Julia (1987) *Soleil noir: dépression et mélancholie*. Paris: Gallimard: 1987.

Kristof , Nicholas and Sheryl WuDunn (2001) *Thunder from the East: Portrait of a Rising Asia* . New York: Vintage.

LeFanu, Mark (2005) *Mizoguchi and Japan*. London: British Film

Institute.

Lifton, Robert Jay (1967) *Death in Life: The Survivors of Hiroshima.* London: Weidenfeld and Nicolson.

Linhart, Sepp and Sabine Frûstûck, ed. (1998) *The Culture of Japan Seen through its Leisure.* Albany: State University of New York Press.

Littlewood, Ian (1996) *The Idea of Japan: Western Images, Western Myths.* Chicago: Ivan R. Dee.

Lupton, Catherine (2005) *Chris Marker: Memories of the Future.* London: Reaktion Books.

Manso, Peter (1994) *Brando: The Biography.* New York: Hyperion.

Marchetti, Gina (1993) *Romance and the "Yellow Peril": Race, Sex, and Discourse Strategies in Hollywood Fiction.* Berkeley: University of California Press.

McClain, James L. (2002) *Japan: A Modern History.* New York: Norton.

McLaughlin, Robert L. and Sally E. Parry (2006) *We'll Always Have the Movies: American Cinema during World War II.* Lexington: The University Press of Kentucky.

Mes, Tom and Jasper Sharp. (2005) *The Midnight Eye Guide to New Japanese Film.* Berkeley: Stone Bridge Press.

Metz, Christian (1974) *Film Language: A Semiotics of the Cinema.* Translated by Michael Taylor. New York: Oxford University Press.

Michener, James A. (1954) *Sayonara.* New York: Fawcett.

Miyao, Daisuke. (2007) *Sessue Hayakawa: Silent Cinema and Transnational Stardom.* Duke: Duke University Press.

Monaco, James (1979) *Alain Resnais.* New York: Oxford University Press.

Morely, David and Kevin Robins (1995). "Techno-Orientalism," in *Spaces of Identity: Global Media, Electronic Landscapes and Cultural Boundaries.* London: Palgrave. 147-72.

Morris, Ivan (1975) *The Nobility of Failure: Tragic Heroes in the History of Japan.* New York: New American Library.

Napier, Susan J. (2007) *From Impressionism to Anime: Japan as Fantasy and Fan Cult in the Mind of the West.* New York: Palgrave Macmillan.

Nathan, John. (2008) *Living Carelessly in Tokyo and Elsewhere.* New York: Free Press.

Nornes, Abé Mark (2007) *Cinema Babel: Translating Global Cinema.* Minneapolis: University of Minnesota Press.

Nornes, Abé Mark and Aaron Gerow (2009) *Research Guide to Japanese Film Studies.* Ann Arbor: Center for Japanese Studies.

Nygren, Scott (2007) *Time Frames: Japanese Cinema and the Unfolding of History.* Minneapolis: University of Minnesota Press.

Quandt, James, ed. (2001) *Kon Ichikawa.* Toronto: Toronto International Film Festival.

Ray, Robert B. (1995) *The Avant-Garde Finds Andy Hardy.* Cambridge: Harvard University Press.

Ray, Robert B. (2007) *How a Film Theory Got Lost and Other Mysteries in Cultural Studies.* Bloomington: Indiana University Press.

de Rham, Edith (1991) *Joseph Losey.* London: André Deutsch.

Richie, Donald (1974) *Ozu.* Berkeley: University of California Press.

Richie, Donald (1974) *Japanese Film: An Introduction.* Hong Kong: Oxford University Press, 1974.

Richie, Donald (2002) *The Inland Sea.* Berkeley: Stone Bridge Press.

Richie, Donald (2004) *Japan Journals 1947-2004.* ed. Leza Lowitz. Berkeley: Stone Bridge Press.

Richie, Donald (2005) *A Hundred Years of Japanese Film.* Tokyo: Kodansha.

Rosenstone, Robert ed. (1995) *Revisioning History: Film and the Construction of a New Past.* Princeton: Princeton University Press.

Rosenstone, Robert. (2006) *History on Film/ Film on History.*

Harlow: Pearson Longman, 2006.

Said, Edward (1979) *Orientalism.* New York: Vintage.

Schilling, Mark (2007) *No Borders, No Limits: Nikkatsu Action Cinema.* Godalming: Fab Press.

Schrader, Paul (1972) *Transcendental Style in Film: Ozu, Bresson, Dreyer.* Berkeley: University of California Press.

Schrader, Paul (2004) *Schrader on Schrader* Ed. Kevin Jackson London: Faber.

Scott, Ridley (2005) *Interviews.* ed. Laurence F. Knapp and Andrea F. Kulas. Jackson: University of Mississippi Press.

Seidensticker, Edward (1983) *Low City, High City: Tokyo from Edo to the Earthquake.* New York: Knopf.

Seidensticker, Edward (1990) *Tokyo Rising :The City since the Great Earthquake.* New York: Knopf.

Shahat, Ella (1997) "Gender and Culture of Empire: Toward a Feminist Ethnography of the Cinema," in *Visions of the East: Orientalism in Film,* ed. Matthew Bernstein and Gaylyn Studlar. New Brunswick: Rutgers. 19-66.

Smaill, Belinda (2010). "Women. Pain and the Documentaries of Kim Longinotto," in *The Documentary: Politics: Emotion, Culture.* New York: Palgrave Macmillan. 71-94.

Standish, Isolde. (2005) *A New History of Japanese Cinema: A Century of Narrative Films.* New York: Continuum.

Stein, Bonnie Sue (1986) "Twenty Years Ago We Were Crazy, Dirty, and Mad," *The Drama Review* 30:2 (107-26).

von Sternberg, Josef (1965) *Fun in a Chinese Laundry.* London: Secker and Warburg.

Stewart, Susan (1993) *On Longing: Narratives of the Miniature, the Gigantic, the Souvenir, the Collection.* Durham: Duke University Press.

Tay, Sharon Lin (2009). *Women on the Edge: Twelve Political Film Practices.* London: Palgrave Macmillan.

Terasaki, Gwen. (1985) *Bridge to the Sun.* Newport, TN: Wakestone Books.

Tomasulo, Frank P. (2007). "Japan Through Others' Lenses: *Hiroshima Mon Amour* (1959) and *Lost in Translation* (2003)." *Japan Studies Review*, Volume 11 (143-56).

Turim, Maureen (1998) *The Films of Oshima Nagisa: Images of a Japanese Iconoclast.* Berkeley: University of California Press.

Udden, James. (2009) *No Man an Island: The Cinema of Hou Hsiao-hsien.* Hong Kong: Hong Kong University Press.

van der Post, L. (1983)*The Seed and the Sower.* Harmondsworth: Penguin.

Van der Kolk and van der Hart (1991) "The Intrusive Past: The Flexibility of Memory and the Engraving of Trauma," *American Imago* 48, no. 4 448.

Varley, Paul (2000) *Japanese Culture.* 4th edition. Honolulu: University of Hawai'i Press.

Washburn, Dennis and Carole Cavanaugh, ed. (2001) *Word and Image in Japanese Cinema.* Cambridge: Cambridge University Press.

Washburn (2001) "A Story of Cruel Youth: Kon Ichikawa's *Enjô* and the Art of Adapting in 1950s Japan" in Quant (2001).

Wilde, Oscar (1986) *De Profundis and Other Writings* (Harmondsworth: Penguin).

Willoquet-Maricondi, Paula and Mary Alemany-Falway, ed. (2008) *Peter Greenaway's Postmodern/ Poststructuralist Cinema.* Latham, NJ: Scarecrow Press.

Wilson, Emma (2006). *Alain Resnais.* Manchester: Manchester University Press.

Woolf, Virginia (1926) "The Movies and Reality," *New Republic* 47 (4 August).

Yoshimoto, Mitsuhiro (2000) *Kurosawa: Film Studies and Japanese Cinema.* Durham: Duke University Press.

Index

zero
books

Contemporary culture has eliminated both the concept of the public and the figure of the intellectual. Former public spaces – both physical and cultural – are now either derelict or colonized by advertising. A cretinous anti-intellectualism presides, cheerled by expensively educated hacks in the pay of multinational corporations who reassure their bored readers that there is no need to rouse themselves from their interpassive stupor. The informal censorship internalized and propagated by the cultural workers of late capitalism generates a banal conformity that the propaganda chiefs of Stalinism could only ever have dreamt of imposing. Zer0 Books knows that another kind of discourse – intellectual without being academic, popular without being populist – is not only possible: it is already flourishing, in the regions beyond the striplit malls of so-called mass media and the neurotically bureaucratic halls of the academy. Zer0 is committed to the idea of publishing as a making public of the intellectual. It is convinced that in the unthinking, blandly consensual culture in which we live, critical and engaged theoretical reflection is more important than ever before.